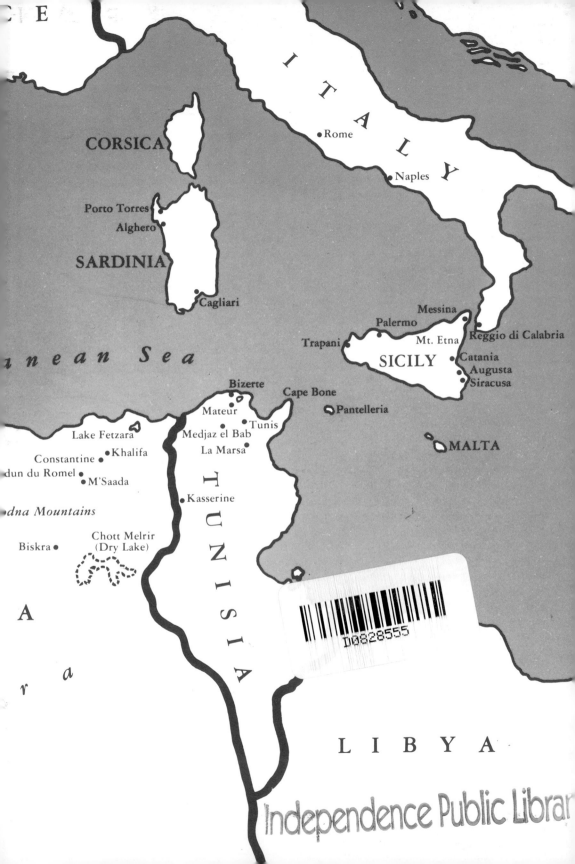

CE

ITALY

CORSICA

• Rome

• Naples

Porto Torres
Alghero•

SARDINIA

• Cagliari

Messina

Palermo

n e a n   S e a

Trapani•

Mt. Etna

Reggio di Calabria

SICILY

Catania
Augusta
Siracusa

Bizerte

Cape Bone

Pantelleria

Mateur

• Tunis

Lake Fetzara

Medjaz el Bab

La Marsa

MALTA

Constantine•

Khalifa

dun du Romel•

• M'Saada

dna Mountains

Kasserine

T U N I S I A

Chott Melrir
(Dry Lake)

Biskra •

A

r   a

L I B Y A

D0828555

Independence Public Librar

DOORKNOB FIVE TWO

FREDRIC ARNOLD

INDEPENDENCE PUBLIC LIBRARY
175 Monmouth Street
Independence, OR 97351
2950 2686

Copyright ©1984 by Fredric Arnold
All rights reserved. No part of this book may be reproduced, stored in a retrieval sysytem, or transmitted, in any form or by any means, electronic, mechanical, photocopying, recording, or otherwise, without the written prior permission of the author and publisher. Manufactured in the United States of America.

First Printing, January 1984
Second Printing, May 1984
Third Printing, December 1985
(Paperback titled "Kohn's War")
Fourth Printing, July 1986
Fifth Printing, February 1987
Sixth Printing, November 1988
Seventh Printing, March 1991
Eighth Printing, February 1992
Ninth Printing, March 1994
Tenth Printing, April 1995

Library of Congress Catalog Card Number 83-062768
Hard Cover ISBN 0-914961-00-4
Printed in the United States of America

S. E. Maxwell
Publishers

For my father—

ACKNOWLEDGEMENTS

This book would never have come to fruition without the loving support of my wife, Natalie. Her strength, her patience, and her forebearance make me realize what an extraordinary person she is.

And to my children, Marcie, Dana, and Marc; they were my inspiration. Their belief in me never wavered, and their encouragement has seen me through some difficult times.

Credits:
>   Photos and Drawings:
>   Fredric L. Kohn, 1943.

>   Cover and Jacket Design:
>   Phillip Schwartz

Publisher's note:
>   Fredric L. Kohn was born in Chicago, Illinois, 1922. The family name was changed to Arnold in 1946.

AUTHOR'S NOTE

In essence, my story is true. The incidents I have written about did in fact happen. I have been careful to avoid reference, by name, to most persons living or dead. In particular, I have disguised the identity of a pilot I flew with whom I met again after thirty-five years, and who threatened to sue me if I wrote a book about the men of the 71st Fighter Squadron.

As he said, "You listen good, Nose. Don't go saying anything about the boys. Just you remember, for a Jewish boy we treated you like a real American."

CONTENTS

CONTENTS

DOORKNOB
FIVE TWO

1

Sicily—July 11, 1943

"STRING OUT! DROP ON THE first pass!" I called, and in the same instant our twelve planes dove at the road, opening fire a few hundred feet away from the longest convoy I had ever seen. We dropped our bombs and pulled out. Some troops tried to run; a few flung themselves prostrate on the ground; others stood motionless, looking up at us as if unable to grasp what was happening.

The combined fire power was devastating. Trucks and mule carts crashed to the sides of the road and were left stranded and burning. There was no return fire. Nothing moved. We made another pass, then headed inland toward Mt. Etna in search of new targets.

We were trained for this, and we were good, strong, powerful. Nothing could stop us. We were going to win the war, and I was playing a part in the victory.

I had come a long way in the last five months. A fighter pilot, ten Air Medals, an ace, squadron leader. Yet I had only one thought—finishing the missions and going home—getting my own noncombat command, training others, planning, strategy, and flying. The consistent drone of the engines, the feel of the throttles and the stick, the pressure of the rudder pedals on the soles of my feet...that was my security, my reality.

A voice blared, "Doorknob Leader, you're losing coolant!"

I jerked my head around to see a vapor trail streaming behind my left tail boom. I had been hit.

"Red Leader, this is Doorknob Five Two." I pressed the mike hard against my throat. "Falzone, I've got troubles. Take the lead. I'm

1

cutting out and heading for the coast. See ya later!"

Foster had seniority, but I couldn't give him the lead. He'd screw things up, I told myself. The real reason was, I couldn't get his name past my lips, I despised him so.

The left engine's oil and coolant gauges quickly climbed into the red. I chopped the mixture control, feathered the prop, boosted the power on the good engine, and trimmed the plane for the flight back to North Africa. No sweat. That's what two engines were for. One to get you home if the other quits.

Flying close to the ground, strapped in a roller coaster, I caught glimpses of the sea from the top of each hill, then grazed valleys, skimmed trees and farmland, villages, and isolated cottages. The left prop stood stiff and straight, its three black blades cutting the air without resistance. The coastline flashed less than a mile ahead. I squinted hard searching the Mediterranean for air space clear of gunboats.

A terrifying jolt reverberated through the frame. Then a blast and the top of the right engine blew off, the cowling hanging back like a peeled banana. The explosion took the right window, the canopy, and the right propeller. Wind slammed my head backward against the padded armour plate and tore at my eyelids. The plane buffeted like a bronco, howling wind in my ears.

The throttle levers moved freely in my hand, without control or effect. The absence of engine sounds startled me, as though God in a single gesture had stopped the steady, throbbing beat of the waves at sea. No longer obedient, my plane took command, ordering the nose to start it's inevitable descent toward earth. The airspeed bled quickly away. A black cloud engulfed the right tail boom and rudder.

Down! I must get down! For an instant, a shadow darkened the reflective surfaces of the instrument panel. Something was above me. Then I saw a Messerschmidt swoop past and pull into a climbing turn, as though the machine itself were looking backward to confirm the destruction of its victim.

Without power, I dropped gradually toward earth in a forced glide. Unable to turn or pick a spot, I was fated to a course straight ahead toward the planted rows of a vineyard and beyond to the land's abrupt end and jagged cliffs overhanging a crashing sea a hundred feet below. I pressed the wheel forward, forcing the plane's nose only inches above a furrow. The wings, like enormous scythes, cut a swathe through bushes and saplings, absorbing excess speed. Still too fast! The end of the field was in sight. A stone wall reached up to grab me. I pulled back on the wheel, barely clearing the nose, but the rudders hooked the wall, ripping the tail booms from the wings and cockpit.

The plane slammed into the bushes and stopped. The black smoke, no longer whipped by the wind, became vicious flames that quickly consumed the right engine, liquefying the paint as they spread. I felt the heat against the side of my face.

I unbuckled my crash straps and parachute harness and leapt out of the cockpit, scrambled over the left wing, stumbled over gnarled vines, and collapsed fifty feet from the burning plane. I couldn't suck in air fast enough to feed my pounding heart. I dry heaved and then laughed out loud. I dug my fingers in the rich black soil. "Fuck 'em all! Fuck 'em all! There'll be no promotions this side of the ocean so cheer up me lads, fuck 'em all!"

The 109 made a low pass and slowly circled the pillar of smoke that now rose a few hundred feet into the hot, still morning air. I got to my feet to move further back, afraid I would be incinerated if the fuel tanks blew.

Then I saw two soldiers walking down the field toward me. They carried their rifles like hunters, slung over their forearms, the barrels pointing toward the ground. I could tell from the bright red and green markings on their uniforms they were Italian. Relieved they weren't German, I waved at them and shouted hello.

They barely noticed me. Instead, they stopped and watched the burning plane, their faces without expression.

"Brucia come l'inferno," the older soldier said, his moustache falling like a loose curtain over his mouth.

"E'vero, brucia come fornace," the other replied.

One tank erupted and the whoosh of hot air brought our arms up in front of our faces. Flames swept the cockpit and the plexiglass canopy melted. Only the nose with its five guns remained intact. The U.S. Army Air Corps insignia on the broken tail boom of my P-38 was obliterated by fire. Mounds of earth and tangled vine obscured the star painted on the wingtip nearest us.

The 109 made another slow circle and headed north. The Italians watched the plane burn.

With casual detachment I noticed that my dirt-stained coveralls, government-issue beige, bore no distinguishing marks. They were the same as all fighter pilots wore. Neither I nor my plane showed our nationality. They must think I'm a German, I thought suddenly. I saw the butt of my .45 peeking out from the plain leather holster under my left arm. They would have searched me, taken my gun if they knew I was an American.

My breath came in short bursts. Should I shoot them? Make a run for it? The ground was hilly and covered with thick vegatation. I would stumble and fall before I could lose them. There was nowhere to hide. I'll only end up with a bullet in my back. Forget it, I told myself. It's finished now. I've made it alive. I'll go along with them quietly, spend a few months in Italy as a POW, and eat spaghetti until the war is over.

The older man took a piece of paper and a tiny pencil from his breast pocket. With an occasional lick of the point, he slowly printed what remained of the plane's letters, LMA, then began to draw the symbols painted on the side of the gondola—eleven white bombs— suddenly his hand froze and his eyes grew wide as the six swastikas and the fascista symbol registered in his brain.

"Fermo!" he yelled at me. *"Non Tedesco! Multa ma sei Americano!"* he said, pointing a finger and gesturing agitatedly. I spread my hands indicating I didn't understand. He pointed to my gun and thumped his open palm against my chest.

"Dammi la pistola!" he shouted.

I handed him my gun and forced a placating smile.

"Grazie," he said returning a smile.

He tucked the gun in his belt and motioned for me to follow. *"Andiamo via da qui!"* Both solders turned their backs and walked ahead of me, their heavy boots stomping through the undergrowth toward higher ground. I followed a few steps behind.

The skies were clear. Only the muffled sounds of distant artillery gave testament that the Allied invasion of Sicily was in progress.

At the end of the field we stepped over a low stone wall laced with cactus and took a narrow trail through prickly brambles and thorns. The sharp spikes tore my skin through the thin fabric of my coveralls. The path was uphill. I had trouble maintaining the brisk pace they had set, the thin soles of my oxfords offering no protection against the sharp rocks and uneven ground. I stopped to catch my breath and they waited until I was ready to continue. I followed them without protest, relieved there were no more decisions to make.

We had walked silently for about thirty minutes when we came upon a congested road. Carts and buggies, wheelbarrows, soldiers and civilians, families and farm animals plodded deliberately north. Creeping trucks and an occasional car slowly passed the migrating column. I was stunned at the sight. This was the type of movement I'd seen from the air, forming a convoy that would qualify as a worthwhile enemy target.

I watched them closely as we reached the road. The women wore black; their dresses, shawls, stockings, shoes, all were a uniform dusty black. The men were gnarled and weather-beaten, too old for military service, the end product of a hard life. Their clothes were torn and their arms and backs were weighted with bundles of clothing, rugs, sacks of produce. And the children. Staccato flashes of scrawny arms and necks, hollow eyes, sallow cheeks, barefoot spindles sticking out of oversized trousers. Tears stung my eyes. I couldn't think about the children. What was going to happen to me?

We blended with the flow of traffic, the soliders now walking behind me in silence. I needed to take a leak. The older soldier flagged an approaching car. The car stopped. The driver was Italian, but inside were German officers. Nauseous fear swelled in my throat at the sight of the insignias on their caps. I swallowed hard and looked straight ahead.

The younger Italian soldier unslung his rifle, holding it at the ready behind me. The older one conversed with the driver. The Germans examined me with their eyes as if I were on an auction block. No sale. The car went into gear and drove off. The old soldier came back and we continued walking.

We hadn't gone far when the old soldier stopped another vehicle, a large command car, its body standing two feet above the pavement. Three officers sat in the rear. All Germans. My heart began to pound again. One officer listened patiently while the older soldier explained something, making broad sweeps with his arms. Then he produced the piece of paper on which he had recorded the facts about my plane. The German glanced at me, then leaned over and spoke to the driver, who pressed a hand mike to his mouth and delivered a radio message in German.

So they were the enemy, I thought. They're old men! Even the youngest I guessed was over thirty. I had fired at them, killed them, yet never really seen them. Everything was dreamlike. I felt no hatred for them only some fear. I waited for two old men to decide my fate.

A half door opened on the command car and the Italian soldier nudged me with the side of his rifle. I squared my helmet and adjusted my goggles over my forehead, trying to hide the Jewish star sewn onto my helmet. I pulled the zipper to the top of my coveralls as though concerned about my appearance. Then I climbed into the rear of the car. A jump seat faced the three officers. I sat down carefully, angling my legs to keep from touching theirs. We drove off in silence. I toyed with the loose end of the radio jack that hung from my helmet, looked at my hands, at the landscape, at the columns of people we passed on the road. All the while, I felt their eyes on my prominent nose, the way Foster looked at my nose. My ethnic identification. No U.S. insignia. No officer's bars or Squadron number, but a Jew; like Foster, they'd understand that. I tried to console myself. They're officers, like me, they'll follow the rules, treat me like an officer, a prisoner of war. Everything's going to be all right.

An hour later we arrived at the German detention camp at Acireale for allied prisoners of war.

2

My Counterpart

THE COMMAND CAR CAME TO a stop in a small clearing in front of a stable. A lone burro munched on a pile of hay, his tail sweeping rhythmically across his hind quarters. A German soldier, a rifle hanging over his shoulder, pushed open a large wooden door and motioned for the car to enter. In the distance were several soldiers stacking rifles and ammunition boxes. They moved about their tasks quickly, without wasted motion. There was a sense of urgency. Two soldiers dressed in full combat gear loaded the equipment onto a truck.

The soldier with the rifle motioned for me to get out and follow him. The back of his neck and his shirt were streaked with perspiration. I followed in the wake of his body odor.

A loud command in German pierced the air. Men ran for cover. The soldier with the rifle and I dropped to the ground. From where I lay, my head in my arms, I could see a squadron of P-38's sweep in from the south over a small hill. They followed the road we had just come from, passing low off to our side, the sound of their guns blending with the roar of their engines, hundreds of spent shell casings pouring from ejection shots. A moment later the ground shook, followed by a loud explosion. Small bits of debris dropped lazily into the clearing. A few twigs and pieces of straw fell onto the roof of the stable. Then it was quiet, except for the muffled sounds of the burro's chewing.

I had never seen a P-38 attack from the ground. It was frightening. As quickly as it had happened, the soldiers returned to their duties, and I followed my escort about a hundred yards to a white stucco cottage.

Under the eaves of the buildings three men arranged files and neatly tied bundles of documents on a long narrow table. A German officer stood at the door watching us approach. He exchanged salutes with the soldier, words were spoken, and a slip of paper changed hands. Again they saluted. The soldier did a brisk about-face and marched off. The officer studied the paper and then slowly looked me over. Uncertain whether I should salute, I stood there, not quite at attention, and focused my eyes on an imaginary dot beyond his head. I could see his face. His skin was the color of richly tanned leather, his eyes light blue behind gold wire glasses.

His neat attire made me acutely aware of my dusty shoes and baggy flight coveralls, stained and covered with bits of straw from my recent contact with the ground. Even in the heat of the day, he looked cool and proper in his heavily decorated uniform. His black leather belt and shiny boots contrasted sharply with my empty sweat stained shoulder holster and leather flying helmet with its dangling length of radio cord, and my goggles with their cracked lens. Over the months I had put layer on layer of adhesive tape over the protruding earphones of the helmet in a futile attempt to muffle the engine noise. Now the adhesive was dirty and peeling, the male jack disconnected and out of place.

The officer reached out, slipped two fingers inside my collar, and withdrew my dog tags. The little metal tags had hung on a neck chain since the day they were issued, and I hadn't given them a thought until that moment. One of them, I had been told, would be used as a grave-marker and the other jammed between my teeth as positive identification for reburial. Important details about me were embossed on them—name, serial number, rank, blood type, and religious affiliation. Would he know, I wondered, "H" meant Hebrew?

I felt a pressing need to urinate. I had wanted to relieve myself immediately after the crash, but with each new distraction the need had subsided.

The officer studied the information on the tags, let them slip back down my chest, reached out and touched my helmet, examining the yellow star stitched and painted over the forehead. The color of his eyes mirrored mine and his blonde crew-cut was the same as mine.

"Jude?" he asked.

It was suddenly quiet. Background noises of the soldiers working at the table, the occasional comments and paper shuffling, stopped. My focus went back past his eyes to the imaginary dot beyond his head.

"*Jude?*" he asked again.

My hands went weak. I understood his question as if it had been asked in English. I worried I would wet myself and be ashamed in front of them. Seconds passed in silence, then abruptly he looked toward the soldiers at the table. The sounds of work resumed. He looked at me again, pointed, and spoke quietly. "*Sie koennen jetzt gehen.* Go...now."

I walked through the open door behind him into a cool room, empty except for a small table and three stools. There was an open window facing west. The sill was low enough to urinate over but in clear view of the soldiers I had seen when I arrived. I decided against it. Now they were dismantling and packing up military and administrative equipment. An evacuation appeared to be in progress.

Beyond them the dusty clearing was bordered on three sides by groves of olive trees. A group of allied soldiers sat at the clearing's edge to the north, guarded by two German soldiers. Most of the area was fenced with wire mesh. The compound was arranged for supply storage and not for detention of prisoners. Somewhere there would be a latrine, but I didn't want to ask. I looked for a butt can. The room was empty. I considered urinating in my helmet, pouring it out the window, then drying the leather on the sill in the hot Mediterranean sun. It wouldn't matter if I ruined it. I didn't need it anymore. I took it off and turned it over in my hands. Most of the yellow paint had flaked off, leaving small traces along the stitching that formed the star. I pulled it back on. It was the only uniform I had. I couldn't piss in it. I sat on one of the stools and crossed my legs against the pressure. If necessary, I would piss in the corner.

Through the open door, I saw a car pull up and a young German officer jump out before it came to a stop. He spoke to someone, then entered. From the angle of his cap and the style of his coveralls I knew he was a pilot. A small cross hung below an open collar and a stylized pair of wings branched out from an embossed Nazi symbol sewn on his right breast pocket. He slapped the table with an open palm.

"Good! You are not hurt!"

I started to stand.

"Please," he motioned for me to remain seated while he straddled one of the stools on the other side of the table. He smiled. "I am Karl Muenster. *Hauptmann.* Captain, you say. The, ah . . ." he searched for the word, "Commandant, yes? says the transports arrive soon and you will leave. I leave also, with my squadron." He jerked his head north. "Sicily is *kaput.*"

I reached for my cigarettes but he put his hand on mine and handed me one from his pocket.

"Keep yours. You will get no more." I lit the cigarette with my Zippo and he smiled at the huge flame the lighter made. I inhaled deeply, then gagged on the sharp tobacco.

"I am a Messerschmidt pilot." He paused acknowledging my nod. "We have met before. In the air, yes?" He spoke with only a slight German accent.

I held the flame for him. "Was that you behind me this morning?"

"We had been in the air together. It was the beginning of June at Cagliari."

Interrogation, I thought. I don't have to answer that. Just name, rank, and serial number.

"Two planes were lost, a P-38 and a Messerschmidt."

It wasn't a question. I kept silent.

He continued. "After your squadron left the harbor we attacked many times to stop your return flight to Africa." I didn't remember but it seemed important to him that I did. I slowly shook my head and shrugged. He continued. "The aircraft crashed in the water. Your squadron flew away and we returned to our base."

I shook my head. "Sorry, I don't remember."

"Later, two and one half hours later, an English flying boat with a P-38 escort returned and picked up the man from the water!" He seemed anxious.

He saw from my expression I remembered.

"You see, I was right! I refueled and escorted a launch to where the man was, only a few miles from shore, but already you were there flying in circles above him, yes?" He laughed and slapped the table.

I felt a slight tremor in the dirt floor and heard the sound of heavy transport trucks. The Commandant poked his head inside the room, spoke sharply to Muenster, then disappeared. I rubbed the cigarette out under my shoe.

Muenster stood, his palms on the table, and leaned toward me looking in my eyes.

"The pilot in the water was my friend. His name was Deiter. Did he live?"

"He made it."

"He made it?"

"He's O.K. Alive." I circled an "O" between thumb and index finger. So that's what he wanted to know.

"*Dank,*" he sighed. "You are from Doorknob Squadron, yes? You are Doorknob Five Two. I like your names, Crabgrass, Beerbottle, Washboard...Americans have wonderful humor. Not so the English or the Germans. For me, Adler Eins. I am Eagle One. I watched from above while you circled Deiter. You did not see me?"

"No."

"Would you save him if you knew he was German?"

"Sure, why not? Tell me, how do you know our names?"

"That is our business to know these things. Have you many sorties?"

"Forty-six. Four more...and I would have gone home."

"For me, more than one hundred fifty missions...Libya, Tunisia, Sicily. I do not stop until..." He moved his hand simulating an airplane, arcing it over palm up until his fingertips struck the table. Then he touched the wings on his chest. "Still, I love to fly. And I am good!"

I knew what he meant. You had to be good.

The Commandant stood framed in the doorway.

"*Herr Hauptmann!*"

Muenster turned and stood at attention as the Commandant spoke. The very sound of German seemed angry to me. I shuddered. The corners of Muenster's eyes flicked at something the Commandant said. When he was through, Muenster snapped to attention and saluted.

"*Ja Befehlshaber!*" Then, to me, he made a little bow and gestured, "After you. We go now, Doorknob."

I followed Muenster out the door, past the Commandant into the heat of the late morning. We walked past the table where the three soldiers were busy with their papers, turned the corner of the building, and headed across the clearing I had seen from the window.

Muenster rolled his eyes in the direction of the Commandant. "The Commandant is unhappy I talk with you. He does not know about Deiter. We have too many prisoners and the Commandant must transport them to the aerodrome for flight to Germany before tonight. There are troop landings at many places, both English and American."

I said nothing. It was still early in the day. I would be in Germany by sunset.

We approached the group of allied prisoners. Most were British paratroopers and foot soldiers. Their flared brim helmets were like the ones worn by American soldiers in World War I. I wished I had a metal helmet. My flimsy leather was no protection against another strafing attack.

A British officer sat on the ground with his back against one of the fence posts that marked the camp's perimeter. Behind him, two German soldiers were removing lengths of wire mesh from the fence posts, rolling, tying, and packaging them into large bundles, stacking them like bales of hay for subsequent pickup. We stopped several yards from the officer.

"I leave you. The Commandant instructs you sit here, not with common soldiers," Muenster said indicating the British officer. "This is respect, yes?"

He looked at the symbol on my forehead. Blood pounded in my head. Stupid, I thought, stupid to have sewn a Mogen David on my helmet. How do they treat Jewish prisoners in Germany? I wondered.

Muenster looked at his wristwatch and glanced at the sky.

"It was you who shot me down, wasn't it?" I asked suddenly. There was a moment before I crashed he could have killed me. I wondered why he hadn't.

"This is not important," he shrugged. "You survived. For you it is over, Doorknob, but not for me. Goodbye."

I leaned back against the fence post, slid to the ground, and nodded to the British officer. He glanced at me and touched the brim of his helmet.

I pressed my back against the post, shifting my weight onto my elbow. The callouses on my bony ass had split from the crushing G forces sometime during the last mission, and now I felt the pain.

3

Escape

THE COMMANDANT STOOD, LEGS SPREAD, thumbs tucked in his belt, watching the prisoners being loaded into large transports. They were uncooperative, straggling toward the rear of the open truck. One prisoner turned and shoved the man behind him. A minor skirmish started, quickly controlled by the pressure of the guards' rifles. Another group waited their turn to board, and a second transport idled nearby. The prisoners cursed over the idling of the truck's motor.

The British officer cradled his knees in his arms. Light glinted off his eyeglasses. The single diamond-shaped pip on his shoulder was the equivalent of my rank, second lieutenant. "Royal Lancers" was embroidered on a red and yellow triangular patch on the upper arm of his jacket. I admired his narrow, well-trimmed moustache and wondered how he would maintain it as a prisoner of war.

The area behind where we sat was free of barbed wire, and formed a border of clear, hard packed soil for some thirty feet, where it met a densely planted orchard of olive trees. It was the outer edge of the camp. There were no guards.

What am I waiting for? I asked myself. I can't go to Germany. How can a Jew survive there? My eyes met the British officer's for an instant. Please don't give me away, I asked silently. I looked back at the row of legs and feet shuffling past to fill another empty transport. Our eyes met again. Not a word passed between us.

I rolled onto my hands and the tips of my shoes and scampered on all fours past the first row of trees, then dropped flat into a shallow depression, my face buried in the dirt. The officer hit the earth next

13

to me, expelling a great gush of air. There were shouts in German and English. Had we been seen? I waited for shots to be fired. *SCHMUCK!* What a stupid thing to do! Maybe I could raise my hands and surrender. Then the voices were absorbed by the roar of aircraft engines. I felt the planes' vibrations in the ground as they flew over.

"NOW!" I hissed. Again we were up, running in a crouch, past one row, then another of the trees. I dove into the shadows at the base of a tree. The officer dropped alongside, almost touching me. My heart pounded in my throat like a giant piston pumping hot air in and out of my lungs. My body shook as it had on my first mission. Warm liquid spread through my coveralls and over my thighs. I thought I lay in an irrigation ditch, but my fingers dug into dry soil. I was urinating. Finally. I relaxed and breathed easier.

Neither of us dared move. With my left cheek pressed flat against the ground, I saw the second flight of planes rake by at treetop level. They were P-38's.

"What now?" he whispered.

"I don't know."

"Can you see them?"

"No."

"Neither can I."

"I don't think we should move," I whispered, "Let's just lie still, O.K.?"

"I'm for that."

The planes didn't return. I heard the first transport move off, than another. We lay motionless on the ground, listening to the sounds of motors starting, brakes screeching, exhausts roaring, backfires, and shifting of gears. When the sounds became less frequent and more distant, he said, "They've gone." It was almost a question.

"Maybe," I said. My left hand and wristwatch were cramped under my ear. We lay motionless while the sun beat down on exposed parts of our bodies.

"I don't do this kind of thing," the officer whispered. He sounded tearful. "Communications, that's my specialty. Can't imagine why I came with you."

Toward late afternoon, only a few isolated sounds came from the camp. The shadows were long now. Slowly I raised my head. I had a clear view of the compound through the trees. No one was in sight.

"Let's go," I said, crawling toward the next row of trees. About a hundred yards further and we were well concealed in the grove, protected by the darkening shadows of late afternoon. At last, we stood and stretched, stepped over a waist-high stone wall, and sat down.

The British officer looked old and tired. He fidgeted with his collar, scratched the back of his neck, and pulled at the stubble on his chin.

"Guess we ought to wait for it to get a little darker before we go any further," he sighed. "Bit of a mess, right? I wager they'll shoot us if we're caught. What's the plan?"

"I don't have one," I said. I had hoped he would. He was older and more experienced. He rubbed his eyes. I realized he had lost his glasses. He adjusted his helmet and brushed at his stained trousers, then looked at his fingernails. "This area has heavy concentrations of German Panzers. We've been indoctrinated that in a situation like this, making an escape and all that, we'd best go our separate ways."

I didn't like that. For the first time since I joined the army I didn't want to be alone.

He squinted at me. "You do present a problem, you know. How is it you're not in uniform?"

"Fighter pilots aren't expected to be in a spot like this," I answered, annoyed. I was tired and depressed.

The sun dropped below the horizon. It grew dark rapidly. The British officer got to his feet, pulled at his ear, and said, "I'm going south. That way, would you say?" he asked, pointing.

"Yes, but pick a star to head for, or if you can see the big volcano, keep it at four o'clock, a little behind your right shoulder," I added.

He started to walk away. "A word of caution, lad. You're not in the air shooting astros out of the bomb bay. No holiday down here. If the Germans catch you out of uniform and with that yellow star on your helmet, they'll blow your bloody head off."

"Take it easy," I called after him. Then he was gone.

I picked my way along the stone wall as it curved west until it ended abruptly. Ahead were plowed fields and beyond, total darkness with occasional flashes of artillery fire on the horizon. Although I had flown over that area many times—Mt. Etna to the north and the sea to the east made navigation simple—on the ground, I was lost. If I could find south, I could find the advancing

British 8th Army.

Concentrate! I must keep control. Panic would set me up as a target. Compose yourself, I scolded. All you have to do is retrace your steps. You were facing south when you entered the field, so retrace your steps. It's easy. Think. You can figure it out, even without a compass. A compass! All at once I remembered the survival lectures during training. There was a compass concealed in my coveralls.

A long zipper ran from the crotch to a snap fastener and two buttons sewn at the collar. They appeared to be ordinary black buttons, fastened with thread through four holes, but there were no facing buttonholes. I pulled. The threads broke easily. Even in the darkness I saw the small white dot painted on the edge of one button. A sharp point protruded from the center of the other. I placed one button, point facing up, on a flat stone. The button with the dot fit neatly on top of the first and started to spin. When it stopped, the white dot pointed north! I dropped the buttons into my pocket and headed south, almost at a run.

My course was dictated by the terrain. I passed through citrus orchards, olive groves, vineyards. Each field, separated by a stone wall and a cactus hedge, forced me in a slightly different direction from due south. And rising terrain dictated that I go east. What if I can't head south? I wondered frantically. How will I find the main road between Catania and Augusta? I knew the British would have reached Augusta. My chest started to ache as though my skin had shrunk, squeezing my throat and my bladder. I urinated in a furrow and continued walking for more than an hour.

The sounds of war were amplified by the darkness and seemed to come from all directions at once. I had never heard big guns and exploding shells. My war was only the sound of my engines. I had smelled the gunpowder that seeped into the cockpit, but I had never heard my guns fire. On dive-bombing runs, I saw the explosions made by the bombs dropped ahead of me, I saw the faint shock wave that preceded the explosion, but I'd never heard the sound. The mushrooming black and white clouds rising from the target, the flak bursting off my wingtip, tracers from my guns pouring into enemy aircraft, incendiaries and cannon shells finding their marks —all were silent pictures to me. Dismembered segments of planes blown apart in the sky or gracefully pirouetting into the sea. Hundreds of silent pictures. But I had never heard the cries of their occupants. Now I was stunned by the sounds. Each explosion startled me, distracting me from what I had to do.

As I walked, enormous cactus plants, their spiked arms reaching out to stop me, ripped through my coveralls, and my arms and legs were scratched and bleeding. A weight pressed against my lungs, forcing me to take quick, short breaths. The path went downhill. In the distance, etched against the night sky, I saw the outline of a village. I heard the drone of truck motors and the deeper rumble of heavy tanks. On coming closer, I saw the trucks stop in their movement north and wait until the tanks passed ahead of them.

Somewhere down that road, perhaps only a few miles, was Montgomery's 8th Army causing this evacuation. All I had to do was find them before the Italians or the Germans found me.

For some time I followed a stream that skirted the village, stumbling over rocks and walls in the dark. Then the stream became an irrigation ditch and disappeared into a narrow tunnel under the main road above me. I started to climb the bank to cross the road when I heard a voice, a quiet statement spoken in German, by a man not more than a few feet from me. I felt faint. My blood retreated, leaving my skin cold. I squeezed my stomach muscles, desperate to remain conscious. I didn't move. Another German answered. The conversation was taking place just above my head. Slowly I turned, and over my right shoulder I saw the backs of two soldiers sitting on a wall. In front of them was a monstrous tank, the first in a string of tanks parked along the road.

I sank into a crouch and crawled a foot inside the culvert. My shoes were full of water. I forced myself to breathe quietly. This was a mistake. I should never have left the detention camp. At least I would have been safe there. The sound of exploding shells unnerved me. I remained motionless listening to the voices above me until the two men left. But I heard others farther down the road. I needed a place to hide. The risk of stumbling into someone in the dark was too great.

Quietly I moved away from the road, exhausted by fear, and retraced my steps toward houses outlined in the distance a hundred yards away. I waded through shallow, stagnant water to the side wall of the closest cottage and leaned heavily against it. The wall was still warm. Walking softly again, aware of every twig that broke under my shoes, I followed a path toward the front of the house. A truck rumbled by to the north. Suddenly, I heard footsteps clicking on the pavement, then laughter and men speaking German.

I froze in my tracks and held my breath, willing the darkness to absorb me. A muffled conversation in Italian, a cry of a small child followed by a woman's angry reprimand, made me tremble. I must hide. I cautiously felt my way back to the rear of the house. Stone and cactus walls blocked my retreat. At the far side of the house was an open shed, reeking from the odor of freshly cut hay. I peered into the darkness, forcing my eyes to check the interior for safety. I slipped inside.

A pair of donkeys dozing on their feet ignored me. At the far end of the shed, I collapsed onto the ground between some wicker baskets filled with produce and bundles of hay. Sporadic sounds of shelling filled the night. I wanted to sleep. I could go no farther now. I was cold and shivering. I pulled at a loose piece of burlap thrown carelessly over something, and uncovered an ornately decorated donkey cart with large spoked wheels and brightly painted side panels. In the dim moonlight I could make out paintings on the panels—scenes of the crusades—armoured knights and elegant ladies. The wooden spokes were hand carved and imbedded with ornamental wrought iron. On the shaft of each spoke, delicately detailed angels flew after each other in a never-ending race. How out of place it all seemed.

I tried to think clearly. I needed a plan. I would wait in the shed until morning and then decide what to do. No, that was too dangerous. With the local population browsing around in the morning and the road crowded with evacuation Italian and German soldiers, I'd be sure to be discoverd. My coveralls, helmet, and goggles gave me away. Then I remembered the Sicilian refugees on the roads making their way north. If I could make myself look as starved and ragged as they . . .

I stuffed my helmet and goggles inside my coveralls. The legs were already torn and stained. The leg pocket, ripped from its seams, hung from a few threads. I took off my wet shoes. I pulled down my right sock and felt the knife strapped to my shin. The Italian soldiers had taken my pistol but they had never searched me. No one had. They'd all missed the compass and the knife.

With the long sharp blade, I cut the bottoms off each pants leg about six inches below the knees and severed the sleeves a few inches below the shoulders. Next, I emptied the wicker baskets and bound them together with a piece of leather from the strap of my shoulder holster. I scuffed my shoes against the coarse ground and cut holes over the toes. I rubbed dirt over my coveralls, arms, and legs, and reversed my dog tags so they hung down my back, leaving only a thin silver chain visible around my neck. This costume, I told myself, should make me indistinguishable from the other migrating villagers.

I knotted the ends of my socks together and tied them around my forehead, like the sweatbands I had seen on the Sicilian workers. I readjusted the garter around my thigh and slipped the knife into its sheath, out of sight. If I carried the baskets over my shoulder it would hide the top half of my coveralls.

I heard men's voices close by, speaking Italian, and the sound of footsteps passing frightening me. The curtain of darkness that hid the surrounding fields and winding roads was threatening— unknown and imagined dangers lurked, draining my resolve to escape. I pressed deep into a corner, rigid at the thought of being discovered. Trembling at every sound, I sat upright waiting for dawn. In daylight, I can avoid people. In darkness I'd be shot. I thought of my father, my mother, my brother. I can't get killed. They don't even know I'm a fighter pilot. Things will look better in the morning.

I heard the rumble of trucks and felt the ground move. For them, it was safer to move in the dark.

How did I get in this spot? What did I do wrong? Only four more missions to go and I would be finished. Why hadn't Falzone or Foster called out the 109?

Then the disorderly sounds of many boots, out of step, pounding on the cobblestone road, punctuated with German words. Even after they had gone, I couldn't relax.

Dad had said, "Never wish ill of any man." For months I had prayed Foster would get his ass shot off. I would fall asleep dreaming of ways he would get killed. Now I'm being punished because I wished Foster dead. But I didn't really mean "dead." I only wanted him to suffer for his unprovoked malice. He suffocated me, wouldn't let me live, and probably all the time he was wishing me dead. Now he thinks he won. I could see the son of a bitch moving my cot out of the tent. I vowed to make it back just to see the look on his face.

Hating Foster gave me strength.

4

Patriotism And Prejudice

EVEN BEFORE I LAID EYES on Foster or knew his name, I felt his malice. It was the day we enlisted, February 28, 1942, almost three months after Pearl Harbor. About twenty of us stood in three rows in a small room on the second floor of the U.S. Post Office Building on La Salle Street in Chicago. I didn't know anyone. We had passed written tests, filled out reams of application forms, and had been accepted as Aviation Cadets in the Army Air Corps.

An officer in his mid-twenties addressed us.

"I'm Lieutenant Garrison. When your name is called, please acknowledge."

"Baker, R."

"Here."

"Allen, S."

"Present!"

"Cominski, M."

"Yo!"

Each man stood a little straighter when his name was called. Feet came together, chins raised, and shoulders pulled back. It didn't register when the lieutenant called "Kahn, F." It sounded like one word, Con-eff.

"KAHN, F?" Still no one responded. Some men looked at one another, curious no one had answered. The officer spelled, 'K-O-H-N,' initial 'F'! Is he here?"

"Kohn, Sir. That's pronounced 'Cone'," I answered. "Here, Sir!"

The Lieutenant continued with the list.

In the row in front of me I heard, "Kahn-eff, Kohn-eff, kinda has a ring to it. How did they let him in?" When they called his name, "Foster, J.," I knew I'd never forget it.

Ten days after we were sworn in I saw Foster again. We were on a troop train heading west. The first night I strolled half the length of the railroad car and paused to watch a poker game in progress. One of the four players was Foster. I took a good look at him. He was stocky, barrel chested, broad shouldered, with thick arms and a short bull neck. His stubby fingers and massive hands, lumpy and calloused, shuffled and manipulated the cards with authority. He looked up as he began to deal.

"Hi there," I said.

"Well, well. Look who's here, little Abie Finklestein." The smile froze on my face. You son of a bitch, I thought. The others looked up from their cards.

"Hi, I'm Curtiss."

"Jeb Peterson, call me J.B."

The youngest looking of the four, seated by the window, reached across and shook my hand.

"Pleased to meetcha, I'm Bob Lynch."

The other two offered their hands. Not Foster.

"I'm Fred Kohn."

No one seemed to notice that Kohn wasn't the same as Finklestein.

"We'll make room for you if you want to join in," Lynch smiled. "We just got started."

"Thanks, maybe later." I looked back at Foster. My dislike for him matched the hostility I saw in his face. I vowed to avoid him for the rest of the trip. It was a big army. Once we reached our destination, I was sure we would never see each other again.

When Foster's group went to the dining car, I waited for the next group to form. When we stopped somewhere and could go outside to stretch, I watched for him. If Foster went left, I went right. When he walked toward me down the aisle, I busied myself with a sketch pad and pencil I always carried, carefully avoiding his eyes.

Drawing had always been my private retreat. Mother said I made my first drawing when I was three. From the low casement window of our second floor apartment, I had seen a horse-drawn milk wagon below and, as if by magic, pencil lines took on the appearance of poles that hung from leather harness, great wisps of hair swirling over large hooves, the big head pushing into a feed bag. I sketched the cast iron anchor tied to the bridle and traced the black blinders that shielded the horse's eyes. I drew in a frenzy, faster and faster, detailing empty milk bottles inside wooden crates stacked on the wagon's rear flap.

When I was finished, I rushed to show my mother what I had done. She said she was busy making dinner. I took the drawing to my father. He hugged me. From then on he carried the drawing in his wallet. Ever since that time, drawing had calmed and comforted me. It even helped me take my mind off Foster.

It was late afternoon of the fourth day when our train rolled into the campgrounds of the Army Air Corps Replacement Center at Santa Ana, California. The barracks were huge with cots lined up dormitory style, to be taken on a first-come, first served basis. Private possessions placed on a cot indicated it had an occupant.

I walked down a long center aisle and discovered a number of unclaimed cots in the corner of the barracks. I chose the one nearest the window and tossed my valise on the mattress. Peterson and Lynch followed. Then Curtiss and another cadet. The only cot left was next to the rear door.

Lynch spread a sheet over his cot. "This is class! Enlisted men don't have it so good." He opened another sheet and a blanket, handling the bedding with expertise. The firm mattress was transformed into a neat package, the sheet at the corners folded to a perfect forty-five degree angle, the top part, folded back, formed a six inch border over the top edge of the blanket, with all three sides tucked tightly under the mattress. He struck the striped pillow with the side of his hand, pinched the corners together and slipped it into a fresh pillow case. He obviously enjoyed what he was doing.

"Where did you learn to make a bed like that?" Peterson asked, stretching out on his cot, his back against the wall.

"My old man's regular army, stationed at Kessler Field. He's a Tech Sergeant, a mechanic on a B-17. But I've always wanted to be a pilot."

"What's a B-17?" I asked.

Lynch put his hand to his forehead in mock horror. The others looked at me. "What's a B-17?"

"Is that the one with the four engines?" I asked.

"You're kidding, aren't you?"

"No."

"Don't you know anything about aviation?"

"Not much."

"How come you volunteered to become a pilot?"

"I'd like to learn how to fly, and it's the only way I can become an officer without having a college education."

"Well, there's no guarantee any of us'll make pilot," Lynch said. "This is only the beginning. I hear less than one out of ten pass the intelligence and aptitude tests and you haven't even seen an airplane yet. They sign up as many as they can so they'll have plenty left over as navigators, bombadiers, and gunners.

"Did you know that if you don't solo in Primary in less than twelve hours, you're washed out? Only three out of five make it through Primary. And Basic and Advanced are tougher." Lynch wasn't smiling anymore. "I gotta make it. Everytime I think about washing out I get the shits."

"Relax," I smiled. "Take it one step at a time and it won't be so tough."

Suddenly, Foster's broad frame filled the doorway. He looked past me.

"There you are, J.B."

He sat down at the foot of Peterson's cot. I picked up my toilet articles and went to the latrine. When I returned, I found my bed had been made and Foster was lying on top, eyes half closed; a smirk on his face. My valise was on the floor near the doorway. My heart pounded. I clenched my fists and breathed deeply, imagining that the forthcoming tests would put Foster in the infantry digging trenches. One day he would salute me. That made me smile. "*A shtick flaysh mit oygen,*" was all I could think. My father's favorite expression, "a piece of meat with eyes."

I looked to the others. No one spoke. Peterson shrugged and gestured helplessness. Lynch glanced at me, then down at his feet. I picked up my things and took the empty cot next to the door.

Later, I stood alone on the steps outside the barracks in the fading light. It was a bad beginning. I was overreacting. Foster was just a guy with a clumsy sense of humor. My father would have counselled, "More to be gained with sugar than salt. It's a *mitzvah* to show a gentile we don't have horns." I resolved to make friends with Foster before he transferred to the trenches.

"Fred! What in the hell are you doing here?" A uniformed cadet approached. I was startled to hear someone call my first name.

"I'll be damned. Irv Bloch! I thought you were in Kansas."

"Are you a cadet?" my cousin asked.

"Yeah. Arrived today."

"I don't understand. Why did you enlist? You're only twenty. You're not old enough for the draft."

"You enlisted," I said.

"Sure. To avoid the draft."

"Well, anyway. Here I am. If I become a pilot I'll make more money than drawing pictures."

"I can't get over running into you like this. How's the family?"

"Everyone's fine," I lied. My decision to enlist had caused my parents deep and silent suffering, but Dad had accepted the fact there was no alternative. Our country was at war and all able-bodied men must serve. My brother had enlisted in the Air Corps a few months earlier. Mom wanted me to wait. Don't worry, I told her, I promise I'll be careful and I'll never fire a gun. I'll learn how to fly and become an instructor, I had said trying to comfort her.

"And Bob enlisted too," I told Irving. "He's at Scott Field in Illinois training to be a radio operator."

"C'mon with me. Let's have some chow." Irv put his arm around my shoulder.

The food at the mess hall was dished out cafeteria style. We sat on benches away from the others at the end of a long table.

"Are you serious about becoming a pilot?" Irving asked me.

"Very much."

"What kind of pilot? There are all kinds, you know. You could end up flying bombers, fighters, transports, or you could even become an instructor."

"I didn't know I would have a choice."

"In a way you do. What I mean is, you may not become the type of pilot you want, but you don't have to be the kind you don't want to be."

I must have looked puzzled.

"Okay, let's say you're on your way to becoming a bomber pilot and you change your mind. It's easy to wash out. No one will know the difference. There are hundreds of eager beavers right behind you who can't wait to get their asses shot off. So, if it's not you, it'll be someone else."

"Then why did you become a cadet?"

He smiled as though we shared a secret. "Actually, I'm not a cadet anymore. I washed out in Primary." He didn't seem disappointed.

"Since then, I've been in one kind of school or another for the past eighteen months. If I can stay in training long enough, the war will be over." He laughed. "Hell, you're an artist. A real one. You should be painting pictures instead of getting yourself killed."

He looked at me shaking his head. "Freddy, you made a mistake. With a sick father and dependent mother you could have gotten a deferment. Wise up. *Goyim* fight, Jews survive. Take my advice. Put in for a hardship discharge. Who's going to support your folks while you're flying planes?"

"I'll be entitled to dependent's allowance and flight pay," I answered.

"And $10,000 life insurance and free burial. I thought you were a smart kid. If you can't get out, then apply for OCS. Get a stateside assignment, they'll even send you to college. Leave the bravery bullshit for the *goyim*."

I wanted to tell him I was an American, a real American. The country was at war and I would make a damned good pilot. I wanted to fly and I wanted to do it alone. If I had a choice, I would become a fighter pilot. But all I said was, "Thanks for the advice."

We got up to go.

"Don't worry," he said bitterly. "You won't get past basic. Those fly boys have their own club and it's restricted. If you want to become a pilot, change your name. And your nose."

"The hell with all of them, Irv. I'm going to make it."

I awakened abruptly in the middle of the night. The barracks lights glared like spotlights. Someone barked, "Everybody up! Form two lines in front of your bunks. As you are! This is a short arm inspection. NOW! ATTENTION!"

I stood straight, shoulders back, chest out. My pajama bottoms slid to my hip bones. Foster stood opposite me in his shorts and undershirt. Lynch was naked, shivering in the unheated room. I stared straight ahead. A corporal stood in front of the first man while an officer sat on a short white stool. In less than a minute, the officer moved to the next man in line. The corporal moved the stool and the officer sat. This procedure continued until they were within hearing distance.

"Drop your shorts...skin it back, milk it down! Turn around!

Bend over...spread your cheeks!" When it came my turn, the officer said, "Skin it back...oh, one of those...just milk it down!"
Foster looked at my circumcision and whispered hoarsely to J.B.
and Lynch. "Don't let it fool ya. Just because its shortened, doesn't
mean they can't fuck ya."

It was over as quickly as it had started. I slid back under the
covers and tried to go back to sleep, but my head swam with nightmare images of the state mental hospital where I had worked on
special assignment as a newspaper artist. Frail men with senseless
unseeing eyes scrubbed clean, herded naked from the showers,
pushed and prodded by male attendants roughly examining their
private parts. Even the most simple-minded had clutched at his
crotch in a futile gesture of personal dignity.

For several days I didn't see Foster. All new cadets were occupied
eight hours a day with tests. We sat at long tables writing answers to
hundreds of questions, from logic and math to psychology, breaking
for lunch and going until dinner time.

There was one last encounter with Foster before the test scores
were announced, about a week before leaving Santa Ana for
Primary Flight Training.

Lynch and I were assigned to latrine duty. It was a posted rule the
latrines were off limits during the thirty minutes they were being
cleaned. We started at 0530 hosing down the showers and the uri-
nals, wiping the wash basins and mopping the floors. The toilet
stools had to be spotless with the seats up at attention and no finger-
prints on the stainless steel mirrors. We turned off the water supply
beneath each sink, then carefully tapped each faucet with a finger,
removing the last drop of water before turning it on again. Failure
to pass any one of a list of standards brought a penalty of additional
latrine duty.

At 0540, Foster walked in. We had neglected to lock the door.
Lynch blinked and said, "Sorry pal, latrine opens at 0600."

Foster wore a pair of khaki shorts and had a towel draped around
his neck. He was barefoot.

"Only be a minute, buddy," Foster sang out. "Got an early date
with the medics." He walked over to the nearest basin, set out his
toilet articles, and began brushing his teeth.

Lynch watched in disbelief as Foster spit into the freshly cleaned
sink. A surprise inspection could happen any time between 0550
and 0600.

"O.K.! THAT'S IT!" Lynch shrieked. "Get out of here!"

I had finished hosing down the floor and was mopping up, swinging the mop in broad arcs. I wanted to stay out of it. Lynch pressed in front of Foster, gathered the toilet articles and pushed them up against Foster's bare chest. Foster clutched at the items and took a couple of steps backward at the same time my wet mop slid across the floor. Its dirty grey tails sloshed over his bare feet and curled around his left ankle. He whirled around to face me, his razor and tube of shaving cream falling to the floor. He pulled the toothbrush from his mouth and with the back of his hand wiped toothpaste from his lips, his eyes blazing into mine.

"Come on, Foster." I attempted a smile. "You know that was an accident." I tried to draw the mop away, but he stepped on it and moved close to me, his face inches from mine. "You fucking kike!" he hissed, a fine mist of white droplets of toothpaste spraying my face. Rage welled up inside me. "Watch your mouth," I said quietly, and tugged at the mop.

"You gonna do something about my mouth, Jewboy?"

"What's with you guys, ya crazy?" Lynch said.

"You don't like my mouth? Try changing it!" Foster edged still closer. "You fuggin Jew bastard. Go on, do something about it!"

I stepped back and let the mop handle drop. Foster started to dance around, shadow boxing, jabbing just short of hitting me.

"What the hell you guys doing? I'm getting outta here!" Lynch started for the door.

"Don't leave, Lynch. If this tub of shit touches me he washes out." I turned and picked up the mop.

"Smart-ass Jew," he spat. "Yellow son of a bitch!" That was the first time I wished Foster dead.

When the evaluation lists were posted, most of the cadets were assigned to navigator or bombadier training. I qualified for Primary Flight Training. I didn't see Foster's name. The next day my group left Santa Ana on our way to Primary. We marched along the road past the barracks. I turned at the sound of a whistle. Foster was leaning out a second floor window. He pumped a clenched fist at me, center finger extended, his mouth forming the words, "Fuck you, kike." I smiled up at him. He must not have made the assignment to pilot. It didn't surprise me. There couldn't be room enough in a cockpit to fit his fat ass.

5

The Pawn Shop

IN THE WEEKS THAT FOLLOWED, I fell in love with flying. After ten hours of instruction I soloed a Stearman bi-wing open cockpit training plane. It was a whirlwind romance. I flew every day, sometimes with an instructor, most of the time solo, communicating with the elements, feeling the pressures on the stick, the wind against my face, in the company of enthusiastic eager young men. I flew more than one hundred hours the first month.

Many washed-out. Of sixty-four cadets that started, only thirty-two qualified to go on to Basic. We moved to Taft, California and learned to fly a larger single-engine trainer, four and five cadets per flight instructor. Civilians were rapidly transformed into military pilots. Every week there were check rides, the dreaded moment when a supervisory flight inspector flew with the cadet for proficiency evaluation. With them came disappointments and more names posted for reassignment to navigator, bombardier, or gunnery training. Twenty-three men made it to Advanced, and we transferred to Arizona to learn to fly a more powerful trainer, the AT-6.

When our eyes met, Foster looked away first. He had taken his Primary and Basic Flight training elsewhere. Now we were in the same section in Advanced. Almost all our flying was alone, but the rest of the time there was no way to avoid him.

By the week before we were to receive our wings and commissions, our numbers were reduced to twenty-one. Four more times the ax denied coveted pilot status, and boys, newly become men, shed tears. Unfortunately, Foster wasn't among them. During the six months of training, I checked the daily washout list looking only for my name and his.

On October 30, 1942, eight months after enlistment, I received my wings and became a second lieutenant. There were seventeen of us receiving our commissions in the thinned ranks of Section D, class of 42-J, Luke Field, Arizona. Foster was one of them.

Next morning we transferred to Muroc Dry Lake to check out in the hottest fighter plane of the day. I had never seen a P-38, though I had heard about its extraordinary performance. I went straight to the flight line. There were dozens of them, standing proud and beautiful.

The Lockheed Lightning had to have been designed by an artist in love with flying. The training planes I had flown had a single engine. This plane had two enormous engines jutting out from slender booms that tapered into twin rudders. The pilot's plexiglas cockpit sat on top of a streamlined center section, the gondola, which stood almost ten feet off the ground. The pilot used a built-in, retractable ladder at the back of the gondola to reach the cockpit. The wings stretched 52 feet. Liquid-cooled powerful engines converted the nine-ton aircraft into a formidable fighter designed to climb high and fast to intercept enemy bombers. Everything about the plane wanted to fly, except the four machine guns and cannon sticking out the nose.

The first time you flew a P-38, you flew it alone. If your ground instructor lacked confidence in your ability to solo, you washed out and were reassigned. We discovered there was another way to washout, too. The P-38's two engines developed a total of 2650 horse power and if one quit during the critical takeoff run, the young man at the controls, six months removed from civilian life, had two seconds to perform the correct sequence of steps or lose his life. That was a lot of airplane for twenty-year-old kids with only a few hundred flying hours behind them.

I was in line behind Garcia waiting for my first takeoff. My instructor was spreadeagled on the wing, one hand gripping the leading edge, the other the side of my open window, his head bent against the prop wash screaming last-minute orders over the engine roar. For three days I had performed the checkout tech-niques repeatedly, sitting hours blindfolded in the cockpit locating instruments and controls by touch, mentally running through emergency procedures honing my reaction time to seconds. Now he said I was ready.

Garcia's instructor checked that the window was secure, slapped the top of the canopy, and slid off the wing. Garcia rolled onto the pavement, ran the engines up to full power, and his plane leaped down the runway. Garcia's plane climbed less than a hundred feet in the air, banked sharply to the right, rolled into an inverted dive, and crashed in the dry lake.

My instructor shrieked, "Mixture full rich! Pull her off at 120!"

Damn! Images of a toothy grin, jet black hair, and broad Mayan features paraded in front of me. My knees felt weak, my heart pounded. . .O.K., stop it! I don't want to know them or miss them or feel sorry for them or their families. . .

The instructor's fingers clawed at my shoulder. "What the fuck you waiting for? Take off! Go! Go! Go!" he yelled as he slid off the wing and dropped to the ground. I closed the window and pushed the throttles to the firewall.

At 120 mph I pulled back on the controls and flew through a belching column of black smoke that rose like a giant arm with a clenched fist. The odor of burning oil filled my cockpit. I held my breath, pulled the nose of the plane up, and shot away, the picture of the dry lake receding in the background. My body pressed hard against the seat, weighted by the powerful thrust of those massive engines.

During the next two weeks, four more of our original group were killed in training accidents.

There were times at the bulletin board, which we checked daily for aircraft assignments, or standing behind one another in the chow line, inhaling the other's cigarette smoke, when Foster and I almost touched. Instead, we looked pass each other and never spoke. We were seated silently at the same table one evening when the loud speaker blared: "The United States has successfully landed in North Africa with minor casualties. The Vichy French forces have surrendered!"

Cheers resounded through the mess hall, everyone talking at once. Where was North Africa? What did it mean to the overall war effort? Foster pounded the table with delight. I laughed excitedly with those next to me and Foster hooked two fingers in his mouth and whistled. But we carefully avoided each other's eyes.

Everyday we practiced aerial gunnery and formation flying. I wanted to stay there forever: flying, climbing, diving, and cork-screwing through the air, the airplane draped around me like a familiar cashmere sweater, responding as though the controls were linked to my thought centers.

Three weeks later, with forty hours of flight time in a P-38, twelve of us remained of the original seventeen commissions. We were ordered to meet at Union Station in Los Angeles for transfer to Camp Kilmer, New Jersey. No one on board the train knew any-thing about Camp Kilmer except it was in New Jersey, across the river from New York City.

I was glad to see that there were others from the old bunch on the train. When I climbed aboard Foster waved. I raised my hand to wave back, when I realized he was greeting someone behind me. For an instant, my hand froze, then casually I adjusted my cap. Screw you, you no-class *schmuck,* I thought, and turned away.

*   *   *   *

It was January 1943, a few days before my twenty-first birthday. The sentry at the gate to Camp Kilmer checked my orders and directed me to the Commander's office where the duty officer reviewed my papers.

"You're assigned to BOQ 221, Lieutenant."

"What kind of a base is this?" I asked.

He looked at my wings and smiled. "You won't find any planes here. This is the point of departure for overseas assignments. You won't be here long."

"Overseas? Aren't fighter aircraft used to defend the United States?"

"They are, and our front lines stretch from the South Pacific and the Aleutians all the way to England and Africa. Welcome to Camp Kilmer. All transient personnel are restricted to base, passes granted for emergencies only."

Our group of twelve was assigned to the same BOQ. We took rooms according to where we found our foot lockers. The barracks were standard except that each officer had his own cubicle eight feet wide, ten feet deep, with eight-foot partitions and clear space above to the high ceiling of the larger room. Two pot belly stoves, one at each end of the ground floor, barely warmed the area.

My foot locker had suffered badly during shipment and I struggled with a jammed lid and lock. I sensed Foster standing at the open door to my cubicle. What the hell could he want? Was there no chance I'd ever be rid of him? Of all the guys that got killed or washed out in training, how come he had made it? I avoided meeting his eyes, and breathing hard, gave the trunk a well-placed kick.

"That's pretty good," Foster said. "Maybe you can use that technique in combat."

"I don't think you're funny."

"It's not my intention, Finklestein."

"Move on, buster," I said.

"Well now, there's some backbone in the little sheeney."

"I don't like those kind of remarks."

"Anytime you want to do something about it, you know where I live."

I gripped the sides of my foot locker, my eyes squeezed shut, my arms and chest bursting with rage. I heard the click of his heels as he walked down the corridor. Why don't I smash his ugly face?

The morning began with a crowded schedule of seminars, health examinations, lectures about life in the tropics and the Arctic, more immunization shots and reports from American and Allied returnees from different theaters of operation. Using the East Coast as a jumping-off point didn't rule out assignments to Asia or the Pacific. We were subject to twenty-four hour call and required to check the bulletin board regularly in case shipping orders had been cut.

On the outside walls of every building, in the mess hall, in every room and pasted over the stainless steel mirrors in the latrines, large posters and slogans hammered into our subconscious, "A SLIP OF THE LIP CAN SINK A SHIP!" "THE ENEMY IS LISTENING!" A man carrying a stack of lightweight khakis back to his quarters in the clear cold air of early February didn't mean he was headed for the Pacific. Great pains were taken to create deceptions.

It was the morning of the fourth day. I was dressed and had finished making my bed when I heard J.B. shout, "Let's go, guys. Get the lead out!" He went running past my room. "We're going to New York!"

"Yoweee!" Foster yelled. "The old son of a bitch pulled it off!"

I grabbed my gloves, short coat, took a quick look around to see if I had forgotten anything. . .paper, right! Paper and my drawing pencil. I fell in alongside J.B. and we sprinted out of the barracks. Lynch came huffing and puffing behind us. When we reached the camp's western boundary, everyone's breath was coming fast making white plumes in the cold air, like wordless balloons in the Sunday comics.

"Cold as a nun's tit!" Foster forgot his gloves and was blowing on his hands. An enlisted man was waiting for us at the fence.

"O.K. you guys! Here's the deal." J.B. was talking fast. "We can stay together or you can go off on your own. Your choice. But if anyone fouls up, we all get it. Write this number down, MUrray 2-6754. Ask the operator for Kilmer, New Jersey. Keep a pocket full of change. The number you're calling is a public phone booth right here on the base. Get it? The sergeant here is going to see to it that one of his men stands by at the phone booth ten minutes before until ten minutes after every hour for the next twenty-four hours. They'll cover for us and tell us if our orders have been cut. Right, Sergeant?"

"Yes sir!"

J.B. looked at his watch. "That means we're clear until 0900 tomorrow." He caught his breath and looked around, "Guess we'll stay together. It'll make it a lot easier and we can share a cab back."

We slipped through a hole in the fence fifty feet from a main road and jogged a quarter mile to a bus stop, where we caught a ride to the railroad station. I took an aisle seat for a better view of the passengers and sketched rapid impressions of workmen, elderly men and women, children, and young soldiers; the kind of sketches I had done for Mr. Riddle at the Hearst newspapers in Chicago.

*   *   *   *

My first visit to New York was two weeks after I lost my job. I was depressed. My love affair with Bobbie had ended badly. Dad encouraged me to spend a few weeks in New York. "Go! Be free! Try to forget what happened with Bobbie. When you come home you'll see life with new eyes."

I took a Greyhound bus to New York. It was the summer of 1939, six months before Dad got sick. It was an exciting time for a seventeen-year-old boy. I visited the art museums and filled my days with the sights and sounds of New York and the World's Fair. Dad was right, I saw things with new eyes. Riddle had done me a favor. I didn't want to draw for money. I would become a fine artist.

In the fall, I enrolled at the Chicago Art Institute and evening classes at the Academy of Fine Arts. I learned that Bobbie and her family had moved to a suburb. Her mother answered the phone and told me never to call again.

In December, I received a message to call my Uncle Al. My father was employed at Midwest Industries, my uncle's company. He invited me to lunch.

"You're serious about this artist business?"

"Yes sir."

"It's a shame. The family expected big things from you. With your grades, you should have gone on to University, become a lawyer, a doctor. But an artist? That's no way to make a living."

When we finshed lunch, Uncle Al looked at me quietly and said, "Your father's sick."

"Sick? No, he's fine."

"He's sick." His eyes filled with tears. "He's very sick, I know he doesn't look it and I can't explain it, but he won't be able to work much longer." He wiped at his eyes.

"I don't believe it." I felt confused. My father had always been healthy and strong. There must have been some mistake.

"Your mother and brother don't know about it."

"I'll call Doctor Goldman."

"Call Doctor Stone, he'll see you, he'll explain your father's illness."

I called and insisted I be given an appointment within the hour. I didn't have to wait long. The doctor called me in. He was an elderly man; he looked like a business executive.

"I examined your father several times during the past few months. We've made spinal taps and laboratory tests, and I am sorry to tell you that your father is suffering from a disease called Lethargic Encephalitis with Parkinsonian Syndrome. We seldom see this in a thirty-nine year old man. How old are you?"

I was confused.

"How old are you?"

"I'll be eighteen next week."

"What has your uncle told you?"

"He said my father is sick."

"Your uncle asked me to talk to you. It will be your decision whether your father and mother will be told. You have younger brothers and sisters?"

"An older brother."

"Is he in Chicago?"

"Yes, he works for my uncle."

"Then you must tell your brother and decide. Your father has a degenerative illness. It will worsen progressively. It may take months or years. Right now, he tires easily. He finds he must nap every afternoon and go to sleep after dinner. The middle finger of his right hand trembles...he has difficulty controlling his tongue..."

It seemed that two people were talking. Wait, wait, you're adding more words on top of the others, I don't understand, I thought.

"...Saliva is a problem, there will be weight loss in time due to difficulty in eating.

"His jaw will shake, his teeth will chatter, and he will acquire a masklike appearance. Rarely is the mind affected, but he may lose his ability to speak. And with loss of coordination he may be unable to walk without assistance. He may become bedridden. The illness doesn't kill. However, in a weakened condition he will be subject to other illnesses that could kill him. There is no cure for his condition."

"I don't believe it."

The doctor got up from his chair, came around the desk, and stood in front of me. "This is what your father is going to look like."

He allowed both shoulders to sag, one lower than the other, his head, too heavy to hold erect, tipped forward and tilted to one side, the jaw dropped and a thick swollen tongue, drooling saliva, protruded and lay in the corner of his mouth, his eyes rolled in their sockets becoming riveted in a stare, like the mindless creatures at the insane asylum. His arms hung loose, the fingers of both shaking hands whipped in an involuntary tremor, as though examining the texture of material between fingers and thumb, a constant pill rolling action. His body bent stiffly, he began to move, in a shuffling gait, sliding stifflegged in short jerky steps.

I jumped up and screamed, "Stop it, you son of a bitch! I'm going to talk to Doctor Goldman!"

"Doctor Goldman sent your father to me. I'm the neurologist. I'm sorry."

Dad's condition worsened, and in spring of 1941, he had to leave his job with Midwest. He had worked there for fifteen years. He received no severance or disability pay.

My robust, handsome father became a gaunt, tragic, shambles of a man. His beautifully articulate speech was replaced by a heart-rending guttural moan. He learned to communicate by scribing letters with his fingers in the palm of my hand. Intelligent, alert, still with a sense of humor, he would shake his head in disbelief while I supported him in front of the toilet, joking how bad his aim was. He slept most of the time, getting up only for meals. The tremors stopped only when he rested.

Our family savings began to dwindle. I was desperate. Reluctantly, I went to my Uncle Al.

"I need your help," I told him. "Bob is only making $17.00 a week and I have another year to complete my studies at the Institute. We'll need an additional seventy-five dollars a month just to cover the rent until Bob and I are earning more money. Can you help us?"

"Don't worry, Freddy. I have confidence in you. Your father will never starve," Uncle Al said and paid for my lunch. I never asked him for anything again.

Two weeks after Pearl Harbor, I read an advertisement in the paper: "Become a Flying Cadet. Earn $275.00 per month as an officer in the Army Air Corps." I decided to enlist. If I were careful and didn't spend much, there would be enough to take care of the folks.

*   *   *   *

When the train reached Penn station, we chipped in a buck apiece. The conductor converted a dollar to nickels and Lynch made the first call on the hour from a pay station. He was worried and regretted having come along. J.B. conned him into staying with us and made him responsible for the calls. From then on, every few minutes Lynch peeked at his wristwatch like a Boy Scout and made the calls to check our status.

Times Square was cold and empty that Monday morning. The city's breath rose from iron nostrils in manhole covers; automobiles with frosted windows groped their way through light traffic.

Our first stop was at the Automat. Lynch changed a couple of dollars into nickels and, delighted by the mechanical food delivery, he bought more sandwiches than we could eat. Then we trotted down the street, Foster rubbing his hands to keep warm, all of us pausing at colorful window displays until we were corralled outside a 42nd street theater. A thin man with a hairline moustache and skin that matched his grey suit slapped the side of a wood stick against a greater than life-sized poster of a semi-nude woman. J.B. was mesmerized, Foster was counting his money, and Lynch looked as though he had seen an accident.

The thin man made suggestive sucking sounds and, like a tobacco auctioneer, fired an incessant vocal barrage. "Come on, men, only four bits, one half a dollar for a show of a lifetime, gorgeous girls, beauty queens of America, they'll sizzle, razzle-dazzle you, they take it off, you see it all, featuring Carlotta with the biggest pair of attractions north of the border, all in the price of admission, only four bits, don't miss it! A chance of a lifetime, come on, come on, there's a new show starting now, don't go 'way . . ."

"Forget it!" said Lynch, "I'm leaving! See ya back at the base!"

"Wait a minute!" Foster yelled holding his sides in laughter at Lynch's reaction, "Come back with our nickels!" J.B. took off after Lynch. The hawker tugged at Foster's sleeve, "Don't go 'way, I can arrange something special, only five bucks."

"Go on, Foster," I grinned. "Try it, you might like it."

The laughter sucked out of Foster, leaving a thin brittle seam in place of his mouth. He glared at me and spoke without moving his lips.

"Keep your big nose out of this, you little shit." Then he turned to the man and hissed, "Get your fucking hand off me . . ."

The hand recoiled as if it had touched something hot. "Easy fella, just making a living," he said, and slapped the poster, directing a fresh barrage at several approaching sailors.

Ten minutes later, Foster was still in a funk. "Nerve of the son of a bitch! We're putting our asses on the line while he's back here selling cunt!"

"Look, you guys!" Lynch pointed across the street, "A shooting gallery!"

"The prick probably can't get it up," Foster added.

"What d' ya say? Maybe we can win a prize to send home," Lynch pleaded, trying to tease him out of his mood.

"Sure," I said. "Why not? We need the practice."

"It's probably fixed so you can't win," Foster grumbled. "They're waiting for a hillbilly like Lynch to get their hands on his money."

Next to the gallery, three gold balls hung above the entrance to a gloomy little shop. In the window was a wild disarray of shirts, suits, and dresses; strung across the ceiling were guitars, banjos, violins, brass and wind instruments; stacked on tables were a myriad of cameras, tools, kitchen appliances, watches, and jewelry. Each item wore a price tag hand-scrolled in red ink. On the plate glass window, gold block lettering with black shadows to give depth announced, HARRY ROSENTHAL, and beneath in smaller letters, "Pawn Broker, Established 1936." A reflection caught my eye, "Look at that! A hunting knife for $3.99! Can't beat that."

Lynch rubbed the cold window glass for a better view. "Who needs it?"

"You heard what the RAF pilot said at the briefing, that a lot of Spitfire pilots who bailed out over the Channel drowned because they tangled in the shrouds and had no way to cut themselves loose from the harness. Said they now carry a knife strapped to their leg for emergencies."

"What are the chances we'll be flying over water?" Lynch asked.

"You can count on it," I said, "The South Pacific, the Aleutians, the Channel, take your pick. Even the new front in North Africa is on the Mediterranean. What do you say, J.B., should we get one?"

"Naw, something like that ought to be GI issue. Anyway, over land or water what's the difference in a P-38? They still haven't figured out how you can bail out of one."

"What about you guys?" I asked.

"I'll pass," said Lynch.

Foster studied the window. "I don't know. Don't like the looks of the place. You can't trust any of them. They're all a bunch of Shylocks. Tell you what, Kohn. We'll be in the gallery. But if they got two knives, Jew 'em down to three bucks and I'll take one."

I felt the muscles in my neck swell.

"Can't you speak English, Foster?" Lynch said. "You mean 'Chew 'em down.' "

"Yeah? What's the difference?"

Foster, J.B., and Lynch walked off into the shooting gallery. I took deep breaths, feeling the perspiration that had gathered at my collar. I entered the pawn shop.

A bell tinkled above the door. The shop looked like an animal shelter. On both sides wire mesh formed floor to ceiling cages bulging with merchandise. At the end of the corridor, behind a wire screen, sat an elderly gentleman probing the miniscule mechanism of a pocket watch with a pair of tweezers. Long grey curls spiraled down from both sides of a black hat perched at the back of his head.

"Yes?"

"I wish to inquire about the hunting knife in the window."

"There's a price marked?"

"Yes."

"You want to buy it?"

"Yes."

"So? What is the question?"

"Is it possible . . . ? Ah, may I see it?"

"Why not?"

It was the first time the man looked up. He did this without changing the position of his head. Only his eyes moved to see me over the top of a pair of rimless glasses supporting a small magnifying lens.

"Molly?" he said, addressing a small grey-haired woman seated behind him before an open rolltop desk. "Molly, you'll open the window case and bring here a hunting knife, yes?"

The desk was crowded with papers and stacks of file cards. A framed reproduction photo of Roosevelt, chin high, smiled down from the wall above the desk. The woman completed an entry in a narrow ledger, secured the top of a fountain pen, and laid it on the desk. Pressing a buzzer, she pushed through a wire mesh gate that separated their cage from the rest of the small shop. Her slippered feet shuffled across the wooden floor, her small frame bundled in a heavy hand-knitted woolen sweater. An aura of warmth clung to her, followed her, swept across my face. I blew on my hands.

"Cold day, huh?"

"You expect maybe you'll go swimming in February?" she answered, returning with the knife.

I held it, turning it over, and extracted the stainless steel blade from its snug leather case. I was ten years old the last time I handled a knife while playing "territory" with the other boys in the neighborhood. We would hold the blade at its tip, flipping the knife so it would stick into a prescribed square of ground. If the blade stuck in your opponent's land, and three fingers fit under the handle to ensure its proper depth, the "territory" was yours. It became more difficult to hit the target as your opponent's land decreased in size. I was good at the game. But when my father found out about it, he took the knife from me.

I returned the blade to its leather sheath and snapped the strap over the exposed handle.

"Do you have others like this?" I asked the old woman.

"Not exactly. I have others that fold, curve, snap and do fancy things. You want that?"

"No, but $3.99 is more than I wanted to spend." I withdrew a five dollar bill from my wallet.

"Soldier, it's a bargain. Believe me, you won't find a knife like that under five dollars. It was pawned for $3.50. For a soldier? $3.75."

The old man gave me change. "If you told me you would stick it in Hitler's heart I would give it to you for nothing and everything I own."

"Maybe one day it'll happen."

"From your mouth to God's ears. Not in my whole life did I wish harm to anyone, only good things, and now I go to sleep every night with a prayer that that man should be dead. I think of such ways for him to die! First he should suffer . . . ."

"Harry, stop already, stop it!"

" . . . He should stand naked and the dead would form a line around the world and each one would take from his flesh a small piece, a tiny piece . . ." he shook his tweezers.

"My God! Harry!"

I slipped the knife inside my coat and looked at suits and dresses hanging from overhead racks, "You have clothing too, I see."

"Yes," she said, pleased to change the subject, "Everything, but only for ordinary people, nothing for soldiers."

"Do you have a pair of garters?"

"Garters? *Nu?* What is garters?"

"To hold up men's stockings."

"Molly! Suspenders he means, in the box with the belts."

I rummaged through a box of now-ownerless articles, grey spats, socks, a vest without buttons, a collapsible top hat squeezed flat, coils of belts and trouser suspenders, and at the bottom of the box, one black elastic garter with a brass hook fastener. I held it up.

"How much?"

"You found the pair?"

"No, but I'll buy this one."

"Molly, you'll look for the other one."

"It doesn't matter, how much is this one?"

He shrugged his shoulders, "It doesn't matter, he says? The price is the same for one as for two. Is there someone else in this world who will buy the other one?"

"I only need one, but I'll pay for two."

"*Nu?* You got maybe a wooden leg?"

Molly grabbed at her mouth, eyes in shock, "Harry! Don't give a *kenahora!* You should bite your tongue!"

Harry put both hands to his head, tears came to his eyes, "I didn't mean it! My God, what is wrong with me!"

"Hey! C'mon," I consoled. "It's all right." I put the garter in my pocket and the old man gave me fifty cents change for my dollar.

I slipped the garter through the slots of the leather scabbard, adjusted the elastic to fit snugly under my knee, and from then on wore the knife strapped to my right calf under my trousers.

On a shelf above my head, squeezed between a steamer trunk and a suitcase, I recognized the oily veneer and well rubbed surface of an artist's paint box.

"You see something else?" Squinting, he wiped his glasses with a handkerchief as he followed my gaze, "Ah, hah! You know what that is? Let me show you."

"Don't bother."

"Bother? I'm here for some other reason?" He stood on a chair and called, "Molly? You'll take this from me. I want you should show it to the gentleman soldier."

The woman placed the box on the counter and slid the wire mesh screen aside. She fiddled with the center lock.

"Please?" I asked, helping her open the latch. The wood was warm to my touch. Under the lock, on a brass plate, barely legible, were the initials "R.D.M." I pivoted the brass hooks at the sides and carefully, to avoid spilling the contents, lifted the lid. Windsor Newton oils, sable and bristle brushes, a palette and two small blank canvases fitted inside the lid, stainless steel containers with brass caps for oil and turpentine, little metal mixing cups. My hands played over every surface, lightly touching, sensing the artist's loss at parting with this treasure.

I felt the old man's eyes on my face, saw him clearly without the cross-hatched effect of the mesh between us.

"*Landsman?*" he asked.

"Yes."

"Vi heyst ir?"

"Kohn."

"Ah! Co-hen! *Vu ist dayn tate un dayn mame?"*

"Ikh farshtey nit." I laughed, "That's all the yiddish I know."

"Vaze meir, Harry, *a yidisha yingl,* such a pity!"

"How did you know I was Jewish?"

"How do I know? I know. I also know you're not just a soldier, you are an officer! You are also an artist? So, Officer Co-hen, pictures you paint?"

"One day maybe, but now I make drawings."

I took paper scraps from my pockets and shared my drawings with them, as I would have shown them to my parents. With each sketch they laughed or crooned approval.

"My, my, a *mechaieh.* Such a blessing!" the old man said, "A gift from God!" He slapped his hands together, "Wait! I have something! Molly? The large black folder. The man who brought in the paint box? A big envelope, stuffed with many things, where did you put it?"

"Where did I put it? I didn't touch it!"

"Ah! I know where it is!" Again he balanced on the chair.

"The man is *meshuge.* Always it's what did 'I' do with it? Someday he'll lose his head and he'll ask me!"

"Here it is! I put it inside the suitcase to save space. *Nu?* You can use something like this?"

He withdrew four narrow books from the folder and fanned the pages of one, "See, blank, nothing in them. The man who left them, also an artist, made drawings in them."

"How much are they?"

"Does a gift have a price? Take them, *mit guzunt un glik."*

The books were perfect. The texture of the pages would accept pen or pencil and they were the right size to fit the side pocket of my short coat or blouse. I wanted them so badly I couldn't bring myself to protest.

"Nu? You'll come for supper? We're...." The woman's question was interrupted by the door opening, the jangling bell, and a rush of cold air. Lynch stood in the doorway, gasping for breath. "Kohn! Let's go! Foster and J.B. are flagging a taxi. I just got the word, we're shipping out!"

I turned back to the old couple. "Goodby. Thanks for everything."

We touched hands. I cleared my throat. Mr. Rosenthal's face was soft and round. Great tears rolled down his cheeks. Mrs. Rosenthal put one arm around him. She squeezed my hand and with absolute authority announced, "God will protect you!"

6

Atlantic Crossing

ONE O'CLOCK IN THE MORNING. Val-packs and barracks bags marked and stacked in the halls. The barracks grey and silent in the faint light. Shoulders hunched in our short coats, filtering the cold night air through tight nostrils, fitted out with steel helmets, holstered pistols, and bulging knapsacks, we trotted to the opposite end of the base, only the sound of our heels clicking on the pavement.

Twelve of us climbed aboard a solitary railroad car, each taking a wicker seat in the forward part of the empty coach. Dim light reflected against the train's white-washed windows. I was tired, cold, and depressed. I wanted to tell someone, "I'm no soldier, I'm a flyer. I'm something special. The gun at my side is only symbolic. That's not me. I would never use it. I'm an artist."

A severe jolt shuddered through the railroad car, followed by a series of starts and stops and the sound of screeching metal as we gained speed. The track smoothed out and the men settled down, motionless fixtures blending with the train's interior. Lynch slept. Foster slouched in his seat, arms folded across his chest, the tight straps of his helmet forming deep impressions in his plump cheeks.

How could this be happening to me, a helpless shipment, stamped, wrapped, and bound for somewhere unknown? My stomach was tight. How could they sleep? There must be others who felt the confinement, the loss of identity, and wanted to break free of that steel compartment. But I couldn't find an open eye.

I reread the most recent letter from my mother. The news was bad. Caring for dad was wearing her down. But the income from

45

Bob and me was adequate.

"Your father is getting better. Doctor Goldman started him on a new drug and I can see how much it's helping. You be careful. The Lillienthal boy! It's terrible! His mother received word they don't know where he is. How is that possible? If something happens to you it will kill your father. Thank God you're not in the real war. We worry so much about you and Bob. Did you learn how to fly an airplane? Everytime I see an airplane I think of you. Can you get a job flying an airplane near us?"

I wrote, "I can't tell you where I'm going, but I'll be close enough to New York so I can visit Aunt Sylvia and Uncle Sandy. I have an assignment to study flying techniques. It's part of my training to become an instructor."

I could see my father reading the letter and remembered him the day I left Chicago, the tears rolling down his cheeks. But he didn't protest. He hugged and kissed me. His body shook. He whispered he had made a deal with God, his illness in trade for his sons' lives. It was a bargain, he said. He knew it would keep us safe.

The train came to a stop. It was less than an hour since we had left Camp Kilmer. The car stood motionless, wheezing. I opened my sketchbook and quickly traced the tired lines of sleeping faces. I thought of the drawings I had made of Bobbie, of how my father proudly showed them to his friends.

*   *   *   *

My father got me my first job while I was in high school. He arranged an interview for me with George Riddle, Art Director of the Chicago Evening American newspaper. He looked through my portfolio and said he could use a photo retoucher. Retouched prints, he explained, with improved detail and contrast and extraneous background removed would reproduce better on newsprint.

I was eager for the chance to try it. I was assigned to the night shift. For me to be employed at regular wages during a depression was a lucky break my family didn't take for granted.

Early one evening in September, a Hearst executive visited the art room, spent a few minutes with Riddle, then left. A few minutes before the end of my shift I made a sketch of the executive and dropped it on Riddle's desk. The next night Riddle complimented me on getting a good likeness within so short a time. I explained I did it from memory.

"Take a quick look at Sandy and then draw him," he said, pointing toward the porter sweeping up around two vacant drafting tables. I looked hard, snapped my eyes shut recording the picture in my mind and, without looking at him again, sketched a fair likeness.

"Could you do that after several hours?"

"After a day I lose the exact image, but I can draw some scenes of things I've seen months, even years ago," I said.

From then on Riddle gave me special assignments. After school I visited courtrooms and made drawings of defendants, juries, judges, and attorneys. I wasn't pleased with all of the drawings but Riddle was. Anyway, I loved the work. Even the photo retouching became more interesting. He gave me prints that required more artwork than photo improvement. And I liked the newspaper atmosphere. Someday I would be a political cartoonist, I thought, until an incident occurred that ended my newspaper career.

One night Riddle came to me with a special job for the morning edition. He handed me two mounted photos of F.D.R. It was 1939. Roosevelt had beaten Alf Landon so badly in '36 there was talk of his running for an unprecedented third term in '40. Roosevelt had been president since I was ten years old. My parents were Democrats; in our home Roosevelt's name was said with reverence. The anti-Roosevelt attacks by the Hearst editorial staff were considered funny by most of us in the art department.

One photo of Roosevelt showed him seated at his desk in the White House, his head cocked, smiling, and looking at the photographer with eyes twinkling. He appeared neat, strong, and fully in command. The other photo was a long shot, though it was unmistakenly the president, in a wheelchair, pushed by an aide along a ramp into a waiting railroad car. They were followed by another aide carrying a pair of crutches.

"This is the photo we're interested in, Fred," Riddle said pointing at the picture of Roosevelt seated at his desk. "Sharpen it. I want the wrinkles to show."

"Where?" I asked.

"Around his face, the eyes and neck. The clothes too. I want a loose fit around the collar."

I studied the photograph. It was a sharp portrait and would reproduce with very little retouching. Riddle knew that. He took on a quiet, confidential tone, "You notice the wheelchair, and the crutches in the other photo? It's well known he sits at his desk in a wheelchair, and it wouldn't be all that unusual to see the brake release sticking out. You can get that in right behind the elbow and, if possible, a suggestion of those crutches leaning against the wall." He paused. I kept my eyes on the photographs in front of me. "A little more shadow under the eyes. Boy, they must have doctored him up pretty good for this photo. Soon as possible, Fred. Need it within the hour."

I liked Riddle. I owed him for his many kindnesses. He got me a nickel an hour raise without my asking for it. He gave me my big chance. I looked up and said, "I can't do that."

"Sure you can, Fred, you have the touch."

"No, Mr. Riddle, I won't do that."

His expression didn't change. He shrugged, scooped up the photos, and walked away. That night he fired me.

*   *   *   *

Somewhere forward a door banged open and someone yelled, "Everybody out!" We clambered down the steps, up a loading ramp, and onto the deck of a steamship.

Naval officers at the top of the gang plank checked a roster and quickly assigned each of us deck location and quarters.

"BR fourteen, for'ard, tell the man," he whispered. And when I reached a hooded merchantman thirty feet down the rail, I whispered, "BR fourteen?" He pointed to a brass plate above a door. I stumbled over the high threshold into darkness, holding a door ajar trying to accustom my eyes.

"Close the fucking door!" someone growled from within.

I stepped in and the spring-loaded door slammed shut. Instantly there was a blaze of light. The room was filled with cots supported by iron pipe, stacked three deep, double rows with barely enough aisle to squeeze through. Partially clothed men lay in bunks, inches between their bodies and the bulging bottoms of the canvas bunk above. Others crammed the aisles in various stages of undress. It smelled like a locker room. There was some mistake. This couldn't be the officers' quarters, I thought.

The door opened again and the lights went out. A blast of fresh cold air swept past. The outline of two men, framed in the opening, stood as I had a moment before, peering into the darkness.

"Come on it and shut the fucking door!" came the chorus.

Once in the light, Lynch and Foster stood, awkward and bewildered. "Jesus, Kohn," Lynch said. "Is this BR fourteen?"

A stocky balding man answered, "What'd you expect, the Waldorf? This is the *USS Susan B. Anthony* and you're in her hole." Matted black hair covered his shoulders, arms, and the back of his neck above his khaki undershirt. "There are only three empty bunks in the back, so there'd better not be any more o' you guys. Air Corps, huh?" he added, shouting to the others, "Start the war, men, the flyboys are here." Several voices chanted, "Off we fly, into a wild blue asshole, climbing high, into the bun . . ."

"Any you guys know how to swim?"

"Who gives a shit about swimmin'. I want wimmin'," someone called out.

Silver bars on a shirt draped over a cot caught my eye. Other insignia on coats and caps and painted on steel helmets verified their ranks and corps. They were all officers—commanders of tanks, infantry, signal corps, engineers—sixty men crowded in a space twenty by twenty. Lieutenants to Captains, unshaven old men over thirty. We took the three remaining bunks, so close to the ceiling, we had to sit bent over to avoid hitting our heads.

"Bill, how long you say it's been since we had a piece o' ass?" asked the stocky man carpeted with hair, talking to a man in a lower bunk. "Now take these here flyboys, they got the life. Don't roast in no black iron mother fucking Sherman tank. And how about the girls? They get it anytime they want. That's a fact, isn't it?" he turned to Foster.

"Come on now. The truth. Flyin' an fuggin', flyin' and fuggin', all day and everyday, right? Which do you like best, or are you old enough to know the difference?"

"And we use a joy stick for both." Foster beamed.

Whoops and hollers broke out.

"You got it good, sonny, but you haven't lived 'til you've had a piece of black Georgia cunt, charcoal on the outside and rare on the inside," he drawled.

I could see the blush rising on Lynch's smooth cheeks. I gripped the sides of my cot. Lynch stared at me, his eyes wide. I only smiled and shook my head.

The ship rolled slightly and creaked with sounds of movement. We were on our way.

A speaker blared, "NOW HERE THIS! NOW HEAR THIS! All hands go below! Repeat! All hands below! All decks topside are off limits. The smoking lamp is out."

I slept in my clothes and was awakened in the morning by the speaker's next announcement. B Deck breakfast lines would form 0645 at the forward galley. The ship rolled gently and steadily. Foster's bunk was already empty. Lynch and I dressed for breakfast, pinks and blouses, fresh and smart, feeling like gentlemen in the midst of these rough, loud infantry officers.

The cafeteria line moved slowly past a stack of trays and utensils, and we picked up real eggs and bacon, bread and jam, fried potatoes, and cups of coffee. There was no shortage of fresh meat and the food looked professionally prepared. Lynch and I filled our trays and joined Foster at a table next to six Army nurses. A signal corps officer across the room shouted, "You guys old enough to have a driver's license?" The women smiled at us sympathetically.

I exchanged glances with the most attractive girl and simulated a bow. She was a sport. She batted her eyelashes and smiled coquettishly.

"NOW HEAR THIS! NOW HEAR THIS! Life jackets must be worn at all times outside sleeping quarters. No exceptions! Three long blasts of the ship's horn is boat drill. Continuous blasts is the real thing! Check the bulletins on your deck for important information."

I studied her face while she sipped coffee and talked to the other nurses. I traced mental pictures, watching the way she moved her mouth and laughed and wet her lips as she chewed. I drank in her neatly pressed and pleated blouse, her cap folded and slipped beneath the strap of an epaulette. She saw me watching her. For a moment we looked at each other and I knew I had not intruded.

She returned to her conversation and I contemplated the food on my plate. I looked up again. Pretty girl, cheeks flushed from the warmth of the dining hall, small, shorter than the others, and she caught my inquiring eyes and we smiled.

When the nurses stood and collected their things, I stood too. "Where to, Kohn?" Lynch asked.

"Going to check the bulletin board."

"Good idea. Let's go, Foster," Lynch said.

I timed my exit to fall in behind the pretty nurse and followed her into the corridor. We joined a group of officers crowding around a cork board tacked with dozens of mimeo sheets. I stood directly behind her and I knew she knew I was there. Others coming out of the mess hall jammed in, pushing close for a better view of the notices. My legs pressed against her warm buttocks. "Excuse me," I said, wanting her to know it was unintentional. She said nothing, nor did she move forward. We stood motionless, our bodies touching, listening to the man closest to the bulletin board call out dining hours, orders against smoking or striking matches on deck at night, the risk of submarine attack. I felt a warmth and stirring in me as her buttocks touched me lightly and intermittently, contouring my belly and thighs. Could it be she felt nothing under her heavy gabardine skirt?

"Here's good news," the man continued, "we're a part of a large convoy with a Naval escort of cruisers and destroyers, throw nothing overboard, check the lifeboat chart for the location of your station, the seamen on board are merchantmen not subject to military authority, we are guests and our cooperation is mandatory . . ." My nose touched wisps of hair, breathed her sexuality. I could turn my head and let my lips graze the delicate convolutions of her ear. She turned her head slightly. We were cheek to cheek, sensations of our skin touching. "Anyone, officer or enlisted, found away from his quarters not wearing a life jacket will be put on report."

"Can you see our station, Kohn?" Lynch asked.

"No," I breathed into her ear, close as pressing bodies in a crowded subway.

"Who cares?" Foster said. "If this old tub gets hit, she'll go down faster than a two-bit whore. Whoops, sorry girls."

"Can you see your station?" I asked the girl.

"No, I've never been able to figure out maps and diagrams. What's your name?"

"Fred . . ."

"Freddie Finklestein," Foster laughed and punched Lynch's arm.

"And yours?" I asked the girl, ignoring Foster.

"Peggy Winfield." An almost imperceptible movement, her back and shoulder cradled against my chest, the minute hairs on my cheeks reached out for her.

I suggested we get our coats and life jackets and take a walk around the block. She quickly agreed. We met on the top deck. Our ship was out of sight of land; but we could see the rest of the convoy. Four freighters kept pace with us on the port side, and on the starboard we counted six more ships, including a sleek cruiser. A flock of sea gulls swooped after us, diving into our wake.

"Do you think eleven ships is a big convoy?" Peggy asked.

"I think speed is more important than size," I answered. We leaned on the rail and watched the grey water race past.

"I can't get it out of my head there may be a submarine down there with men inside, watching us," she said. "I couldn't sleep last night."

"We're well protected," I said. "Come on, we haven't been around the block yet."

The outside deck came to an end at a heavy bulkhead. The windows facing front were smeared with salt spray, distorting the deck below and the view of the sea. Five P-38's were lashed to the deck, their outboard wings protruding beyond the sides of the ship, suspended over the onrushing sea as if flying in formation. I wondered if one of them would be mine.

"Are those your airplanes?"

"That's the type we fly. I didn't know they'd be shipped with us."

"Let's go below for a better view," Peggy said. The bulky lifejackets strapped over our heavy coats restricted our movements. We bumped into walls and jostled each other as we made our way, laughing, to the outside cargo deck.

We stood alongside the tail of a P-38. Canvas covered the cargo hatches, but the planes were exposed to the elements, and the plexiglas canopies glistened from the salt spray. Each bore the new Air Corps insignia, a white star with the former red dot deleted to avoid confusion with the Japanese emblem of the rising sun. Peggy noticed the last four digits of a long serial number stenciled on the rudder, 1918, the year she was born. She was twenty-five, I calculated quickly, an older woman.

She took a long look at the P-38's and said, "There's room for only one person in that plane! Do you mean you're in there all alone? I had no idea! I thought there was a crew."

"You're thinking of bombers," I added authoritatively.

A few seconds later, the horn for the boat drill blasted. Lifejacketed enlisted men, up from below decks, swarmed to their stations, some staring in awe at the sight of a woman. We ran to the gangway and, hollering over shattering blasts from the horn, agreed to meet at noon.

Lunch was a frustration. Life-jackets and food trays conspired to keep us apart. Nurses and pilots shared the same table and Foster managed to squeeze next to Peggy. I sat opposite her, too far away to press her knee with mine or to hold her attention. I continually lost the meaning of the conversation, examining her lips as she talked to other nurses at our table, fascinated by the movement of her nostrils and the tip of her nose when she smiled. I imagined her body beneath the heavy uniform, and I traced the lines of her small breasts, narrow waist, and the slight indentations below her hip bones. I had to readjust my trousers to allow for the expansion that crept down my thigh. I didn't want to draw her, I wanted to touch her. She seemed to have forgotten I was there.

"What do you think, Fred?" a nurse said.

"Who, me?" I asked, looking at Peggy, trying to recapture the end of the conversation, something about doctors, not flattering, "Well, I couldn't say."

"You're too nice, Fred. They're a bore and preoccupied with their own importance."

"Yeah, Kohn," said Foster, "just like someone else I know."

"Is your name Kohn, or Finklestein?" Peggy asked.

"Kohn."

"Why does he call you Finklestein?"

"That's his way of letting you know I'm Jewish."

I didn't see Peggy that afternoon and missed her again at dinner. Later I saw her and another nurse standing in the corridor.

"I looked for you," I said.

"Martha and I explored the ship all afternoon and had a tour of the bridge. It's fascinating. We ate early. Want to come along for a walk?"

"Count me out, I'm bushed," Martha said.

I followed Peggy onto the deck. It was cold and dark and the horizon was lost. No lights, no sign of other ships. I gradually made out the figure of an officer walking toward us. He saluted.

"Careful, you guys. It's dark and you're alone out here. Don't strike a light." He wore a belt and side arms and an armband with the letters "O.D." "Sorry, ma'am, thought you were one of the fellows," he added.

"We'll be careful, Lieutenant." I replied.

Peggy laughed and took my arm. The Officer of the Day continued his tour and we walked in the dark to the end of the deck, where we huddled in a corner at the rail, sheltered from the wind by the forward bulkhead. I warmed Peggy's hand in mine and pressed my thigh against hers. She didn't object. We looked down at swirling foam on the black seas, then our heads turned toward each other, and we kissed and embraced, held apart by the cumbersome jackets. I grabbed her hips, pulling her close, and with my free hand tugged at the string ties of our jackets, opening the fronts so our uniformed bodies could touch.

We pressed with open mouths and held each other tightly, and then it wasn't enough and my hands raised her skirt and went further. She leaned back against the steel wall and encircled my thighs with her leg. I fumbled with my trousers and suddenly stopped. "Freddy," my father said, "a man has two heads but only one with brains." Peggy felt my hesitation, "It's all right, it's all right," she breathed in my ear and reached down, directing my eager, mindless, penis until it slipped deep inside her. Then I didn't hear the ocean or see the black water or flashing images of fighter planes lashed to the deck. Apprehension and fear washed from the canvas of my brain.

Afterward I felt the cold and pulled her skirt down to cover her exposed legs. I led her through the bulkhead door into a sheltered lookout station where it was warm and secluded. I drew her down on the floor where we cradled each other, rocking gently with the ship's movements.

*   *   *   *

Even at 0530 there was a long line for the washroom, and it was 0615 when I entered the dining room. J.B., Foster, Layton, and Wagner were already eating.

"Hey there, you seen Lynch? What happened to you guys?" J.B. asked me.

"He's still in the sack. We've got the executive suite next to the Captain," I answered.

"I'll bet. Six of us are jammed in a stateroom that'd be tight for one. Great chow, huh? Here, we'll make room for you."

"No thanks, I'm waiting for someone." The blackout curtains were open to a clear view of the horizon. Layton was talking. "Foster says there are broads on the ship."

"Tell 'em, Kohn. You've been sniffing after one of them since we came on board," Foster said.

"What are they, Foster, WAC's?" Layton asked.

"You better believe it. Wide asses and cunt."

J.B. shook his head. "Any you guys taking bets we're going to the South Pacific? Gotta be. That's where the action is. If it was England, we'd have flown our planes across. Besides, we've been on a course due south toward the Panama Canal."

"Doesn't mean a thing," said Wagner. "Could be we're sailing in the wrong direction just to fool any subs that may be in the area."

"Looky, looky!" Foster interrupted. "Didn't I tell you? Look at the wing span on the little one."

Peggy and Martha approached and stopped at our table.

"Gentlemen," I said. "May I present Lieutenants Krasner and Winfield, Army nurses." All four men jumped at the same time, sending one of the benches crashing. Layton's cheeks bulged with his last mouthful, and a strip of bacon fell from his fork to the floor.

"Lieutenant, sir, excuse me, ma'am," J.B. spluttered. "Why don't you join us? Plenty of room."

"Thanks, but we don't want to crowd you," I said, taking Peggy's elbow and ushering her to an empty table. J.B. followed with his tray and sat alongside Martha, opposite Peggy and me.

"How do you become an Army nurse?" he asked, nervously toying with his coffee.

"For us it was easy. We were nurses and the Army gave us direct commissions," Martha answered smoothly. I noticed she looked older than Peggy. She wore her hair in a bun, glasses, no makeup. Even next to J.B. she looked matronly. He was the oldest of our bunch, twenty-four. Did I look so young next to Peggy, I wondered. Martha and J.B. were still talking when Peggy and I finished breakfast and left the dining room.

Peggy remembered the right doors to get us below. We followed ladderlike steel steps a deck at a time into the engine room, passing behind a blue-shirted seaman scanning pressure gauges and recording numbers on a clipboard. The noise level from giant pistons and generators, roaring oil furnaces and hissing valves made talk impossible. We walked across slippery steel plates and into another section of the hold.

"This is as far as I went yesterday," Peggy said. "Did you have any idea all this was down here? Scary, isn't it? Look down."

We seemed to be in the very belly of the ship, looking down an unobstructed shaft to the ship's keel 50 feet below, sloshing with oily bilge water, shielded from the throbbing beat of the ship's engine. I imagined that split second after a torpedo ruptured our ship's side, it's explosion time-delayed to allow greater penetration, the missile's wet steel head stuck like a plug in a cask a moment before it blew, while we rode, lambs to slaughter.

I felt giddy. Peggy had stiffened slightly with fear. I put my arms around her, my life jacket tight against her back, and squeezed her hands around the rail, my lips grazing the back of her neck.

Peggy leaned forward, gripping the rail, her legs parted and stable. My hands and fingers followed the contours of her buttocks, gathering fabric and lifting her skirt until I felt bare flesh. She rose on her toes and I pressed into her, my fears surrendering to physical contact.

By the morning of the fourth day at sea, our convoy had more than doubled in size and we were heading east. It was a bright cloudless day and I counted twenty-eight transports and two destroyers. During the night, the ship pitched and rolled, and in those moments when the bow rose, both ship and men groaned, waiting for the nose to drop again. Inside it was stuffy and dark. The men suffered. So far, I was still O.K.

After breakfast, I climbed to the top deck and joined Lynch, J.B., and Foster. Unable to tolerate the closeness below, they lay stretched out on the deck, wrapped in blankets, faces raised to catch the sun's rays. I sat with my back against a ventilator and a blanket over my legs while I sketched a transport on our port side. Peggy and Martha approached us.

"You fellows feeling all right?" Peggy asked. "I notice those big strong infantry types didn't show for breakfast. Brrrr, it's cold."

Foster pulled down a corner of his blanket and made a sucking sound. "Slip right in. I'll warm you up."

"No thanks," she laughed at him. "I'll get in with 'Finklestein.' Didn't you know the Jews were the chosen people?" She slid under my blanket, tucked the end under her legs, and snuggled close.

"Did you do that?" she asked, appraising my sketch of the transport. "That's a gift. I can't draw a straight line. Draw me, will you?"

"Sorry, I don't draw pictures of people I like. It never comes out right," I said. The ship rolled. Martha grabbed a rail.

"This isn't funny. It must be terrible for the men below. Maybe we can help?" Martha said.

"You gotta be kidding," Peggy pinched her nose. "It's contagious. By now they're all puking."

The rolling and pitching took on a predictable cadence. The *Susan B. Anthony* climbed up and slid down the giant swells of the North Atlantic while cold air swept across our bundled bodies.

"Kohn," Lynch hollered, "Almost forgot, you've been posted for O.D. You start at noon tomorrow for twenty-four hour duty. Better check the board."

The swells were worse during the afternoon. The ship rolled frighteningly, her decks dipping almost to the sea, the bow digging deep, cascading tons of grey water over the forward decks, leaving every exposed surface gleaming from salt spray. Peggy and I made short running bursts along corridors to the dining room, grabbing at pillars and railings for support. Only a handful of pilots and nurses showed for dinner. We slid onto a bench at an empty table bolted to the floor and poured water on the tablecloth to keep the plates and utensils from sliding off. We picked at the food and talked about our families, speculated about the ship's destination and how long the war would last. I said things to her I couldn't say to the men, about my fears of the war and the role I would play in it, my father's illness, my crushed dreams of completing my studies at the Art Institute.

"When the war's over," she said, "I'd like to go back to school, maybe become a doctor, do research. I'm not that keen on people. There aren't that many I like."

I thought about that. I didn't have many friends either. I had never considered that a woman, too, could be a loner. After we ate, we stretched out on benches and through the night drifted in and out of sleep while the ship rolled.

In the morning, the ship looked deserted, the decks and halls empty. A few minutes before noon I found the O.D., an Infantry First Lieutenant, leaning against the wall next to the bulletin board, holding his stomach. He had already removed the armband, belt, and pistol, and pulled a card from his breast pocket.

"Sure glad you weren't late. Stop at all the places marked with a red dot, 'specially the cargo holds. You're on until 1200 tomorrow, and if you want to get any shuteye, just let the bridge know where you are in case you're needed. It's a joke. The merchant marines have their own sentries. Half our men that are supposed to be on watch aren't there. As far as I'm concerned, I don't give a shit." He hurried off holding his hand against his mouth.

Peggy joined me and we made the rounds from bow to fantail, from bridge to engine room. At a checkpoint marked on the ship's diagram, she waited while I opened a hatch and stepped down a gangway expecting to enter the cargo holds. Instead, I went from cold fresh air into the thick, overwhelming stench of vomit. When my eyes adjusted to the darkness below, I saw row upon row of servicemen, hundreds of them, crowded onto tiers of narrow bunks, comatose from exhaustion and seasickness. They were the cargo. I retreated up the steps, past Peggy, gasping for air, lurching for the rail. I hung over it and heaved.

During the days that followed, I lay on a pile of blankets on the deck below the bridge, sucking in great quantities of fresh air. Peggy brought me tea and teased that if I lost any more weight I would weigh less than she did.

We were on deck at midnight after nine days at sea when we passed through the Straights of Gibraltar. That was the first moment we knew our destination was North Africa.

"You're a wonderful person, Peg."

"Yeah, a real Florence Nightingale."

I took her hand. "You know what I mean. You're the only thing that's real. Do you understand?"

"Did it ever occur to you, I needed you too?"

"Maybe there's a way we can stay in touch? I have an aunt in New York. She could forward our letters?"

Peggy smiled and touched my cheek. "You're sweet. When we dock in the morning I have to be with my outfit. Let's say goodbye now, Fred. Haven't you heard of shipboard romances? Well, we've had one. You know we're never going to see one another again. I'll probably be stationed in a hospital far from the fighting. But that airplane of yours looks like one big gun to me. If we agreed to write and you forgot or couldn't, I'd think you had been killed. No thanks. I want to go on thinking of you alive and well." She kissed my forehead and we held each other.

Once we docked, I never saw Peggy again.

7

No Turning Back

"NOW HEAR THIS! NOW HEAR THIS! ALL PERSONNEL REPORT TO THEIR COMMAND FOR IMMEDIATE DEBARKATION!"

Four loud blasts from the ship's horn sent hundreds of sea gulls screaming into a curtain of grey drizzle that hung from the morning sky. The bustling Port of Oran, Algeria looked like the New York waterfront.

On the cargo deck, a great crane fastened quickly to a sling cradling a P-38 and swung the plane into the air. My purpose was once again brutally clear.

On the dock, a troop truck waited just long enough for us to identify our gear, and then we took off in a roar of shifting gears. The truck traveled northeast on narrow roads alongside fertile farmlands and tiny villages. Several hours later we arrived in the coastal city of Mustagonem. The Army had appropriated a few dozen villas facing the sea for officers' quarters. J.B., Layton, Wagner, and I took cots on the enclosed porch of a weather-beaten summer cottage. Curtiss, Anderson, and Elkhorn grabbed the cots in the unfurnished living room, and Foster and Lynch went up to the second floor.

Within thirty minutes after our arrival, barely enough time to unpack, we were ordered to stand retreat. We fell in before a handful of administrative officers and enlisted staff while the flag was lowered against a background of bugle noise. The regular Army brass stood cast in a brace, shoulders squared, eyes fixed on the flag, holding a salute at the approved angle. In marked contrast, the pilots slouched, wearing a haphazard mixture of uniform parts, leather and sheepskin flying caps, trousers tucked into socks that drooped over bulkly flying boots. We hadn't stood reveille or retreat since we were cadets, and our appearances and attitude were calculated to convey guts and talent. We gloated that we were Air Corps and not Army.

The flag was lowered and we were dismissed. Falzone, Cominski, and Smith, who were commissioned with us, were there. They were always together. We called them the three musketeers.

"Hey, Falzone," Foster jabbed, as though to hit him, "Thought you joined the Italian Air Force. Where the hell are we?"

"Used to be a resort for rich Europeans."

"Bet Kohn's old man is real rich. Diamond merchant maybe. Or furs. His folks probably come here every winter."

Falzone sighed. "You guys still at it? Why don't you save it for the real war?"

"Where is the fighting? What are we doing here?" J.B. asked.

Cominski lit a cigarette. "The front's hundreds of miles to the east, in Tunisia. I heard we're getting the shit knocked out of us at a place called Kasserine. We don't join a combat squadron from here. We get checked out in formation flying first somewhere in Morocco. It'll be weeks before you see action."

Good, I thought. I'm in no hurry.

It was a bright morning, the first time the sun had pierced the clouds, and I skipped breakfast and went for a walk. Waves broke on the beach and the receding water left the hard brown sand flat and shiny. Abandoned villas were boarded and shuttered for the winter. Scattered driftwood and piles of seaweed formed skirts around their foundations. Farther west the shore took a sharp turn and I came upon two men busily loading nets onto a brightly colored fishing boat. They raised their heads in a friendly nod. The boat was close to shore, flapping a ragged grey sail. The gunwale dipped in and out of the water. I scooped a handful of worn stones and sat on the sand next to the rotting ribs of an old scow to watch the fishermen.

*   *   *   *

It could have been Lake Michigan, the swells and white caps, the bleached decaying wood of the boathouse, scenes of endless fascination for a skinny five-year-old who raced a half block to the beach every morning, winter and summer, to watch an eight-man crew put out in their long boat.

"Promise you will stand right here."

"Yes, daddy."

"Don't go near the water and if you get too cold, go home."

"Yes, daddy."

"And you must be home in time for lunch."

"Yes, daddy."

"That's a promise?"

"I promise."

"Shake my hand, no, not with your glove on. It is not polite to shake hands with your glove on. Good! That's better, now put your glove back on. We've made a deal."

I would watch, bundled and mittened, wearing a woolen cap and ear muffs and a muffler turned twice around my neck and knotted, while the men dragged the boat from the boathouse, its weight breaking the thin ice covering the sand. They waded in hip-high rubber boots, pushing their boat into the lake. At a precise instant during the momentary calm between the swells, they would climb in, holding their oars almost vertical until the next swell hit. The boat would stand on end and, as the nose began to drop, the oars came down digging deep and powerful, fiercely beating white water.

Sometimes they made no headway, other times the boat was picked up by rough waves and smashed onto shore, but they never failed to break through and row out into the open lake. They were glorious strong men in their shining black boots and slickers, their wide-brimmed yellow rain hats buttoned beneath their chins. Once I felt warm pee dripping down my leg in my excitement.

It was long past the time I was supposed to be home for lunch. When I got there, no one was home. I let myself in and stood in the empty apartment, staring at the cream cheese and jelly sandwich waiting for me on the dining room table, neatly wrapped in wax paper. The key turned in the door, there was a pause, my mother would have seen my beach shoes at the threshold. The door opened.

"Where have you been? I'm crazy with worry. I've looked all over the neighborhood. Why do you do this to me?" She ran past me into her bedroom, her eyes puffed and swollen, and slammed the bedroom door. For a long time I heard her crying.

At the dinner table that night, Bob hissed under his breath, "Boy, are you gonna get it!"

We ate in silence, and later my father patted my mother, "Now, now, Idele. He's a little boy, it's normal to forget."

Dad came to me when I was in bed, "Freddy, Freddy, Freddy. You made a promise. You gave your word. When you break your word you bring shame on your name and dishonor your mother and father."

         *   *   *   *

Wind filled the sail, the fisherman bent beneath the swinging boom, and the squat boat bounced toward dark blue waters. I walked along the shoreline, skimming flat stones into oncoming whitecaps. A steep rise in terrain and jagged boulders diverted my path to the road that led into the village of Mustagonem. A shopkeeper nodded greetings from his doorway; an elderly man touched the brim of his hat as he cycled past. Soon several curious youngsters tagged behind me, laughing and shouting.

I chose a stone bench circling a fountain and sat down, intending to sketch. The children crowded close, speaking rapidly.

"Vous êtes Américain, oui?"

"Oui, Américain," I answered. They laughed.

"Vous êtes pilote?"

"Qu'est-ce que le mot 'Pee-lote'?" I said.

A swarthy boy with jet black hair pointed to the wings on my breast pocket.

"Pee-lote, avion."

He stretched out his arms and zoomed in a circle, joined by others flapping their arms and making engine noises. I laughed, told them I was a pilot, and put a cigarette to my mouth. In an instant a dozen brown arms shot out, *"Cigarette? Cigarette?"*

"C'mon, you kids are too young to smoke!" I reached for my sketch pad, shook my head, and searched the square for a scene to capture. Not far from us, a uniformed gendarme and two middle-aged men stood talking. The policeman carried a hard wooden nightstick tucked under his arm. A perfect subject, but the children pressed too close, jumping on the bench, chasing each other, imitating the sound of machine gun fire.

A dark little boy, the same age as the others, watched from a distance. Bashful, I thought. I flipped the pages of my sketch book. The children crowded to see the drawings and they laughed. The dark little boy seemed so lonely I waved to him to join us. He started to approach, then stopped. I waved again. Finally, he stepped toward us, but the children yelled something at him, and when he didn't immediately withdraw, two boys shoved him. He retreated behind an invisible line, a distance acceptable to the others. I tried to see him, but my view was blocked by bouncing heads clamoring for attention. I beckoned for the boy to come closer. He tried, and again the others set up a howl and raised threatening fists. He stopped.

I raised a hand to the gendarme. He stopped his conversation and came quickly, rapping his stick against the bench to scatter the children. He touched his cap with a two-finger salute, *"Service, Monsieur."*

"No, it's O.K.," I said, waving the children to come close again. *"Bons enfants,"* I said, words dredged up from my high-school French. The children returned and I pointed to the lonely sentry beyond the group, trying to understand why the boy was being ostracized, and asked the gendarme, *"Voulez-vous demander . . .* the little boy . . . *le jeune garçon."*

The gendarme gestured in protest and crinkled his nose as if there were a bad odor.

"Sorry, sorry," I said, thinking the boy must have something contagious. Indeed, some of the boys had open sores, flies walked across their desensitized faces and eyes. I thought of my yellow fever and cholera shots, *"Merci, merci,"* I said, *Je comprends, malade."*

He laughed, *"Oui, oui, malade. Juif!"*

"Shoe-eef?" I repeated, *"Non comprends 'shoe-eef'"*

He took me by the shoulders so I could watch his mouth slowly form the word, *"Ju-if, Ju-if."* I didn't understand. He pointed to a shop window in the shadows across the square, *"Voilà! Juif!"* I saw a vandal's smeared yellow star of David painted on the window.

"Oh, Jewish!"

"Oui, Juif!"

The gendarme laughed, the children giggled, and I nodded and smiled thinly while the children nagged the little boy, *"Juif! Juif!"*

I motioned again to the little boy to come close. He stood his ground. The gendarme clapped his hands, said something in an authoritarian tone, and the dark-skinned little boy lowered his eyes and approached. The children opened a path and then closed in behind, leaving him no chance for retreat. He stared at his feet.

"Comment vous-appelez vous?" I asked. No answer.

I squatted in front of him trying to get him to look me in the eyes, and again I asked his name. The gendarme held up his hands to quiet the giggling children and bent close so as not to miss anything.

"Vous Juif?" I asked. I heard the children breathing.

The little boy showed me his brown face, *"Oui, Juif."* Snickers danced through the group.

I tapped a finger against my chest, *"Moi Juif."*

His expression remained unchanged. I tapped his chest then mine, *"Juif! Shalom!"*

His little finger almost touched my nose, *"Vous Juif?"* I put my arms around him. We held each other and laughed and the children laughed and the gendarme patted the little boy on the head and laughed and said, *"Juif, bon juif."*

*　　*　　*　　*

J.B. met me at the entrance of the cottage. "We got our assignment!"

"Where to?"

"Boy, were we lucky! Elliot Roosevelt's Photo Recon outfit!"

"What's photo recon?"

"They posted it on the board less than an hour ago. They want five volunteers. I couldn't find you guys, but Layton and I are on the list. So if you're interested, make up your mind fast."

"What is it?"

"P-38's. No guns, just cameras. You fly high and alone, too high for flak and too fast to be intercepted, and the C.O.'s Roosevelt's son, a chicken colonel!"

"Sounds great! Any room left?"

"I dunno, you better move."

I ran to operations, searched the board, and found a small notice in the upper righthand corner where I saw J.B.'s name and Layton's. There were two more names I didn't know. I added my name fifth and last on the list. Later, I went to the mess hall.

I could hear Foster all the way from the steam table.

"Gotta hand it to you guys, you're really something. A bunch of fucking photographers!"

"Sorry, Foster, we looked for you," Layton grinned.

"Kiss my ass. Snapping pictures ain't my idea of fighting a war. If you guys wanted a gravy ride, how come you didn't join the Navy?"

I stepped over the bench and slid my tray next to Curtiss. Foster jerked his thumb toward me, "And here's another great Kodak warrior, gonna win the war by taking Hitler's picture. I expected Kohn to chicken out, but not you guys."

I thought of the gendarme, the little boy in Mustagonem. I pounded the table and glared at Foster, "Not another word, you son of a bitch!"

Foster grinned, "Going to stop me, you Jew bast . . ." I leaned across the table and punched him hard in the mouth. Foster jumped up, overturning the bench, eyes bulging, "I'm going to bust your ass!"

Layton and Wagner grabbed Foster's arms and held him back. Falzone ran over from another table and pushed me out of the way. "What in the hell is going on? Did it ever occur to you that along with your commissions, you guys became gentlemen?"

"Now or later, Kohn, I'm going to get you," Foster spat.

"Make it now," my words shot out like steam from a kettle.

Falzone moved in front of me. "Kohn, you've got to settle down. You're too sensitive. Nobody gives a shit you're Jewish. We never held that against you. So you're the only Jew in the outfit, so what? You're an O.K. guy and we accept you." He pointed a finger at Foster. "And you lay off. You've been riding his ass from day one. We don't want to hear it anymore. Right guys?"

"Right," the others said. Foster pushed Layton and Wagner away. The bench was tipped back in place and we all sat down. I stared at my plate, unable to eat. Falzone slapped my back. "What do you say, you guys? Shake hands."

Foster jabbed a cigarette in his mouth and turned to Layton. "Let me have a light."

I shook my head. "Not on your life."

"All right, don't shake. But you guys better learn to live with one another."

"Guess you haven't heard, Falzone," Layton interrupted. "We're going to miss you. Some of us are transferring to photo recon."

"You could'a put my name on the list when you signed up," Wagner said quietly. He didn't look up from his plate, but Layton knew he was talking to him.

"The Major wouldn't allow it. He said a man's own signature was required to accept the assignment."

Wagner's face was grey and sullen. I felt sorry for him but lucky that I'd made it on the list. Photo recon was a natural for me. Drawing, photography, I'd probably be good at it, better than as a fighter pilot. And the higher the altitude, the better. Best of all, I'd be flying alone and I'd never see Foster again.

"Maybe you can switch with one of the other guys?" Layton sounded genuinely sorry. Wagner chewed silently and said nothing.

That night I lay awake in the dark long after the others had fallen asleep. Against a background of deep breathing and the sound of the surf, I tried to visualize high-altitude flights over the Mediterranean, mapping the southern coast of France, swinging down the boot of Italy, alone and invincible. I felt calm now. News of combat losses and odds against survival didn't apply to me. I was lucky.

"Kohn?" I felt a tug at my shoulder.

"What time is it?" It was dark and I couldn't see who was shaking me.

"Change with me, will yah?"

"Who is it?"

"I can't make it, Fred, it's Wagner."

Odd hearing my first name. Wagner must have seen it on the bulletin board.

"I wanna stay with J.B. and Layton. We been together since the beginning. You're a real fighter pilot, Kohn. I'm not. I can't handle it. I know I'll be no good. I'm still having trouble flying the goddamn plane! Please, it'll be a piece of cake for you and, oh shit, I'm scared." He made little sobbing sounds and his damp breath brushed my ear.

Damn it! I thought, he's crying. How could he have come along so far and chicken out. You made a deal, you punk! What good are you if you don't keep your word?

"Please?"

"Change it."

"You mean it?"

"Yeah, go ahead."

When he left, I had second thoughts. *Schmuck,* why the grand gesture? I asked myself. I couldn't sleep. For hours, a debate raged in my head. It's done, forget it, I thought. But I couldn't.

In the morning, the major's voice crackled over the speaker system. "The request for five volunteers is rescinded. The newly activated Photo Recon Group is complete and additional pilots are not needed."

Before noon the next day, my name with eleven others was listed under orders to report to the 327th Combat Training Wing in Morocco. We were transported to an air strip twenty kilometers from Mustagonem, given a terrain map of North Africa, and told to take our pick from a line of new P-38's.

"I figure a heading for 220 degrees to Marrakech," said J.B.

"Why bother?" I asked. "Let's follow the coastline."

Foster traced a finger along the multicolored aerial chart. "Two twenty degrees is about right. This side of the Atlas mountains. And look at these elevations. They're in meters instead of feet. What do you say we make two flights of six, J.B.? You lead one, I'll take the other and meet you there."

"O.K. with me," J.B. said.

"Anybody check the weather?" I asked.

"There are no weather stations or weather reports. What do you say, Kohn? Want to join my flight?" J.B. asked.

"No thanks. I'll take the coastline. All I have to do is follow my nose."

Foster slung his chute over his shoulder and muttered, "With a nose like his, that ought to be easy."

I took off before the others. I matched the shoreline of Algeria to the map, curved down to avoid neutral Spanish Morocco, picked up Fez as a checkpoint, then landed at the air base in Marrakech. I had clear skies all the way. The plane handled beautifully. I felt good.

A few minutes later, J.B.'s flight landed. Two planes short. He had lost them during a descent through a thick overcast near the Atlas mountains. Three days later the wreckage was spotted. Wagner and Lynch were dead.

8

The Sphinx

THE ACCIDENT SOBERED US ALL. Foster and the others kept to themselves, and everyone worked hard refining his flying techniques. At briefings, we listened carefully to our flight supervisor, a twenty-year-old second lieutenant named Snell.

"Practice all you can while you're here. If planes are available, fly every morning and afternoon. You won't get another chance. Make up flights of four, trade positions every fifteen minutes from leader to tailend charlie. Wring it out. Hang in best you can. Tight formation. If you can't stay in there, you're going to get your ass shot off.

"There are three supervisors. We've all flown some combat and one of us will tag along for evaluation. It's simple. Fly good, you're in. Drag your ass, you're out. I know you're eager for combat, but if you can't hack it here, you better fly puddle jumpers."

Or maybe I'll fly a few missions like you, Snell, and become a supervisor, I thought. As far as my parents knew, I was a flight instructor anyway.

Four days later, J.B. and Layton left to join the 14th Fighter Squadron. Seven days later, the rest of us were assigned to the 71st Fighter Squadron with orders to be packed and ready to leave for Algeria in four hours.

Light turbulence and a steady vibration in the DC-3 made it impossible to sketch. I relaxed and let my eyes do the drawing. The lashed cargo strained against heavy ropes and pulled at the cleats when the plane fishtailed. Several enlisted men draped themselves over an assortment of barracks bags, foot lockers, and blanket rolls. Up front, Foster's thick torso, framed in the narrow passageway, hunched over the two pilots. Falzone, Cominski, and Smith were in the rear. The rest of us were strapped into the trough of bucket seats against the sides. Curtiss and Andy dozed, Elkhorn gazed out a window perfectly motionless. I wanted to sketch. It would keep me from wondering how I'd perform in combat and what kind of track record the 71st Fighter Squadron had.

It was pointless speculating. Even the transport pilots didn't know anything about the 71st, although they had been there before with replacement pilots. Who was I replacing and what had caused the vacancy? How often were fighter pilots replaced? All we knew was that the Squadron was based close to the city of Constantine, within striking-distance of German-held Tunisia. The pilot said it was too far to reach before sunset, so we would have to spend the night in Algiers and continue in the morning. On the approach to the airport, Foster sat down next to me and buckled his belt.

"Listen, you guys," he announced. "I've taken care of everything. The pilot says we can leave our gear on board and spend the night in town, as long as we're at the airport for takeoff by 0900. He says the Army took over all the hotels for the officers. Room service and real chow, maybe even a bath! How 'bout that? No sense missing the bright lights of Algiers. Who knows? We may not come back this way again."

Elkhorn looked up, "Very funny."

"Oh hell, you know what I mean," Foster said.

*   *   *   *

It was dark when the truck pulled up in front of the El Cabib, a dreary, climate-scarred building, distinguished from others along the street only by an M.P. standing under a red sign painted with white letters, "B.O.Q. U.S. ARMY." Elkhorn, Curtiss, and Anderson took turns ribbing Foster about how bad the place looked. I kept quiet, not wanting to jeopardize the temporary calm between us.

Inside the lobby, Elkhorn held his nose, "Whew! The French Foreign Legion died and are waiting for burial! Real great, Foster. It's what I call class. See if they have a room with a view."

Foster looked around, "You see, men, this is one of the advantages of being an officer."

The corporal at the reception desk assigned us bunks. Anderson and Curtiss went up the stairway first. The three musketeers stayed together. I followed Elkhorn and Foster to a room on the fourth floor. The room was small, crammed with two three-tiered metal bunks separated by an aisle wide enough for only one to pass through. Foster slammed his hand over his mouth.

"I'm going to puke! This is for the birds, and I mean vultures. Come on. Let's get out of here. The co-pilot said there's another place called the Sphinx, not far, one block back and two to the left. Says they got eats, drinks, and dancing girls."

"What makes you think it'll be any better than this?" Elkhorn asked.

"Can't be worse. Maybe we can hang around there 'til morning. We don't have to meet the truck 'til 0800."

"Yeah," I agreed, "There's no way I'm going to sleep here."

Foster looked at me in silence, surprised I planned to go with them.

"C'mon," he said finally, "Let's get out of this sewer."

A light drizzle put a high gloss on the cobblestones. The street was dark and deserted. It was a relief to be out in the fresh night air. We turned the corner of the second long block and I sucked in my breath at the sight of several shop windows smeared with yellow stars, stars like I had seen in newsreels on armbands, identifying Jews in countries invaded by Germany. Sharp glass slivers hung from the window frame of a kosher butcher shop. The bastards! But Algeria was occupied by the French. The Vichy French were obviously no better than the Germans. We walked on without comment.

A few yards past the next intersection, two M.P.'s stood in front of the entrance to the Sphinx. They saluted as we approached. An over-dressed middle-aged French woman received us in the entry.

"Welcome, gentlemen, we are honored. Please hang your coats and put your caps on the table. The salon is on the left." She smiled with painted red lips and fingered a double-looped pearl necklace that hung below her waist. The heavy, dark walnut sideboard contained an assortment of officer's caps from every allied armed service. We added ours to the array. A bevelled mirror rose from the polished table top to an ornate plaster molding at the ceiling. Elkhorn straightened his tie, Foster squared his shoulders and puffed out his chest. I wondered what the three adolescents I saw reflected in the mirror were doing there.

"What do you think?" Elkhorn whispered.

"You ever been in a place like this?" I asked.

"Christ, no! What about you, Foster?"

"Always a first time. C'mon, I smell food!"

We followed Foster into the salon. He stopped, pulled something out of his pocket, and handed each of us a package of condoms.

"Here, you guys, a present. Compliments of Uncle Sam. The corporal at the El Cabib said we might need these."

I put them in my pocket.

The muscles in my stomach tensed. When I was fifteen, my brother said I had been drawing naked women long enough and now it was time I learned what to do with one. He took me to a prostitute. She was thick and fleshy, stretched out on rumpled grey sheets, her knees bent and thighs spread wide. I watched her dip her fingers in a jar, then push a yellow glob of petroleum jelly in the hole between her legs. I knew what was expected of me but I couldn't do it. I left without taking off my coat.

Filaments flickered throught the clear glass light bulbs of a crystal chandelier. Clusters of middle-aged officers, some standing, others seated comfortably on couches and in soft armchairs, engaged in quiet conversation. Everyone held a cocktail glass. An Arab boy fussed at a tea table preparing sandwiches and pouring straight shots of whiskey.

I looked around and breathed easier. Foster was playing a practical joke. The Sphinx was an elegant Officer's Club, not a whorehouse. Foster went straight for the food bar, scooped three tiny sandwiches onto a porcelain plate, grabbed a handful of dainty rolls not much larger than his stubby fingers, and stuffed them in his mouth.

"Flyers, right?" The accent was Scottish.

"Yes, sir," said Elkhorn to a middle-aged British officer. I was unfamiliar with the insignia but guessed his rank was high on the ladder. A coiled piece of braid looped through an epaulet, embroidered pips perched on his shoulders, and above his breast pocket lay four impressive rows of medals and campaign ribbons. Foster stiffened, stopped chewing, his cheeks bulged.

"Are you newly stationed here?" the officer asked.

"In transit, sir, on our way to join a fighter squadron." Elkhorn's voice was an octave higher than the officer's. A blush spread across

Elkhorn's smooth cheeks. I rubbed my chin unconsciously. None of us shaved regularly. Foster's blond stubble disappeared an inch below his sideburns.

"Fighter pilots, aye? Good show! American tanks broke through El Guettar into Tunisia today. Only a question of time before Rommel calls it quits. That calls for a drink."

"Excuse me, sir," Foster swallowed and waved a half eaten sandwich. "How do we pay for this?"

"Quite simple. Food is on the house, supplied by the combined hospitality of the Allies. Keep a tally on beverages, the honor system, you know. Settle with Madame Durant at your convenience. There is a charge of fifty francs for the exhibition; optional, of course, but I dare say you won't want to miss it."

"Do they have rooms for overnight?"

"I should inquire about that, might be two hundred francs. I suggest you make those arrangements as soon as possible. Oh yes, it is customary to leave a gratuity of ten francs in the bowl next to the stair before you leave."

"Is this a private club?" I asked.

"I expect so, in a manner of speaking, an Officer's Club you might say. Come on lads, join me for a drink.

"You know, laddy, you'll never take a piece of German soil with an aeroplane," the officer said after a sip of his whiskey. "That's not to say the RAF didn't do a fine job over Britain, but it proves my point, you see. With all their bombing, the Germans still couldn't set one foot in England. Needs the infantry to take and hold land."

"Yes, sir," Foster rolled his eyes.

I edged past a group of officers at the piano and settled in a frayed easychair against the wall. I pulled my sketchbook from my pocket, found a blank page and quickly drew the rigid posture of the British officer, tracing the thin lines of his face and absorbing myself in the decorations of his well-tailored uniform. Glancing up occasionally and indifferently surveying the room, I convinced myself no one could detect I was drawing.

"Hey, Kohn!" Elkhorn motioned for me to follow. I slipped the sketchbook in my pocket and came up behind Foster and the British officer as we entered a wide corridor into another salon as large as the lounge we had come from. Eight women sat on chairs against the left wall and two women sat alone on the right.

"The ladies on the left are spoken for," Madame Durant said with a sweep of her hand. "However, a few ladies are available after the midnight curfew, *n'est-ce pas? Michelle? Charlotte? Qui sont les autres filles pour ce soir?*"

A few women looked up, half smiling. One buxom woman, heavily powdered and rouged, ran her fingers through henna-dyed hair. A moist, curled tongue slid across her upper lip as she opened her mouth toward Foster.

"Look at the boobs on that broad!" Foster said. "I'd like to squinch my toes in those melons!"

Elkhorn stepped forward and reviewed the two rows of women, pausing in front of those who had indicated their availability. He stopped at a small, dark-haired girl, younger than the others. She raised her chin and smiled.

"Madame," Elkhorn asked, "Would you ask her to stand?"

"But of course! You may ask her yourself. You see, Michelle understands English. All my ladies understand English!"

Michelle stood, the outline of her slight frame clearly defined beneath a tight, low-cut cotton sweater and a wrap-around skirt that stopped above her knees. Michelle cupped her hands under her breasts and pushed them up toward Elkhorn until they spilled over the top of her sweater, two red pupils staring from ivory white globes. Elkhorn studied them like a government inspector I had seen at Swift & Company examining white hog bellies. I felt a rush of blood spread through my cheeks and down my scalp.

Elkhorn looked back at us. Foster's thumb and middle finger formed a circle. The British officer held a match to a deeply stained meerschaum, sucking and puffing until the flame burst up and down in clouds of smoke.

"Aye, lad, a proper choice."

Michelle sat down again, crossed her legs, and resumed a conversation with the woman seated to her left.

My breath was shallow. I felt lightheaded. I didn't want to be here. Images started to blend and swirl. The women formed a Toulouse Lautrec tableau of shapes and colors, flowered prints and bright silk robes, partially buttoned and tied, casual displays of thighs and bellies and breasts, painted indifferent faces, shades of tinted hair, braided, bundled, knotted, curled, and smooth. Chalky white arms draped over backs of chairs, legs crossed and raised and spread, framing the darkness beneath. The air heavy with perfume and stale odors of unwashed bodies.

"Et vous, Monsieur?" Madame interrupted my thoughts.

"Thank you, later, perhaps." I felt weak.

"Pardon, Monsieur. There are few rooms for overnight guests. If you wish to stay until morning, you must advise me as soon as possible. *Voilà!* Michelle et Jacqueline, rooms nine and eleven, *n'est-ce pas?* And, *Monsieur* Lieutenant, you will decide before too long, no?"

Madame Durant led us back to the main lounge. Elkhorn tapped my shoulder.

"If you're short, Kohn, I'll loan you the dough."

"He's short, all right. Had it clipped before he knew what it was used for." There was an edge in Foster's voice. "Does *'kosher'* mean you can only have Jewish ass?" he continued.

"Not at all," I said. "Haven't you heard, we have a reputation for screwing gentiles?"

"Yeah I know. You're experts." Foster pulled at his crotch. "Let's get at it, Elk. I'm ready now! I've been ready for months!"

A beautiful French landscape hanging near the piano caught my attention. I stopped to admire it. The British officer sucked on his pipe, the bowl fashioned into a powerful Turk's head, its turban appearing to unravel in swirls of smoke. "The Sphinx has been an attraction dating back to the first World War. You'll find paintings in the rooms, if that be your interest. G'bye laddie. G'luck to yeh."

I returned to the armchair to put little touches to the sketch of the British officer, radiating crow's feet and lines around the mouth I had not previously seen. I felt calmer now. Suddenly I was aware of a strong perfume, then I sensed her presence so close I felt her breath.

"Fantastique! Le Field Maréchal!" She was one of the women I had seen in the other room. *"Un artiste, non?"* she asked.

"An artist, yes."

"May I see?"

She turned the pages of the sketchbook stopping occasionally to study a drawing, rapidly passing others, commenting to herself in French. I watched her closely. There was a glossy bump where eyebrows should have been, replaced with thin black-painted arches that gave her a look of anticipation. Her lashes were so thickly matted they seemed to be one piece. Above and below her eyes traces of mascara caked in dots and dashes. She wore a sleeveless dress with a low-cut square bodice pulled tight to force full breasts into a sharp cleavage. Splits in the seams of the dress exposed discolored areas of flesh, rashes, and old insect bites.

"You are too young to be an officer," she said.

"The Army doesn't think so."

She placed an index finger on my chin, pressing my head to one side and then the other. As she did this, her other elbow bent and hand on hip, plumes of black hair peeked out from her armpit. She cocked her head, eyes gliding slowly over my features.

"You stay with me." Her thigh bulged over the armrest of my chair and pressed against my shoulder. She placed a firm grip on my knee. "I make you happy."

I swallowed and smiled with clenched teeth.

"You have been with a woman. I know. Yes?"

Foster and Elkhorn were drinking, laughing and talking loudly. I thought to excuse myself and join them. The woman tapped the hard cover of my sketchbook.

"I am an *artiste* too."

"That's wonderful, do you paint?"

"No."

"What is your art?"

"Fockeeng!"

"Of course, but you see I am not well, you know what I mean. I'll be back, I promise, and I'll ask for you. What is your name?"

"Rodelle."

"Rodelle? Good. I leave in the morning and when I come back I'll ask for you. You are very nice."

"You don't like me?"

"I do. Please understand. I do not feel well."

"I am better than a young girl, you will see."

"I'll sleep here," I patted the armchair. "If I feel better during the night, I will come to your room. O.K.?"

"But you cannot sleep in the lounge. Madame will not allow it. I will be good to you. You pay two hundred francs to Madame and fifty francs to Rodelle, yes? It is settled! Come to room fourteen at eleven o'clock, yes?"

Few officers remained in the lounge. Most had drifted to the floor below where the "exhibition" was to take place.

Foster broke away and came toward me with a drink in his hand.

"Hello there!" he said to the girl. "Think you're able to handle this?" he asked me while his eyes traced the contours of her body.

"I take care of your friend," she said.

I cleared my throat. "As a matter of fact I feel a little punk. Think I picked up a cold from Andy."

"Cold feet, huh?" he said.

"I am very good," Rodelle said, with a knowing smile.

"Looks like you could take care of the three of us." He slapped Rodelle's rear. "Too bad there won't be any women like you where we're going. C'mon, Nose. Elk says it's time for the exhibition."

Rodelle put her hand on my shoulder. "Please, do not go to the exhibition. At eleven you come to my room. You will not like the exhibition."

"Why?"

"You will not like it. I know. Go to my room now and wait for me. On the second floor, yes?"

She nodded at Madame Durant. "I must go now. I am good for you, you will see."

She walked away, her worn heels accentuating a sensual rolling movement of her broad hips.

I caught up with Foster and Elkhorn and started down the stairs into thick humidity blended with the odor of stale tobacco. We found ourselves in a small room with several rows of folding chairs facing a curtain. Half the chairs were occupied. The men smoked and sipped warm drinks. We took seats in the first row. The curtain remained illuminated and the rest of the room darkened. Amidst isolated whistles and hand clapping, the curtain parted to reveal two naked women on a raised platform. They lay motionless, locked in an embrace. In seconds the curtain closed briefly and opened again to reveal the women in a different position. The curtain opened and closed a dozen times. Each time the poses were more daring, frozen pictures of erotic sex.

The men watched silently for several minutes until a voice in the dark called out something in French. Others joined in whistling, stomping feet, and clapping in cadence. The women became distracted and fell out of position. Awkward attempts to remain graceful turned into comic distortions. The curtain jerked shut and Madame Durant pushed through a slit in the center, making an announcement in French that was drowned by cheers and applause.

When the curtain opened again, the same two women had

assumed a half-crouching attitude, holding on to one another in mock terror, while a tall figure in black beret, sunglasses, and a moustache, stood stationary, arms folded across the chest and legs spread wide. The costume did not disguise a women's body. A tight leather waistband with two leather straps pressing into the folds of her thighs supported a stiff greased leather erection, a foot long and thick as an axe handle. The embracing women moved in slow motion, changing positions, then stopped the action.

The curtains remained open. The audience was silent. The women rubbed and caressed one another, kissed and licked the other's body, and the action gained momentum. They gyrated from one pose to another, breathing loudly, groaning. One woman supporting herself on her knees, spread her legs. I slumped lower in my chair, turning my head but not far enough to take my eyes from the scene. The other woman led the huge penis into the kneeling woman and the pumping began, each time deeper, the men joining in with encouraging calls, beating a progressively quickening rhythm, cheering each time the glistening leather penetrated deeper. The breasts of both women swung in unison, whipping back and forth, creating an illusion of creatures not found in nature.

The straining legs driving the penis were covered with tiny white scars etched on olive calves, discolored with old insect bites and pimpled areas irritated by leather rubbing against flesh. I imagined the woman's hair free of the beret, cascading over her back and shoulders, the glasses and moustache gone.

The performance ended in a wild writhing of heads, hands, arms, and legs, each woman, legs spread, poking her fingers inside the other, each trying to upstage the other in sexually arousing the audience. My genitals shrank, I could look no more. I wanted to leave but was afraid my departure would be a criticism of the others. Too late I closed my eyes, knowing it would be a long time before I could purge those images from my mind.

When at last the squirming stopped, the men broke into catcalls and applause, throwing coins and paper money onto the platform. The women dropped to their knees, slapping flat hands to stop rolling coins, bunching paper money in their fists. Some of the regulars skidded coins to stop against the back wall, forcing the women to line up on their hands and knees to burrow and scramble, their asses facing the audience like cows at a trough.

Madame Durant stepped forward, clapping and smiling approval at the three naked women who were now taking bows at the front of the stage. With a flourish, the tall woman removed her beret and allowed her hair to tumble down her back. When she took off the glasses and stripped away the moustache, the audience rose to a standing ovation.

Foster jabbed me with his elbow. "Jesus Christ, Nose! That's your girl! Wow, are you going to get fucked tonight!"

The men's laughter, amplified by the barren walls, drowned Madame's last announcement, the curtains yanked shut, and the house lights came up.

I made my way back up to the salon. It was nearly eleven. Foster was the first to leave the lounge.

"One of you guys leave an early call, I want to get in a quickie before we go."

One by one the others left, disappearing behind many doors. Elkhorn said goodnight. I was alone. I felt dislocated. What was wrong with me? I had so little in common with any of them. I didn't belong here. I didn't share their pleasures. I saw myself inside the frame of an ugly picture.

The Arab boy wiped his table clean, switched off the lamps, dimmed the chandelier, and waited respectfully for me to leave the room. He closed and locked the massive lounge doors after me and padded down the hall pushing a large cart. I put ten francs in the bowl next to the stairs, picked up my cap and coat and opened the door to the outside. The M.P.'s huddled to protect themselves from a downpour.

"When did this start? I asked.

"Ten minutes ago, sir."

I lifted the shawl collar of my coat and pulled my visor down.

"Don't think you'll be going far, Lieutenant. The water's ankle deep in the street and up to your knees in the gutter. Besides, it's less than five minutes 'til curfew. Our relief will be here at 0400 and we could drop you wherever you want to go."

"Four hours from now?"

"Sorry," the M.P. glanced at his watch, "Even if the rain stops, we can't let you walk the streets."

"Then I'll have to spend the night here."

"Yes sir!" he smiled, "That's sure a whole lot better than standing out here in the rain."

I went back inside. Rodelle was waiting at the foot of the stairs. She leaned against the bannister, relaxed in a red silk robe and bare feet.

"You come back because of the rain, yes?"

She accepted a cigarette.

"You cannot imagine how difficult it is to entertain so many officers. Why are Americans so impatient?" There was a great crash of thunder and the lights dimmed. "But you are not like the others? You will have a coffee with me?"

"Do you have tea?"

"Of course, come with me."

A faded print of Van Gogh's Sunflowers was tacked to the wall of her room. I looked out the window to see if the rain had let up.

"No!" she cautioned. "Do not open the curtain while the light is on!"

She picked up a bowl of water and a towel that had been set outside her door and placed it on a chest opposite the bed.

"You wait. I come back."

I stood uncertainly, not knowing where to sit. Next to the chest were two unmatched wooden chairs flanking a low circular table. The blanket on the double bed was turned down, the sheet and pillow on one side wrinkled. The other pillow was puffed and propped against a tubular brass headboard. A light blue painted clothes cupboard completed the furnishings. She returned, closed the door behind her, and placed a tray with cups, a milk pitcher, and a steaming teapot on the low table.

We sipped tea silently, audibly inhaling when we breathed the hot liquid. Rodelle leaned back in the chair, her head against the wall, legs crossed at the ankles. She balanced the cup on her stomach with one hand, her body relaxed, her eyes half closed. I wondered if she had fallen asleep. Her robe, parted by one knee, exposed her leg from thigh to bare foot. The overhead light bulb dimmed, then brightened, followed seconds later by a crash of thunder. Rodelle remained motionless.

I reached in my side pocket for my sketchbook and quickly drew the significant line of her posture, the folds of the robe revealing the tired contours of the spent body underneath. I drew quickly and economically, wasting no lines, detailing the hair that spilled over the shoulders and I watched the features take shape. The chin rested on the chest, hidden in the soft robe; strong features emerged through the surface makeup. I was pleased with what flowed from the tip of my pencil.

Rodelle's eyes moved under her lids. She pulled back her legs, drew her heels up onto the chair, encircled them with her arms, turned and rested her head on her knees and again became motionless. Then again, through half closed eyes, seeing I had stopped drawing, she took a new pose and waited, hardly breathing, until I had finished the second sketch. Soon she stood, threw her head back, raised her arms and hands as though she were combing her hair, and waited. She held the pose until I said "Very good!"

Encouraged by my approval, she dropped her robe and assumed a series of poses, natural, simple movements, disrobing, standing before a mirror, sitting on the bed, crossing a leg and studying her foot, lying on her side with her head on her hand. Insatiable, I sketched for hours, revising a pose with a gentle push on an arm or a leg, improving the form, brushing aside her long hair, placing a hand to establish a new center of gravity; and whatever I did, however long I kept her in one position, she remained motionless and silent.

When at last I had finished, I said quietly, "That was wonderful!" And when she did not move, I knew she was asleep. I gently pulled the blanket over her sleeping form and, without removing my clothes, lay down beside her and slept until morning.

9

Don't Lose Me, Boy

"WELCOME GENTLEMEN. MIGHTY GLAD TO see y'all," the captain said ignoring our salutes and shaking hands with each of us.

The eight of us stood holding our caps and covering our eyes against the dust stirred by the propwash of the departing DC-3.

"I'm John Wallace, your Commandin' Officer. Everyone calls me Tex. Say hello to Master Sergeant Garrett, personnel and squadron historian." The captain looked too old and too tall to be a fighter pilot, almost six feet, wiry, and in his late twenties. He wore senior pilot's wings.

The captain referred to a clipboard and a sheaf of papers.

"Anderson? *Svenska,* yah?"

"Yes, sir!"

"That's the trouble with havin' a name that starts with A. Puts you first in line." He laughed. "Like to fly?"

"Yes, sir!"

"Y'all will get your share, and there's a good chance each of you will get your own plane. Cominski?"

"Sir!"

"Polish, right?

"Yes, sir!"

"Guess you have a good reason to be here. Curtiss?"

"Yes, sir!"

"Let's see, that's two of you from Minnesota and the same town, too."

"Yes, sir. Anderson and I went to the same school," said Curtiss.

"Falzone."

"Sir!"

"We have ourselves a regular League of Nations. And which one of y'all's Elkhorn?"

"I'm Elkhorn, sir."

"Nice to have you with us."

"Foster?"

"Sir!" Foster squared his shoulders and tucked in his chin.

The captain studied Foster and smiled. "You're kinda built for bombers, not fighers, aren't ya?" The muscles in Foster's ass tightened. "Good thing ya got an extra engine to carry that weight." With our laughter, Foster relaxed. For some reason he didn't take offense.

"Ko-han?"

"Kohn, sir!

"Is that German?"

"Jewish, sir!"

"That's kinda nice. You're the first Jewish fighter pilot I've had in my outfit. Welcome aboard."

"And Smith?"

"Yes, sir."

"Men, you now belong to the 71st Fighter Squadron. I know y'all are interested in what your flyin' duties will be, but first a word about the ground rules.

"Y'all will find life on the base pretty easy, but there are some things I'm fussy about. On occasion you can get a pass. Four to six hours restricted to the nearby town of Chateaudun du Rommel. In a few weeks, we hope to get you passes to the city of Constantine. There'll be no talkin' about our activities off the base, not even the name of our outfit.

"We permit a few locals on the base, some KP duty, garbage detail, laundry pick up. Nobody else! If there's a strange Aay-rab within fifty feet of one of our planes, or our supplies, or anyplace he's not authorized to be, we'll shoot him. For five bucks he'd drop sugar in your fuel tank. Another thing we don't take kindly to is black marketing. Give away cigarettes and chewin' gum all you want, but don't sell anythin'. Our Intelligence Officer will give y'all a booklet of helpful Aay-rab phrases and talk to you about appropriate behavior off the base.

"And don't be surprised if y'all see Italian POW's walkin' around the base. They're useful and willing workers. Once in a while there'll be a German pilot here on his way to a prison camp in the states. Intelligence tries to learn about their planes and their tactics."

"How about the local wine or booze sir?" Foster said.

"The wine is better'n the water. There is no local booze."

"Beer?"

"There is none."

"Captain, any rules about making home brew?" Elkhorn asked. Foster and the others laughed.

"No, but if you've had any alcohol twelve hours before a mission, I'll put a bullet through your head."

"How much advance notice before a mission, sir?"

"None. Kinda like playin' Russian roulette, isn't it? Another thing. Be nice to your ground crew. Right, Sergeant? Rank doesn't mean a helluva lot out here. I have more respect for a mechanic than a brigadier general. Pilots come and go, but the ground crew are the heart of the outfit. They keep our planes flyin' and the guns workin', so you better believe they're the best friends y'all will ever have.

"Now, I need three men for tent number six. Anderson, Curtiss, and who else?"

I raised my hand, but Elkhorn beat me to it by shouting, "Me, sir!"

"O.K. That leaves Cominski, Falzone, Kohn, Foster, and Smith. You lucky fellows get tent number eight. Y'all live together and eat together, and the better you get to know one another, the better you'll fly together."

I was depressed by the thought of being in the same tent with that son of a bitch Foster. Somehow it will work out, I hoped.

"Leave your gear. Sergeant Garratt will bring it over on the jeep. Your tents are within walkin' distance. You can see them from here.

"Y'all can take it easy for the rest of the day, and tomorrow I'll take each of you up for a practice flight. Get y'selves some chow first thing in the mornin' and..., let's see here..., Ko-han, you first. Meet me at my tent at 0800. I'll see the rest of you after we land. Formation flyin' is what it's all about. We start you out as wingmen, so if ya stick close enough to count the hairs on the back of my neck, y'all are ready for the big time. That's it."

*   *   *   *

Early the next morning a jeep was waiting in front of Captain Tex Wallace's tent, parachutes draped over the hood. The C.O. ambled out, smiling, and he pointed to me, "O.K., let's go."

I climbed into the back seat. Tex's large frame filled the passenger seat and his knees pressed against the windshield. He had a nice easy-going manner. I was glad he was the Squadron Commander. We pulled to a stop in front of his plane, he slid off the seat and drawled, "Just a little formation. Wanna see what they taught ya. Now, don' lose me, hear?"

Painted on the nose of his plane in big yellow letters was "The Alamo," and to the right of the name, three swastikas were lined up like a scoreboard. He'd shot down three planes. My heart began to pound. Damn, I should have taken the time for one more leak before I left the camp. The jeep bounced along on the dirt track leaving a large cloud of dust, then over the open field to the far end where other P-38s were parked.

"The Captain's pretty good, huh?" I asked the driver.

"The greatest! Got his wings at Randolph." I heard the pride in his voice and the subtle comparison of credentials. His C.O. was a real pilot, not a bird hatched from civilian life. "Two more and he'd have been an ace 'cept Wing doesn't let him fly much. They're saving him for a desk. Any day now he'll be getting oak leaves."

The driver braked hard and skidded to a stop in front of a dark, dirty green P-38G. The letters LMA were printed on the side of the coolant radiators. Two members of the ground crew were wiping the plexiglas canopy. Two others were removing their tool boxes from beneath the left engine. I got out of the jeep, slung my parachute over my shoulder, and walked toward the plane.

A short, well-built man with smooth cheeks ran to meet me. "I'm Sergeant Chad Jessup, crew chief." He reached out and shook my hand. "Here Lootenant, let me help you," he drawled, taking the parachute from me. He climbed up the little ladder to the cockpit, and slipped the chute over the seat. I followed, adjusted the harness over my shoulders, and buckled myself in. Chad helped me tighten the crash straps.

"Wow! That's hard!" I slipped my hand under my butt and felt the seat pack. "Where's the seat cushion?"

"Removed to make way for an inflatable life raft."

"It's like sitting on a stone slab."

"I could put the cushion back but you'll hit your head on the canopy for sure."

"O.K.," I nodded, "Guess I'll have to live with it. By the way, whose plane is this?" I said, running my hands over the polished control knobs.

"Mine, sir." Chad reached in, set the throttles, and checked the ignition switches.

"I mean, who's the pilot?"

"It's unassigned," he answered quickly and looked over his shoulder. "Better hurry, the C.O.'s taxiing out. Start anytime... don't energize, you're plugged into a battery cart." He signalled to one of the men on the ground and all the electrically operated instruments suddenly came alive. Chad kneeled on the wing waiting until I started both engines. As each engaged and fired, he reached in, adjusted the throttles, and checked the fuel mixture. His eyes swept the instrument panel and the position of every lever in the cockpit. Satisfied, he waved to the man to disconnect the battery.

"She's all yours." He slid off the wing, stowed the ladder, and joined the others. The crew smiled and touched their caps as I released the brakes and started to roll from the parking space. I taxied slowly, checking temperatures and pressure gauges as the plane swayed over uneven ground, creaking and groaning. The purr of the engines sounded good and I was eager to fly again. The cockpit was spotless. The plane was meticulously cared for.

I pulled alongside Tex. His shoulders and arms pressed against the side windows and his head was tilted slightly forward under the canopy. His plexiglas capsule looked like the transparent skin of an overstuffed sausage. I would have laughed, but I had other things on my mind. Tex smiled and nodded and we rolled out onto the steel mesh runway. I was to his right and slightly behind. We held the brakes and ran the engines to full takeoff power. I used all my strength to keep the quivering plane from moving forward. The instant Tex got off the brakes, so did I, my back pressing hard against the seat as our planes leaped ahead. I was determined not to be left behind.

We raced down the runway and left the ground at the same time. Tex pulled back on the stick, I followed, and we began a long, hard, steep climb. I expected him to level off and reduce power, but it didn't work that way. He kept pulling the nose higher and higher. I didn't take my eyes off him for a second for fear of losing position. The altimeter passed through 10,000 feet, then 15,000, and at

18,000 feet he pulled up sharply, rolling over onto his back and I followed. With airspeed dropping rapidly, risking an inverted stall, it was the last thing I expected him to do. I was a half a beat behind and the surprise lost me several feet. And then down we roared, full throttle, crowding the red line.

His steady voice came through my headset. "Don' lose me, boy."

Frustrated, only minutes after takeoff and wanting desperately to show him how well I could fly, I was already in a sweat fighting to hold position. I dove after his wing hoping to pick up a few feet when next he reduced throttle. But he didn't. Then we were all over the sky, climbing, diving, skidding, slipping, alternating sharp turns left, then right, the scene beyond his head continually changing from sky to ground, then back again. I watched his aileron for warning signs of a turn. No luck. He flicked his rudders and ailerons left, then broke sharply to the right.

I lost several more feet. Sweat trickled down my ribs. The G forces from tight turns pressed my boney ass against the life raft's wooden paddle. I hunched forward, squinting through sweat-drenched eyes, left hand on the throttles, wet right hand on the control wheel, glaring at that son of a bitch who was making a fool of me. He had no intention of giving me a break. I couldn't regain the lost distance. I saw him grinning from two plane lengths behind.

He flipped into a turn, exposing his belly. "Ya still with me, boy?" he asked. I didn't reply, conscious that whatever was said on the air was broadcast by loudspeaker to those on the ground. We dropped lower with each maneuver, and he pressed further down in a long arc that swung back toward the base, cutting through narrow valleys at treetop level.

"Look alive," he drawled.

We barrelled across the tent tops of the squadron, men diving to the ground. The distance between us stretched to three plane lengths. It looked like a city block. Suddenly I had him. I was closing in fast and would catch him on the next turn. Instead he pulled up, banked right in front of me and called, "Careful, boy." Then without warning, he chopped throttles and I caught up to him in a vertical climbing turn, in tight formation. His gear doors opened and the wheels appeared. I hadn't caught him, the flight was over and we were in an approach for landing. Automatically I reduced throttle, extended the gear, and lowered flaps. Our wheels touched the runway at the same time.

Tex rolled on to the end. I swung off and headed to my parking space. He was too good for me. I was disgusted with myself. The ground crew was waiting and Chad was on the wing before the props stopped turning.

"Gee, Lootenant, that was terrific!"

I was surprised he thought so. I knew how inadequate it really was.'

"Great plane, huh, Lootenant?"

"Handled real well. I enjoyed it," I said with a forced smile.

"The two of you looked real good up there. Did you notice the right supercharger? Did it cut in ahead of the left?"

"I was too busy to notice, but I'll watch it next time."

"Then you're our pilot?" Chad asked. His plane and his pilot. The other three mechanics crowded close, waiting for my answer.

"I don't make those decisions. That's up to the C.O."

"This plane's a virgin, Lootenant." He pointed to the nose. "No name and never shot down an enemy plane. We talked about it before you landed. We'd like you to be our pilot."

Tex's jeep pulled up. His right boot rested on the fender. "Wanna ride back?" he was smiling. It was all still a big joke to him. I was disgusted with myself.

"No thanks, I'll walk back," I said, glancing at Chad, and hoping Tex wouldn't make a wisecrack about my poor showing in front of the crew. No harm in their thinking I was good.

"Come to my tent tonight at 2100 for a briefin'. I'm sendin' you on a mission in the mornin'," Tex said. "And thanks for the ride. That was mighty fine flyin'. Do like that tomorrow and you'll be awlright."

I looked at him and swallowed, "Can I use this plane?" I asked.

"Use it?" he laughed, "Hell, it's yours."

10

Easy Combat Time

I PUT ON CLEAN KHAKIS and at exactly 2100 walked to the C.O.'s tent. Tex smiled from his cot and waved me in. Two other men were there, a baggy pilot and a lanky administrative-type first lieutenant.

"Meet Earl Stodder, Intelligence," Tex said. "We call him 'Shorty.'"

Shorty sat on the floor, knees bent and folded like a grasshopper's, his eyes magnified behind thick lenses. He put down a pad and pencil, reached up and shook my hand.

"Delighted to make your acquaintance, young man. We of the 71st are honored. It would give me great pleasure were you to call upon me for guidance during your sojourn."

"That's Shorty," laughed the pilot. "Ask him where the latrines are and you need a Ph.D. to understand the answer." He jabbed out a hand, "My name's Sadler." His short-cropped red hair matched the color of the freckles that spread from his pug nose across his cheeks. He looked like an Iowa farm boy. I liked him.

"Make y'self at home," Tex said motioning for me to sit on the cot. Sadler had squatted on his heels to study a large terrain map that he'd spread over the dirt floor.

"Nice to have you with us, Ko-han," Tex said, making my name sound Irish. "Like I said, we're informal around here. In town, y'all will get a salute from every gendarme."

I lit a cigarette.

"Nervous, huh?"

I nodded.

"Relax, you have nothin' to worry about. You fly real good so you won't have any trouble. It's a job. You like to fly, don't you?" He didn't wait for an answer. "Well, that's what y'all will be doin' tomorrow, lots o' flyin'." He pointed to a red circle on the map in front of Sadler. "That's home base, the course runs out to Sardinia, down to Sicily, over Too-nee-ja, and back again. Recon, maybe three hours. Memorize the headin's and the times. Carry no maps, y'hear? No paper scraps, nothin'. In the mornin' mark the numbers on the palm o' your hand. That way it comes off easy with sweat. Any questions?

"What are we looking for?"

"Any kind o' movement, somethin' happenin' in the harbors. Most important, we want a careful weather report so Wing can plan the bombin' missions. Just 'tach y'self to little ol' Sadler's wing and don' let go, just like y'all did today."

"Just the two of us!" I blurted, losing what superficial calm I had mustered.

"Yep, just you and Sadler. Y'all will be over 30,000 feet most of the way, so no one's goin' to bother you. Used to take new pilots with the squadron, but no more. Y'see, no one wants an inexperienced wingman in a combat situation. A recon flight is a gravy run, high and fast, no flak or enemy aircraft. Take a look-see and come home. It's the best way for a new pilot to get his feet wet."

I looked at Sadler. Nothing would shake me loose from his wing.

"In case we get separated, how do I find my way back?"

"Hold those headin's," Tex answered. "That'll put you in the neighborhood. Then call 'Washboard' for homing, tell 'em you're Doorknob, that's the name of our squadron. Shorty, what's his number?"

"Five Two. Doorknob Five Two. That's you, Lieutenant."

"Washboard'll vector you to Constantine forty kilometers from here," Tex added, "two-six-zero degrees for five minutes will put you over this tent."

Shorty referred to a manila folder. "You'll be in a fast descent over Tunisia. That's the only place with heavy concentrations of anti-aircraft fire." Tex leaned back against a mountain of skeepskin jackets, fur-lined boots and assorted articles of clothing, his eyes fixed on the ceiling, where the tent's center post and the four canvas sides formed the inside of a pyramid. Sadler rocked on his haunches making designs with his finger in the dirt floor. No one spoke.

"Is there anything else?" I asked.

"Nope."

Did they wonder whether I would go? It was happening too fast. Somehow I didn't think this moment would come. The blood drained from my cheeks. I needed more time.

"When can I check out my plane?"

"You have all night."

"What time's takeoff?" I heard myself ask, as if I had separated from myself. Sadler scooped up the map and punched my shoulder.

"0615! Someone will wake you at 0530. You're tent's number eight, center cot, right?"

"Right. Anything else?"

"Oh yeah, dress warm. It's cold up there."

The man poked his head through the open tent flap and asked in a loud whisper, "Ready, sir?" The luminous dial on my wristwatch read 0530. I had slept in my coveralls and double socks. In less than a minute I was completely dressed—flying boots, shoulder holster and gun, jacket, Mae West, helmet, and goggles. I slipped a sketchpad and a package of Tootsie Rolls in my leg pocket. Foster and the others were sleeping soundly. I wanted someone to wish me luck.

Outside it was chilly and dark. I made my way to the chow tent wondering if I had forgotten anything. I hadn't pissed! At high altitude, thirty below zero and parachute leg straps jammed in my crotch, trying to pluck a cold shrunken penis out of my overalls and bend it into the relief tube would be impossible. I'd tried it during training. Better do it the last minute behind the plane.

Sadler was alone sipping coffee. He nodded in the dim light of a small bulb that pulsed in time to the wheezing of a distant generator. I tasted the bitter black coffee and set down the stained aluminum cup. Sadler smiled, "It's hot."

"No tea?" I asked.

"We're lucky to get this."

At 0545 we drove in silence to our planes like bus passengers commuting to work. Sadler had an air of experience that I envied. When we reached his plane he grabbed the jeep's windshield post and swung out of his seat.

"How many missions have you flown?" I asked.

"This'll be my fifth...takeoff will be to the east. Be out on the runway by six ten." Then, as an afterthought he added, "Punch in Channel A, two hits on the mike button for radio check. No talking after we're airborne, O.K.?"

"O.K."

At 0555 the driver came to a stop in front of my plane. Sergeant Chad Jessup, bundled in a heavy jacket and a wool cap pulled down to his eyebrows, ran to meet me. The other three members of the ground crew huddled under the nose. I was glad to see them. Maybe they'd wish me luck.

As I ducked under the wing, I felt heat from the engine nacelle. The plane had been pre-flighted and the engines run. Chad had to get up early to do that. I was grateful. I handed my sketchbook to him. "Please hold this, Sergeant. I'll want to make some sketches when I land while the mission's still fresh in my mind." Chad shrugged and nodded.

Inside the cockpit, the fluorescent lights glowed and the iridescent instrument dials shone brightly. Chad adjusted my parachute harness and shoulder straps, scanned the settings and levers in the cockpit, checked the canopy latch, and slapped the plexiglas with the flat of his hand. "Good luck, sir. Good hunting!" He slid off the wing and stowed the ladder.

A chill ran up my spine. Good hunting! I thought of rabbits and squirrels. I had never hunted in my life. I cranked the window closed to within an inch of the top, leaving an opening to hear Chad if he called.

It was quiet in the cockpit, dark and lonely. Three of the ground crew, barely visible in the dark, stood in front of the left engine. Another man waited at the left tail boom ready to disconnect the battery cables. Time to start, no mistakes, double check everything. The procedure had become second nature. I heard myself reciting the checklist. It was comforting to talk out loud. A bomber pilot could talk to his co-pilot or his navigator or bombardier or to his gunners. I had only myself.

My father had taught me to do everything with care and precision. He would keep me from doing anything foolish. I broke off a Tootsie Roll segment, popped it in my mouth, snapped the oxygen mask on, and called out, "Oxygen lever, Auto-mix...Generator ON, boost pumps ON..." Everything checks out, Dad. I reached for the primer and called to Chad, "CLEAR!" Chad signalled to Ted and yelled, "CLEAR!"

I waited as the needles on the temperature gauges rose. Takeoff was at 0615. At 0605 I released the brakes and rolled out of the parking space. Sadler was waiting on the runway. I fell in behind. He wiggled his ailerons. I completed the run-up and returned the signal. It was 0612.

I straightlegged the toe brakes, pressing the pedals with all my strength to hold the plane and pushed the engines to full throttle. The plane quivered and shook. The tires skidded on the steel mesh. In front of me, Sadler's exhaust turbines glowed red hot. Then together we released brakes and leapt into a running start. My eyes scanned the gauges. Everything's O.K., Dad, no turning back now. I remember how you had a thing about turning back. You said it was bad luck. And the time you forgot your briefcase, you poked your head inside the door and yelled for one of us to get it. You wouldn't put your foot past the threshold.

Half a sun peeked over the mountains to the east. We climbed almost into its rays, reaching 31,000 feet as we crossed the coast of Africa, instruments saying all was well, engines pounding steady and strong, outside temperature forty below zero. The heater couldn't offset the heat loss and cold stabbed at my knees and gloved fingers.

But I hung on Sadler's wing, looking only at the sea and sky beyond him and to the sides. For a wingman, a glance backward was an invitation to a mid-air collision. I submitted to blind, unquestioning faith that Sadler would see any attack from the rear.

Vapor trails churned a white cloud behind Sadler's plane, skywriting our positon to anti-aircraft batteries below. We dropped to 29,000 feet and put an end to the message. Continuous cold drained my body heat, cutting into my bones. My hands and feet throbbed with pain. I stamped my feet one at a time, warming my hands, first one, then the other, in my crotch. My thinly padded butt ached, and I shifted my weight in my seat. Sadler set a stiff pace for a long flight, obviously in a hurry to get out and back. That was fine with me.

The coast of Sardinia appeared on our left and Sicily emerged from the haze. I imprinted the shoreline and harbor in my mind, a quiet painting of soft brown hills and purple sea.

The illuminated gunsight was a constant reminder of the purpose of our flight, but nowhere was there evidence of war. We flew toward two suns, one rising straight ahead and one reflected on the water below. Ten minutes more and we were close enough to make out Palermo. The city slept and our presence went unnoticed. Sadler kicked right rudder. I followed, and we came out of a steep bank, an end to our squinting into the sun. An hour and a half to go.

Reconnaisance, Dad. . . ECT, easy combat time.

Now Sadler dipped the nose of his plane, the air speed crowded the red line, and the coast of Africa came to meet us, catching me by surprise. I hunched over in the cockpit as we flashed over the city of Tunis at four hundred miles per hour, feeling a thousand eyes counting the rivets on my belly. I stuck close to Sadler, refusing to be left behind. A sense of danger set me on edge.

Past the city, at a greater angle downward, Sadler pushed faster than I had ever flown. The sounds were different, unfamiliar creaks and nervous vibrations. The terrain changed from flat coastal sand to rolling foothills. Somewhere below, unseen and unheard, great battles raged. See, Dad? It's safer up here than down there. Only twenty-five missions. I'll be home in no time, safe and sound.

I was comforted to see Sadler always looking past me, checking the sky behind, his head constantly sweeping in all directions. A disciplined flier, his course never varied. This is fine. I can handle it. No need to be apprehensive. We dove below 10,000 feet, low enough, I knew, to remove our oxygen masks, but I'd wait for Sadler to remove his first. Then I'd light a cigarette and reward myself with a piece of candy.

Almost directly ahead, I saw a large, slow-moving twin-engine transport, a black cross clearly marked on each wing, a swastika on it's rectangular tail. In a minute our paths would cross. Sadler's voice crashed through my head set, "HIGH! AT FIVE O'CLOCK! BREAK RIGHT!" Sadler's belly tanks whipped away from beneath his plane, freeing him of drag, and he pulled ahead. I hit my tank release buttons and flipped into a right vertical climbing turn. Then I saw them. Escorts for the transports. Two Messerschmidts, side by side, diving on us. Sadler's voice jarred me, "TAKE THE ONE ON THE RIGHT!"

We pulled in tight and climbed to meet them head-on. The hair on my scalp pressed against the inside of my helmet. My plane shuddered on the edge of a high speed stall, pressing my chin to my chest under crushing G forces. The 109 pushed down to meet me, his plane growing larger in my windshield as the distance between us closed. I pushed the throttles harder against the stops in a futile effort to make the plane go faster. My pores oozed warm moisture, my mask dragged down my cheeks, and my vision dimmed as I strained against the control wheel.

The 109 was dead center. I pressed both trigger buttons blanketing his plane in yellow streams of tracer shells. Flames flashed from his wings, bits and pieces fell. Thank God, I thought. He was on fire. I squeezed the trigger buttons harder and harder. But still he came, filling my windshield, his nose and wings spurting flames. Now I could see he wasn't burning; I hadn't hit him. Those were his guns firing at me. The bits and pieces were spent shell casings. The son-of-a-bitch was trying to kill me!

He roared over, showing a white oil-stained belly that blotted out the sky, and I rocked in the turbulence of his propwash. Untouched, the 109s circled the German transport, continuing their protective vigil. I closed in on Sadler and we headed for home.

"We did O.K., Dad," I shrieked. "Calm down! Control! Get hold of yourself!" My legs shook and my feet bounced on the aluminum floor. I took deep breaths to slow my speeding pulse. It had happened so fast! Maybe five seconds. Sadler was good. If he hadn't seen the attack we could be dead.

I felt warm liquid oozing in my pants. I reached down. My seat was soaked with blood. The tremendous G forces pressing me down had ruptured the thin skin on my ass through to my pelvic bone. I forgot about the cigarette and candy. I was wet with perspiration when we landed. Chad was rapping on the top of the canopy.

"Hey, Lootenant, you still got your oxygen mask on."

11

Tail-End-Charlie

"WHAT DO YOU SAY, SADLER?" Tex asked, "what's it look like? Sadler had joined Captain Wallace on a low platform in the squadron briefing room. Large aeronautical terrain maps hung from the canvas walls. Shorty and another captain sat in the front row. Pilots occupied the other three rows of benches. Sadler's coveralls were sweat-stained and rumpled like mine. Great dark blotches spread from his armpits. He was calm and expressionless now, but he must have been scared too.

"Weather's good. Nothing special going on," Sadler answered.

"How did it go, Ko-han?"

"O.K., I guess."

"What do you mean, 'You guess'? "

I looked at Sadler.

"What he means, Captain, is during our letdown we kinda surprised a Ju-52."

"Hope you surprised him permanently," said one of the pilots.

"Nope. He had company. A couple o' 109's. They made a pass at us, missed, and we came home."

Sure, I thought, that's the way it happened. Sadler made it sound so simple.

"How'd our new boy do?"

"Stuck to me like a dog in heat."

"How do you like that, men? Ko-han here went on his first mission this mornin'. Supposed to be a gravy run, but it seems like it didn't turn out that way."

99

"You lucky bastard," Cominski said, "Did you get a shot at 'em?"

Tex interrupted, "You boys did the right thing. The mission was weather recon and a look-see at enemy activity, bring back information and don't screw around.

"Ko-han, I suppose you would have liked to tangle with those 109's?"

I looked at him with disbelief. Tangle? He must be crazy, a real *meshugeneh.*

"Well, goddamn it, that's not the way it's done! Good thing you stuck with Sadler. Your mission was to find possible targets for the bombers. Bombs do more damage than knockin' down a few planes. And, suppose y'all got yourself killed—or traded one for one? That's no good! We're short of planes and pilots. There'll be plenty of chances to mix it with enemy fighters during escort. It's the bombers they want and they have to get past us first. Screw off after a fighter and a dozen more will knock out some of our bombers.

"That's why we place so much importance on good formation flyin'. It's the best defense for the bombers and the greatest fire power against the enemy. But we do it the hard way, in broad daylight, no surprises, mostly medium to high altitude. We can be seen and heard, so expect a reception committee everytime you go over there.

"All daylight! Y'hear? We don't fly or fight at night. Remember that. Return after dark and there's no way we can get you down. Can't talk you down, no instrument approaches, and no lights on the runway," he paused.

"There's no mission scheduled for today, so get yourselves some sack time or do whatever you want. Ko-han, you'll go with the squadron tomorrow. Probably bomber escort. Fly Sadler's wing again. He'll lead an element so that'll put you in the tail slot. . ."

Too soon, I thought. I need time to think about this. I was lucky with Sadler. I'll think about it later. I must listen to what he's saying. It could be important.

". . . you new men, talk with your flight leaders every chance you get. They have an average of ten combat missions. They've met the enemy and can give you firsthand accounts of what it's like.

"Before you go, Captain Mulvaney, our Flight Surgeon, wants a few words. Doc?"

Captain Mulvaney stepped forward. "I'll be brief. The dispensary is open to pilots any time, night or day. No waiting, go to the head of the line. Those who need cholera or yellow fever booster shots, check next week. We expect supplies by then. Each man will take two Atabrine tablets a day. It may not prevent malaria, but it could keep it mild. Africa is hot. You're going to sweat a lot and lose body salt. Take salt tablets to supplement your diet.

"And speaking of food, army chow may not be tasty but it provides a balanced diet. Don't drink local water, or eat uncooked fruit and vegetables. Primitive cultivation techniques allow potentially dangerous levels of harmful bacteria.

"You men must maintain good health to stay on combat status. When you're not flying, you're free to do whatever you want. You will be given physical examinations at regular intervals, and you cannot fly if you have a cold or any condition that would congest your sinus cavities, since flying at various altitides subjects you to extreme changes in pressure that could split your eardrums. Disobedience to this rule could endanger the lives of other pilots and will be cause for permanent grounding."

The doctor glanced at his watch and said, "Any questions?"

"Being on oxygen most of the time, is it true it can make a guy sterile?"

"Hey, Cominski, first you have to get it up!"

Everyone except the doctor laughed. "I have no medical evidence to substantiate that claim. Yes? You in the back?"

"Most of the targets will be on the other side of the Mediterranean, two or three hours away from the base. If we're hit during a mission, I mean wounded, bleeding, and in pain, what do you recommend?"

"There's morphine and a tourniquet in your emergency backpack, but I doubt you could administer it in the confines of a small cockpit. Yes??

Smith stood. "I can't sleep."

"When you get tired enough, you'll sleep."

Smith remained standing, looking like he had something more to say. At nineteen, he was the youngest pilot in the squadron, a Baptist from North Carolina. Every night in the tent Smith read from his Bible and wrote in his diary.

Tex spoke. "Listen, Smith, and this goes for y'all. If you have somethin' personal you want to talk about, see the doc. Shucks, that's what he's here for. We're lucky to have a top surgeon for a fighter outfit even if the only problem we have is an occasional case of the runs. You want to see a chaplain, let me know. There's one stationed with the 332nd Bomb Group and we can get him here. Any questions? No? Thanks doc."

I wandered out of the briefing room. Maybe I am coming down with a cold. If I were sick, that would risk lives. Maybe I needed a few days' rest. I stopped at the dispensary.

Without bothering to get up from his cot, Dr. Mulvaney asked, "What can I do for you?"

"It's my rear end. I can't sit." I turned around, dropped my coveralls, and bent over.

"How'd that happen?" he asked without much interest, mechanically reaching above his head into a cabinet and tossing me a tube of zinc ointment. "Eat more. You need some padding." I noticed he slurred his words and shook his head like he was trying to concentrate. Then, he sat up, swung his legs onto the floor, and sighed. "How many missions have you flown to tear the skin like that?" I smelled whiskey.

"One."

"You've got a way to go, son."

Tears welled in my eyes. I wanted to confide in him. How could I fly twenty-five missions like this one? I'm no fighter pilot. I'm a fake. I wanted to tell Mulvaney about my fear. I wanted to talk to him like I had talked to our family doctor, tell him how scared I was when I saw those tracers. I was afraid of getting killed. Maybe he would understand.

"Here, take some bandages and tape. Fold it double thick on your buttocks. It'll give you some relief."

I nodded thanks and left.

I went through the chow line at lunch but didn't eat. Instead, I took two large pieces of dark bread to eat later in my tent. I felt drained. I wanted to sleep. I'd have to be sharp to fly with the squadron in the morning. They'd made me tail-end-Charlie. Not bad jumping to number four position so soon. Tex must have thought I could handle it.

I got into my cot and pulled the blanket tight around my neck, burrowing my face in the fur lining of my leather jacket. I won't think about the mission. Think about good things or I'll never fall asleep.

My hand tunnelled into the folds of the bedding, searching for the smooth warm texture inside Bobbie's thighs. I imagined her hand tracing a path from the small of my back, across my hip, and then down as she cradled and fondled my testicles. No, it's going too quickly. I'll start again. I stood her in front of me, fully clothed. Slowly, very slowly, I had her take off her jacket, unbotton her shirt, and expose her beautiful white breasts. A warm flow spread across my abdomen. Then suddenly her breasts grew hazy and joined, one overlaying the other until the two nipples became one and the breast grew, expanded, covering my field of vision. It started to spin, faster, the reddish purple nipple diffused, swirled into patterns of orange and pink, a yellow blur framed by a black angular wind- shield, wings, and oil scoop, encircled by flame and smoke, spewing white hot shells. The heat from incendiaries scorched my temples. The son-of-a-bitch was trying to kill me! I screamed at him, dodging, ducking, diving violently to evade him. My plane shuddered and shook, my crash straps tugged at my shoulders. I tried to break free. A voice on the radio said, "Hey, Kohn, take it easy. You all right?"

Smith was standing over me, shaking me, his hands gripping my shoulders. I was breathing hard. Foster stood at the foot of my cot holding his mess kit. "Talking ain't so bad, but if you walk in your sleep too, we'll have to dig you out of a foxhole."

"What did I say, Smitty?" My breath came in short gasps.

"Who knows? Sounded like you had a fish caught in your throat. Come on, Kohn. Time for chow," Smith said.

I turned on my back, trying to free myself from the tangled bedding. The blanket was soaked with perspiration.

Falzone was waiting at the entrance to the mess tent when we got there. "What did the doc say? 'Army chow may not be tasty.' Cold, cruddy, beans. Just what we need at 30,000 feet. Gas pains. Foster, you fart, you're sleeping outside the tent tonight. Here, Kohn. Mail's in. One for you."

"You guys go ahead. I'll catch up with you," I said, and turned the envelope in my hands. It was my first letter since I arrived in Africa. It was from my brother:

March 20, 1943

Hi boychik,

Just spoke to Mom. Dad's holding in there, but it's not good. He's lost a lot of weight. His body and jaw shake so much he can't chew or get any food down. Mom's trying to get him to take vitamins. Dr.

Goldman says there's nothing else that can be done. They're getting our allocations like clockwork.

Your address doesn't tell me much. If you can, let me know where you're stationed. I'm with a crew that delivers B-17's to England and C-54's to the South Pacific. I could get on a delivery to North Africa and visit you. It would be a treat to piss in the same urinal as an officer.

I hope you teach your pilots how to fly better than some of the green ones I get stuck with. Met a returnee bomber pilot who saw action in North Africa. He didn't know there was a school for P-38 instruction over there. But he says, keep 'em coming. They need all the fighters you can send them. He gave me a poem for you to pass on to your students.

> Oh, Hedy Lamarr is a beautiful gal
> And Madeline Carroll is, too;
> But you'll find, if you query, a different theory
> Amongst any bomber crew.
> For the loveliest thing of which one could sing
> This side of the Heavenly Gates
> Is no blonde or brunette of the Hollywood set,
> But an escort of P-38s . . .

Don't be a wise-ass. Take care of yourself.

Love,
Bob

Bob believed my story about being an instructor. I knew my parents would too.

The next morning I sat in the briefing tent with the other pilots.

"That's it," Tex pointed to the map. "Reggio Callabria, the Straits of Messina, affectionately known as flak alley. B-17 escort. Get'em there and get'em back. Pick'em up on the coast at 12,000 feet. They'll cross Cape Bone at 0648 on a climb to 30,000. That's a course of 027 degrees, takeoff 0610. You'll hear 'em on channel B. Their code name is 'Workshirt.' Any questions?"

I glanced at Sadler and caught him looking at me. We were a good team. I could follow any move he made. He winked.

"You new men have to understand bein' a fighter pilot is different from what people think," Tex continued. "They have the idea we're crazy, wild, and fearless. Well, that's a lotta shit. Fighters are defensive weapons. It's hard work and unrewardin' and no one's goin' to kid you. You can get yourself killed. Since we arrived in Africa, we've lost eight planes and destroyed six. We're not up to full strength yet. For the time bein', it's tough gettin' a full squadron of twelve planes in the air. But what we lack in equipment and experience is more than made up by good ol' yankee guts and ingenuity.

"Today, Shaker and Rayburn will be Flight Leaders. Brooks will lead the squadron," Tex gestured to a pilot in the front row. "Lieutenant Brooks."

The pilot stood, motioned toward the black board with the names of all the men. "There'll be two new men in my flight today, Foster and Kohn. Foster on my wing and Kohn, tail-end-Charlie on Sadler's wing. That way, Sadler and I can keep an eye on them."

I stood, "I've only flown one mission. Maybe I need more time in number two slot before taking on tail-end-Charlie."

Tex interrupted, "M'daddy used to say, 'When does a boy become a man?' Then he would answer, 'When a man is needed.'"

"I'm ready, sir," Foster said. "This is the day I've been waiting for."

"Jus' give your leaders a little breathin' room."

"You new guys," Brooks continued. "Remember the calls. We're White Flight, the lead flight. Always in the center. The flight on my left, is Blue. On my right, Red. I do a lot of weaving. You're going to be switching back and forth all the time. Just remember, right is red. Left is blue. And a word of advice. If there's a hotshot in this bunch, he'd better stay off my wing. I've had my share of eager beavers. You guys are replacements. No one in this outfit has finished twenty-five, so you guys are filling vacancies. You get the picture?"

I listened to Brooks, remembering Bob's letter and thinking about my parents. I had to keep them thinking I wasn't doing this. Why was I doing this?

"I don't want any daredevils, but you can bet your sweet ass I can't afford anyone who's going to chicken out. Fuck up and you can take another man with you. Just keep your head out of your ass and on a swivel and you'll be all right. They say you never see the one that gets you. Check your guns, your engines, and your radio right after takeoff. If they're not working right, GO BACK! And burn this in your head, an empty belly tank is full of explosive fuel vapors. If it won't release when the order comes to drop it, turn around and go back!

"Wingmen, stick close to your leader. No stragglers. Fall behind and I'm going to leave you. When I give a call, I mean MOVE! and right now! We don't take a vote, you hear? And stay off the goddamn radio unless it's absolutely necessary. That about covers it. Now, let's get the show on the road."

This is it, Freddy boy, no turning back now. *'Tuchis afn tish,'* my father would say. I couldn't think of my father now.

The squadron shaped up fast in good formation and joined the bombers on time. I sat on Sadler's wing, throttled back, keeping pace with the slower bombers a thousand feet below. When we approached the slot between Sicily and Italy, my heart started to pound. As cold as it was in the cockpit, perspiration ran from beneath my leather helmet. The sky was clear, then suddenly, flak burst ahead, as if coming from nowhere. The flak was meant for the bombers, but stray bursts rose to our altitude, and Brooks turned the squadron away and climbed to get out of range. Like a pilot fish under a shark's snout, I slid along with Sadler, keeping a constant distance from his light green belly. In the next instant, his forward motion stopped. Sadler and his plane were gone, replaced by a black and orange flash. I swung my head around to look behind me. There was nothing there.

"Sadler's gone!" I screamed. "He blew up!"

"Get off the air!" Brooks yelled. "This is Doorknob Leader. Enemy fighters two o'clock diving on the lead bomber. Let's go!"

He called the bombers. "Workshirt. Watch for us. We're coming through."

I jammed my throttles forward and pulled opposite Brooks and Foster, feeling naked and alone in third position where Sadler had been. Now I had a clear view of six German fighters as they attacked the bombers. We dove after them, twisting through the bomber formation, causing the 109's to break away.

Rapidly, we closed the distance, coming within firing range of the last two fighters. Whiskers of smoke trailed around the nose of Brooks' plane and his tracers found their mark. The engine of the German fighter on the left burst into flames, the canopy separated, and the German pilot stood up in the cockpit as if to reach for cool air. His torso, bent back under the force of the wind, stood in full view behind the blowtorch of his engine. Brooks fired again. The upper half of the man, cut clean, tumbled past the tail and shot like a cannon ball over the top of Brooks' plane.

My sights were dead center on the Me-109 on the right. I heard myself screaming, "Kill the son-of-a-bitch," while I pressed the trigger buttons and watched the right wing of the 109 break away. The plane did a crazy flip, cartwheeling in pieces like a clay pigeon. My God, I thought, I've shot down a plane and killed a man. He disappeared in seconds, just like Sadler.

I heard Foster. "The lucky bastard."

"Good show," someone said.

"Doorknob Squadron, this is Workshirt Leader. Looked mighty fine from up here. We thank you much. My mother thanks you, too."

I slouched deep in my seat, my face buried in my mask. I didn't kill that man, I told myself. The squadron did.

12

Impossible Odds

AFTER BREAKFAST ALL PILOTS REPORTED to the briefing tent. I sat alone on a long bench, sketching memories of the previous day's mission. The squadron historian, Sergeant Garrett, took notes. Shorty rose to address the group.

"Thank you, gentlemen. Make yourselves comfortable." With his middle finger he pushed his glasses up on his nose. "I see new faces. I'm Capt. Earl Stoddard, your Intelligence Officer. But I warn you not to be fooled by my title. All the answers don't come with the job. By the way, you can call me Shorty. Now I have a few announcements.

"To begin with, any day we're not scheduled to fly, we meet here at 1400 for general indoctrination. In addition, all pilots, scheduled or not, are required to attend all briefings and debriefings..."

"Why can't the briefings be briefer?" someone asked.

"...Check the bulletin board outside the mess tent for announcements of special events and war communiques.

"A tour of duty for a fighter pilot in this theater is twenty-five combat missions. If you were in the Pacific or the Aleutians, it could be one hundred. The number varies in different theaters of operation and is based on many factors. For one, there is a direct relationship between the frequency and type of combat a pilot is subjected to and his efficiency. A loss of efficiency is called 'combat fatigue.' You could suffer from it and not even know you had it."

"That's what's wrong. I'm fatigued!" another pilot blurted.

Shorty ignored the remarks. I was surprised at the levity. The more experienced pilots even appeared to be dozing.

"When you complete twenty-five missions..."

Twenty-three to go, registered in my brain.

"...you'll be sent to R and R. You could be sent sooner, if in Doc's opinion it's necessary."

"R and R sir?" asked Smith.

"Rest and recreation."

"Then do we return to this squadron?"

"No. You might get another tour of combat duty in a different theatre or you might become an instructor. There's a big demand for instructors who have had actual combat experience. Only ground personnel are permanently attached to this squadron. Consider your time here temporary."

"Yeah, temporary and expendable," added Brooks.

"Any questions?" Shorty looked around.

"Sir, this 'combat fatigue,' what is it?"

"What's your name, Lieutenant?"

"Falzone, sir."

"There's a town in Sicily with that name."

"Doesn't surprise me. Where there are Italians, you'll find Falzones. It's common like Smith or Jones."

"Speak for yourself," said Smith.

"Well, Falzone, there's no clear-cut definition of combat fatigue. It's subtle changes. Reflexes aren't as fast. And that's deadly for a fighter pilot. He deliberately puts his life on the line every day. A foot soldier is a pawn, others decide his fate. *'Alen est lacta'*—The die is cast. He becomes fatalistic. But every day a fighter pilot makes a personal choice, each day brings a reconfirmation, a new dedication..."

"Sir? Wouldn't each day reconfirm the reasons we're here in the first place."

"True, but it's like old age, you get tired, things aren't as important as they used to be, there are fewer tomorrows to look forward to. And in the next couple of months, even weeks, some of you boys can become old men. The toughest part is that every time you climb in that cockpit, you know you don't have to go. No one's ever been court-martialed for refusing to fly."

"What he means, Falzone, is if you quit, they make you a foot soldier," said Foster.

"No...it makes you something special." Shorty paused. "Now,

gentlemen, by order of the commanding officer, Directive AR-5412 shall be read to all flying personnel. . . ."

"Here we go, another lecture on VD."

". . .Subject: Medals, Awards, Citations, and Field Promotions."

". . .every box of Cracker Jacks contains a Congressional Medal of Honor. You too can be an instant hero," someone said under his breath.

"Gentlemen, your attention please." Shorty waited until the mumblings subsided. "Thank you, gentlemen. You are serving in the Mediterranean Theater of Operations, which entitles you to the appropriate campaign ribbon to which you may affix battle stars for specific engagements to be determined at a later date. An airman who completes ten sorties against the enemy will be awarded the Air Medal. . . ."

"Show us your medal, Brooks!" said Shaker.

". . .and, for every ten sorties thereafter, the airman will be awarded an oak leaf to his Air Medal."

"Hey, Cominski! How did you get that oak leaf you wear on your dingus?" Foster asked.

Shorty looked around for help, but Tex was smiling. Shorty began again.

"The confirmed destruction of an airborne enemy aircraft earns an oak leaf to the Air Medal."

"You mean we have to wait for him to take off before we shoot him down!. . ." Smith asked.

"Wait 'til he has one wheel off the ground," said Shaker.

"The D.F.C. . . ." Shorty began, and the talking ceased. "Thank you, gentlemen. The Distinguished Flying Cross is the highest award given by the Army Air Corps to a flyer for valor, bravery, or for service above and beyond the call of duty. Lindbergh got one for flying the Atlantic. Two pilots of the 71st Fighter Squadron have been awarded the DFC, posthumously."

It was so quiet I could hear the men breathing. Someone cleared his throat.

Tex took the floor. "Any questions?"

Foster raised his hand. "Sir? What establishes a 'confirm'?"

"There are three possibilities: Damage, probable or destroyed. Confirm refers to the destruction of an enemy aircraft. If y'hit the enemy but he gets away, that's a 'damage.' The engine of an Me-109 is held on with four bolts. If he can limp back, the engine can be changed in an hour. If y'see fire or pieces fly off, that's a 'probable.' The destruction of an aircraft will be considered 'confirmed' if someone else sees the plane crash, blow up, or the pilot bail out. If y'all are alone, there's got to be some convincin' footage from your gun cameras to back it up.

"Those were confirms for Brooks and Ko-han yesterday. No doubt about that."

Foster stood, "I was on Brook's wing and fired the same time he did."

"Don't matter, your leader gets the credit. With Sadler gone, Kohn became the leader. That's the way it works."

Foster, slowly moving his head side to side, slumped down on to the bench.

"Ko-han, you're an Element Leader now. Y'earned it. Y'ought to be proud o' y'self, boy."

I sat with my hands pushed deep in my pockets and nodded at Tex. Element Leader meant I would have my own wingman. That extra protection could mean a lot. Not a word about Sadler. As though he never existed.

"Let me remind you men," Tex went on, "destruction of enemy aircraft isn't a sport. We're not interested in who gets the highest score. Accurate information is necessary for Intelligence to estimate enemy strength. Sergeant Garrett here keeps the records. And headquarters maintains a gain and loss tally from fighter groups, aerial gunners, and photo reconaissance. Based on that information, missions are assigned and we are able to make reasonable estimates of what we may expect from the enemy. Yes? You have a question?"

Smith stood. "Why not count the ones destroyed on the ground?"

"Can't be confirmed, and it's safer not to underestimate their strength...

"I have a few more things to say, then I'll let you go. First, put to rest that crap about how a P-38 spins. It's a lot of bullshit! It won't flatten out. I've even tried it with no ammo in the nose and still haven't been able to get that bird to flatten out. Standard recovery technique will get you out of a spin as easy as possum shit sliding' off a pine cone. O.K., that's it. Dismissed!"

Sergeant Garrett stopped me outside the tent. "Excuse me, Lieutenant, what's the name of your newspaper in Chicago?"

"You selling subscriptions?" I asked.

"Just for the record. A little PR for the folks back home."

"I don't get it."

"You get an Air Medal for shooting down that 109 and that's news."

"No dice!"

"You don't want the medal?"

"I don't want my name published in Chicago. Ever." Garrett looked puzzled. "Sergeant, I want your word you won't make this public. News like that would affect my father's health."

"I don't know if I can keep it quiet, sir."

"Why not? There's one less enemy fighter, and that's all that matters. Give headquarters the count. They don't need my name on it. Right?"

"Well, I suppose. . . ."

"Is it a deal?"

"I guess it's all right."

We shook on it and I went back to my tent. This time I'd been lucky enough to stop the news release. Next time I might not be around to prevent it. That night I wrote a letter.

North Africa
March 28, 1943

Dearest Mom and Dad,

I hope you will never read this letter.

I am not a student. I am not learning to be an instructor. I am a fighter pilot engaged in aerial combat. I didn't tell you before because I wanted to save you from worrying.

Now I must tell you I have failed to return. I want you to hear it from me before you receive government notification.

It is possible I may never come back. Whatever happens, I want you to know I have done what I wanted to do.

Your loving son,
Fred

I sealed the letter, addressed it, and taped it to the bottom of my mattress. Then I went to Garrett's tent and made another deal with him. He would mail the letter if I failed to return from a mission within four days.

13

A Bitter Pill

"FUUUCK," CHAD EXHALED THROUGH HIS teeth, "Here comes chickenshit."

A jeep bounced toward us in a cloud of dust. A captain, neatly dressed, pleated shirt, squared cap, was out of his seat before the jeep came to a full stop. He ducked under the wing of the plane and started up the ladder. The plane moved slightly, creaking under his added weight. Chad moved forward on the wing, making room for the captain to crouch alongside, the officer's knees bent just enough to keep his kakhi trousers from touching the plane's dusty surface. He didn't seem to notice me sitting in the cockpit, bare from the waist up, the sleeves of my coveralls knotted at my waist. The captain's eyes met Chad's.

"Damn it, Sergeant, I'm gonna bust your ass!"

"Sir?" Chad looked surprised.

"You've gone too far this time. Parker's plane's been picked clean. I warned you that Parts and Maintenance will do the cannibalizing, so keep your friggin hands off those planes. I decide who gets those parts. I want 'em back. Every last piece."

"Captain, sir, I don't know what yer talking about."

"Shit ya don't." The captain's voice was up an octave. "I want it back, all of it. Carburetor, fuel pump, a transmitter and receiver, an artificial horizon . . ."

He shot a glance at the open doors of the gun compartment.

". . . and one 50 caliber machine gun!"

Ted was standing on the ground, his arms inside the gun

compartment, his head hidden behind ammo trays and belts of machine gun shells. I heard him busily fussing, oiling, cleaning and adjusting the guns. I knew nothing about armaments. They either worked or they didn't. I wouldn't know if anyone had changed a machine gun.

"I didn't take nothing." Chad stared the captain in the eye, his voice unwavering. I believed him. "Someone *tell* you I took that stuff?" he asked. "Not a chance!"

The captain wasn't listening. "Sergeant," the words came slow and steady, "I don't know where you stash the stuff you take, and I don't care. Get it all back to Parts by tonight or you won't be crewing this plane."

A small vein pulsated on Chad's left temple.

"Do you understand, Sergeant?"

"Yes, sir, I understand." Chad measured each word.

"No later than tonight!"

"No, sir, can't do that, sir!"

"What do you mean?"

"Don't have the parts and don't know where they are."

"You're off this plane, Jessup, as of now! Report to MacMillan for reassignment." The captain climbed down the ladder, ducked under the stabilizer, and headed for his jeep. I got out of the cockpit and followed.

"Excuse me, Captain, may I have a word with you?"

He turned, apparently seeing me for the first time, pointed a finger and barked, "As you were, soldier!"

"I'm Lieutenant Kohn. This is my plane."

"Cohen?" He looked from me back to the ground crew. They puttered with the plane as though they hadn't heard, except Chad, who stood on the wing, arms folded across his chest, watching and listening.

"Sorry, didn't know you were a pilot, no uniform and all. . . Willard. Jess Willard, Chief, Parts and Maintenance. You want something?"

"Pleased to meet you, Captain. I joined the squadron a few weeks ago."

"So, you got LMA? It's an early model. When we get delivery on the H series maybe we can trade you up."

"Thanks, I like this one. Handles real well and no problems."

"Good, that's what I like to hear. Not much sense keeping these birds flying if it weren't for you fellows." He turned to go.

"It's about Sergeant Jessup, sir," I began, a little unsurely.

He looked back. "Yes?"

"I overheard what you said about removing him as crew chief."

"What about it, Cohen?" he snapped.

"I'd appreciate it if you wouldn't do that."

He squinted. "Something you know?"

"No, sir. I just want Jessup as my crew chief."

The captain looked at the plane, the open cowlings, and the men at work. "You can have him 'til the end of the week."

"That's not what I had in mind," I said. "I guess I'm superstitious. I want him until I've finished my missions or until I don't make it back."

"You're new here, Cohen." He pronounced my name with special emphasis. "That's not the way it works. Maintenance is my responsibility, and that includes assignment of mechanics. No exceptions. I'll have a crew chief for you next week with more experience than Jessup. That's what you want, isn't it?"

I lowered my voice. "No, sir. I want Chad Jessup as my crew chief as long as I fly that plane. Like you said, Captain, 'Keep 'em flying.'"

A few seconds passed. The captain remained unblinking and expressionless. I looked at my wristwatch. "I'm scheduled for a straffing mission in forty-two minutes. Sorry I bothered you," I shruggged. "The C.O. said whatever I wanted, all I had to do was ask. I'll talk to him."

Willard's eyes darted from me to Chad, then back again. He called to Chad, "O.K., Sarg, she's all yours. Your Lieutenant Cohen is gonna win the war all by himself." The captain left without saying goodbye.

Ted's hands remained inside the gun compartment but I couldn't hear him doing anything. Chad contemplated the grease under his fingernails, then looked up. "Thanks for what you said to the captain. He blows a lot but he don't mean no harm. Gives me stripes and takes 'em away so often I don't bother sewing 'em on anymore. You see, Lootenant, this ain't like taking care of a bomber. Their mechanics get to go on missions sometimes. We don't know what it's like for a fighter pilot. Captain Willard forgets it takes more than a bunch of parts to get this baby up in the air." He ran his hand over the horizontal stabilizer.

"He always talks about losing planes and being short of parts, but everyone in a fighter squadron knows, you lose a plane, you lose a pilot."

Chad sighed, "I'd do anything to keep this plane flying, Lootenant, even steal if I had to. But I didn't take the stuff he's talking about. I swear I didn't!"

"I didn't ask."

"I say the captain's got troubles with those creeps back at supply. They're always losing something. Hey, Lootenant, you got a girl back home?"

His question caught me by surprise.

"Well, not really. Why?" I asked.

"Now that you're an Element Leader, maybe you'd like to give our plane a name. Some pilots name 'em after their wives or sweethearts. I'm going to paint a swastika on the nose for the plane you shot down. I could paint a name at the same time."

I thought for a moment. "Name it, 'Mr. Arnold.'"

"Mr. Arnold?"

"Yep, it was the name my father used in business."

Chad shrugged. "O.K., it's yer plane, Lootenant."

The mission started badly. Ten minutes after take off, Brooks sprung an oil leak and turned back. I moved ahead to lead the fight and Brook's wingman slid in behind me to tail-end-Charlie position.

"This is Shaker. I'm taking over Doorknob Squadron. Who's leading Brooks' flight?"

"Kohn, Doorknob Five Two," I answered.

"You're Red Leader now."

Shaker's flight swept overhead with Foster as Element Leader.

O.K., Dad, hang on. We've been promoted. Here we go. We crossed the Mediterranean fifty feet above the water and roared over a small village perched on a coastal cliff of Sicily. Our target was a German figher base at Enna.

"Close it up, Doorknob, nice and tight. Looks like Caltagirone. What do you think, Blue Leader?"

"Maybe. There's the river. The airfield should be forty-two miles on this heading."

"Keep your eyes open, Red Leader."

"Roger," I said.

The sky was clear. The land seemed quiet. The river narrowed and disappeared into a tangled blanket of dense trees.

"How about it, Shaker. Where's the fucking field?" Blue Leader said.

"Give it another five minutes," Shaker said.

"We should have been there two minutes ago."

"Knock it off, Blue Leader."

Three minutes later, Shaker turned the squadron and we started to crisscross the countryside. The terrain changed to short choppy hills and sharp canyons. The son-of-a-bitch was lost.

"Doorknob Squadron, this is Doorknob Leader," Shaker said. "We'll go back to the coast to get our bearings and re-enter. Any of you guys have to switch to reserves, give a holler and we'll head back to base." Shaker turned east and we followed the shore. At the southeast corner of Sicily, where the coastline turns north, he got his bearings. "O.K. Doorknob. I know where it is. Let's go."

The squadron took a heading inland. Ten minutes later I heard a new voice, "Doorknob Leader. This is Blue Four. I've got ten gallons left in my mains."

"I'm running low too. Red Three. Over."

"The field's dead ahead. Let's wipe 'em out," Shaker yelled.

"Doorknob Squadron! Fighters four o'clock. Break right!"

I wrenched my plane around to the right. There was nothing there. I was breathing hard. There was another call. "Enemy fighters! High, six o'clock to Blue Flight!"

I flipped back to the left. Someone had screwed up the call. I saw them. Three German fighters in a dive. My wingman and tail-end-Charlie had slipped ten plane lengths behind. The enemy fighters broke off their dive and came after the fragmented remains of my flight.

"Doorknob Squadron! Fighters at three o'clock!"

"Jesus!" someone screamed, "Five more at twelve o'clock!"

We were under a hail of attacking aircraft. Every plane in our squadron turned and dodged to avoid colliding. We were scared rats in a cage.

I skidded onto the tail of a Focke Wolfe, got in a quick burst of fire, almost overran him. He showed no signs of being hit but continued in a straight line into the crest of a hill and blew up.

Radio calls piled on top of one another, fragmented, some unintelligible. I couldn't distinguish one voice from another.

"Fights at three o'clock to White Fl. . .!"

"Where are you, Blue Leader?"

"I got him! I got him!" someone yelled.

"Aaaagh!"

"Let's get the hell out of here."

I was alone, ducking in and around shallow valleys, trying to sort out the radio confusion when suddenly it was silent. My chest throbbed, my breath burst in and out of my throat like a razor, my legs vibrated, and I ordered myself to relax my grip on the control wheel.

"Doorknob Squadron. This is Doorknob Leader. Don't regroup. Lean out your mixtures and refuel at one of our bomber fields on the Algerian coast. We'll meet back at our base. Anyone in trouble?" There was no answer.

I seethed with anger, pounding my feet on the metal floor of the cockpit. Damn you! Shaker, you idiot! You fucked up, screwing around, then all that talking on the radio.

I remained low during the return flight across the Mediterranean, all the time thinking how awful it had been, how Shaker had groped around looking for the target, and then the whole thing fell apart. I landed on reserve tanks at a B-25 base thirty miles inland. A mass of men on four wheels raced toward me. The driver pointed to the swastika on the nose of my plane.

"Hey, look at that! Got one, huh?"

Two of the men took their shoes off and crawled over the plane like kids in a playground.

"How about a favor?" I asked the crew chief.

"Sure, lunch?" asked a husky sergeant with a New York accent, "Spend the night? A lube and a wash, maybe?"

"I need some fuel."

"Is that all? You got it!" The sergeant pointed a greasy finger at one of the men. "You heard the man! Get the lead out!" The jeep raced away in high gear and in minutes came barrelling back across the field, a gasoline truck trailing behind.

"O.K. men, fill 'er up," the sergeant ordered. "Hey Lieutenant, what's that?" he asked, pointing to my right wing. I climbed onto the wing and saw two gaping holes and a series of jagged rips, as though a giant fist had punched up from below through the top skin, inches from a fuel cell. I had never felt it. A fraction closer and the plane would have exploded. I could have disappeared like Sadler. Suddenly I felt weak. I waited in the shade under the wing. The sergeant handed me a piece of cheese from his rations and a canteen of coffee. I nibbled at the cheese and watched.

When they had finished refueling the plane, the sergeant said, "After take off, maybe you could fly low across the field so we could see this baby in the air? We've heard a lot of rumors about how good they fly. It'd give the men a kick."

It was their fuel. I owed them a pass. I raced down the runway and pulled into a steep climb. I was flying again! I'd survived six missions. Nineteen to go. I can do it, I thought, and I relaxed into the feel of the plane again. At 6,000 feet I turned the plane on its back, pulled it through the loop, and roared back down to the runway. The airspeed indicator hit the redline as I shot across the boundary a few feet above the ground, the men waving wildly from their jeep. Two jumped off the hood as I hurtled a few feet above them. The others scattered, unable to hold their balance in the prop wash. I climbed straight up and rolled the plane, once, twice, three times. I loved the sensation of plunging through space and I was happy to be on my way home. Over my shoulder I watched the diminishing figures dance and wave their arms. Then they were gone and all I could think about was how that Shaker almost got me killed.

I levelled off at 6,000 and set my course. It was almost noon, and the heat at low altitude was intense and oppressive. The canopy absorbed the heat and held me in it, transforming the exhilaration I had just felt to nausea. I felt queasy. I tasted the cheese. Damn, I was getting sick. I reached for oxygen. The air holes in the mask triggered a stream of associations. I saw the holes in the wing. Sweat burst from my pores. There could be structural damage. Stupid *schmuck!* God-damn showoff! I could have torn a wing off in those rolls!

I dropped the mask and pressed my hand across my mouth, afraid I would vomit. Settle down. Breathe deeply through your nose. It'll pass. A sudden pain, searing, agonizing, gripped my stomach. I forgot the nausea, hunched over and clutched my stomach with both hands. After a moment the cramps subsided, but I was afraid to move. The plane somehow maintained its attitude.

The magnified rays of the sun drilled through the plexiglas. Perspiration followed the contours around my nose and dripped from my chin. My coveralls were soaked. The cramps returned. The outside air temperature was 103 degrees at 6,000 feet and hotter in the cockpit. I cranked down the right window below my chin, creating a suction in the cockpit so that if I vomited, the mess would be drawn out and not make a disgusting clean-up for Chad. But the opening disturbed the air flow. The plane porpoised, gained and lost altitude, then drifted twenty degrees off course. I was too sick to be concerned about navigation. I'd re-establish my course when I felt better. At least I had a full load of fuel.

The terrain below was unfamiliar. I suspected I had drifted south of the course to my home base. Landing in the mountains would be impossible. I was afraid I would pass out.

I punched Channel "B" and called Washboard. No answer. I tried again. Still there was silence. I must be too far inland and too low to be heard. I would try again later.

My fetal position had relieved the searing stomach cramps. Finally a moment of peace; the nausea too subsided. I willed it away. Probably it was the cheese I'd eaten. Now to get home. I began to ease into an upright position when a new pain struck, low, deep in my bowels. I straightened my feet and ankles under the rudder pedals and squeezed my buttocks together to keep from unloading my bowels. The pain gripped me. I was bunched too low in my seat to see outside the cockpit. I was in trouble. Over the panic rising in my throat, I called Washboard.

A voice boomed through my headset. They heard me! "DOORKNOB FIVE TWO! THIS IS WASHBOARD! OVER!"

"A homing," I choked, "Give me a homing...over." My voice was barely audible. I was concentrating on keeping my body stiff. The voice came back, no longer detached and professional. "Give me a long count, please, over."

"One, two, three...four...five..." my voice tight and strained, "...six, seven...eight, nine..." I fought the pressure, "ten!" Then downhill fast, "Nine-eight-seven...six-five-four," I squeezed, "...three-two-one-over!"

Silence for some seconds. "Doorknob five two, we're getting it now, stand by and, let's see, here it is, you're nine zero miles from base...Take a heading of two seven four degrees. Over."

Only ninety miles from base. It was broad daylight and I was lost! I was humiliated. I corrected to 274 degrees. Minutes passed and Washboard came in again.

"Doorknob five two, short count, please. Over."

His voice was solicitous, apologetic. I gritted my teeth, squeezing hard not to dump in my pants. I didn't answer immediately. His voice blasted in my headset, "DOORKNOB FIVE TWO! DOOR-KNOB GIVE TWO! You O.K.? Come on fella, come in, over!"

I answered, "Won-two-ree-hor...ive-ix-even-ate...ya get it? Over."

"Just fine, Doorknob, read you loud and clear, easy now, let's see..." He kept up a steady commentary, stalling while he finished the computations. "You're doin' fine, jus' fine...we have it! Seven five miles from base, left to two four nine degrees and you'll be over Constantine in eight minutes."

No wind, seventy-five miles from base, and I can't hold course? He must think I'm bleeding to death.

"Doorknob! Off your right wing! Constantine! See it?" he asked hopefully.

I jerked the wheel hard to the right in a vertical bank. No Constantine. I spun the wheel into a sharp bank to the left. There it was, off my left wing tip.

"Thanks, Washboard, got it! Out!"

To see Constantine was to be home. You could cut the engines and glide to our landing strip. I turned my head and stretched my neck for a better look at the city. I sighed with relief. For a second, only a second, I relaxed. Quickly it came. No amount of squeezing would stop it. I didn't care. I let it come. The cramps, the pain, the nausea disappeared. It seemed cooler in the cockpit. It kept coming. The parachute would be ruined. I felt better.

A different voice called, "DOORKNOB FIVE TWO! You're flying right over the field! Can we help? This is Doorknob Ground Control. Over."

I called to the man in the radio shack, "I'm O.K. I just need some toilet paper."

As my wheels touched the runway, jeeps, an ambulance, and a command car from Wing chased alongside my plane. I swung the plane into my parking space, flipped the switches before the props stopped, and threw open the canopy. Chad, having spotted the damage, jumped up on the wing to help.

"Lootenant, can I...?"

The odor hit him like a club. He staggered backward and almost lost balance. I dragged myself out of the plane. Chad helped me down and, without a comment, produced a pail of gasoline and a handful of rags. The assorted vehicles circled the plane. Mindless of an audience, I dropped my flight coveralls and cleaned myself in the hot African sun.

Nobody laughed.

*   *   *   *

The mission had been a disaster. By the end of the afternoon, only nine of the original eleven planes to reach the target had returned. Ground crews watched the sky until nightfall, hoping theirs wasn't among the missing. Two planes from Shaker's flight were lost.

At the de-briefing the two names left unaccounted for were LMD-Wade and LMJ-Kearns. I didn't know them.

Tex sighed. "Well, Shaker, let's hear it. What are the chances they made it?"

"I saw LMD get hit."

"See a chute?"

"No, but we were too low anyway."

"What about the other one?"

"I don't know."

"How about the rest of you? I want to know what happened." No one answered. "He didn't just disappear. Falzone, you were in that flight. When did you see him last?"

"Just before we got jumped. I was too busy after that."

"Yeah!" said Shaker, "Some asshole calls for a break right and we get jumped from the left. Who made that fucking call?"

"Jesus Christ!" came a whisper from the front row. I saw two unfamiliar faces, two replacement pilots sitting crosslegged on the ground in front of Tex. It was a bad first briefing for new pilots to hear.

"What happened, Shaker!" Tex asked.

"We were outnumbered and they were just sitting up there waiting for us. We ended up in a dog fight, every man for himself. It was a lousy break."

"Bullshit," I said.

"What did y'all say?" Tex asked.

"Bullshit," I answered. "The Germans had plenty of time to know we were coming."

"What do you mean?"

"We spent ten minutes looking for the field!"

Shaker was looking at me, slowly shaking his head. "It was more like three."

"And what about radio silence? We sounded like student pilots on a navigation flight!"

"Listen, Buster, it was my ass on the line," Shaker said.

"What about our asses? With all that yapping, you invited every German to our party."

"I was there too, Nose," Foster growled. "And that's not the way it happened."

I ignored Foster. "Shaker, we were lost and you know it. We missed Enna by fifty miles."

Tex looked doubtful.

I walked up to the chalk board and rapidly sketched a map of Sicily, retracing the various courses we had flown and diagramming the position of our squadron when we received the first order to break right.

"That's a lot o' shit," I heard someone say. "What's he, some kind o' fuckin' expert?"

I continued the drawing, my back to the group, when I heard Foster say, "The closer you get to combat, the fewer Jews you find. Now you know why."

The chalk broke in my hand. I turned and glared at his soft putty face. Words caught in my throat. I wanted to hurt the son of a bitch. He was painting yellow stars.

Only Falzone was looking at me. The others stared at their hands or the walls of the tent.

Foster pointed his finger at me. "I say you're gutless. Just like the rest of your scummy tribe. It's all right when you're doing the shooting or ripping a sucker off, you're a big hero. But when there's a plane on your ass . . . you're yellow! Don't go blaming Shaker . . . "

Tex cleared his throat. "O.K., that's enough."

" . . . Get him out of my tent. Throw him out of the squadron, Tex. He's not one of us."

Tex talked down at the floor in a low steady voice. "Not one more word, Foster. Don't even breathe too loud." He raised his head and spoke to everyone. "There's jus' no place for that anti-Jew talk in this squadron. It's un-American. What do you think we're fighting this war for? Take my advice and put that hate where it'll do the most good. We got an enemy out there that's big enough for all of us."

Falzone stage-whispered, "Boy, you guys sure put on a show."

"You heard that prick," said Foster. "Made it sound like old Shaker cost us two planes."

"That's not what I meant," I said aloud.

"Sure as shit sounded like it," Foster answered.

"I meant, it was his fault we lost two *men*."

"OK, OK. That's enough," Tex said, and picked up where he had left off. "We lost two planes, and as far as I'm concerned, there's no excuse for it. Anyone hear them call?"

"I think one of them was hit. I mean *him*, not the plane," Falzone said.

I shivered involuntarily. Once a pilot was lost, his name was never mentioned again.

"We're not givin' up on them. They could have made it to the water and ditched. Y'all remember, particularly you new men, ditchin' is a good option. You're flyin' the finest fuckin' machine ever built. It's strong, powerful, and dependable. It can do anythin' you ask it to. If you gotta ditch, keep the nose high and jettison the canopy just before she hits the water.

"Keep callin' Mayday all the way down so Washboard can get a fix. The plane ditches easy in a calm sea. Fortunately the Mediterranean is never rough. Y'all have a Mae West and dinghy, so if either of 'em ditched they stand a good chance of bein' picked up by a British Sunderland flying boat."

"Sure, after they've had their afternoon tea," grumbled Brooks. "Come on, Tex. Let's call it like it is. We've never had a successful air-sea rescue of a downed Lightning. As for me, I'll bring that crate back to dry land even if I have to carry it on my back."

"O.K., Brooks, so nobody wants to get wet. But the primary reason for puttin' it in the water is poor fuel management. If you don't watch your mixture, you won't make it back. And the Germans know all the angles. Just when you're ready to head home, that's when you can expect enemy fighters. They try to keep y'all busy 'til you run empty. If ya don't think you can make it or you're in trouble, get on that goddamn radio and call 'Washboard'! They'll home in on you, pinpoint where you ditch, and call for rescue."

"'Washboard'?" asked a new man.

"Right. They pick you up by voice transmission, same way the enemy does if we gab too much. Only the squadron leader or someone callin' in an attack is authorized to break radio silence. You!" Tex pointed a finger at Foster, "Say you're in Blue Flight crossin' over White Flight and an attack comes in from 6 o'clock high. How do you call it?"

"That would be 3 o'clock to White Flight."

"Right. Or 'Six o'clock to Blue Flight.' "

Brooks called from the back, "We had one joker used to say, 'Bandits at ten after four.' Drove me nuts."

"You think that's bad? How about the guy whose watch ran slow?" someone added.

"Bailin' out of a P-38 offers some real problems," Tex continued. "Unlike low-wing fighters, the 38 is a midwing and a lotta guys have hit the tail in a jump. I say, if you can't avoid it, pop the canopy, turn 'er over on her back, and drop out."

"Sounds like my girl," said Cominski.

Tex waited for the laughter to cease.

"But that's not the only problem. Say y'all get out in one piece. You won't last three minutes danglin' from a chute at 30,000 feet without oxygen and with enemy fighters takin' pot shots at you."

"The Germans shoot at pilots while they're helpless?" Falzone asked.

"Is there a better time? I wouldn't let a German pilot float down so's he can climb in another 109 and come after me again. So think twice before you bail out. Over water, I'd take ditchin' every time. Over land, if you bail out or crash in enemy territory, say Tunisia, you stand a good chance o' gettin' back. The Germans are retreatin' under heavy pressure. Look for help from Catholic churches or storekeepers with Jewish names. We don't have an underground in Sicily or Italy, so if you go down there, y'all got a problem.

"O.K., fellas, y'all can take it easy today. Maybe there's some chow left. Takeoff's tomorrow at 1450. See y'all in the morning."

Shaker passed me on his way out. "You were right, Kohn. That's just the way it happened."

14

The Covenant

IT WAS AN HOUR'S DRIVE to M'Saada over bumpy roads, but it was worth it even though the water was only lukewarm. A foul-smelling sulphur spring trickled from a crevice in an underground cave and formed a shallow pond. This they called a mineral bath. The hours of use were posted at the entrance, and admission was controlled by a middle-aged British officer. Local villagers used the baths in the early morning hours, enlisted personnel came later in the morning, then officers had exclusive use in the afternoons and early evenings. It was my third visit to the cave and the first time I had found it empty.

The officer looked up as I approached. "This time is reserved for officers."

"I am an officer."

He studied my coveralls.

I pointed to a bundle under my arm. "Fresh uniform."

He tapped a clipboard. "Sign here, name, rank, and serial number. Can't be too careful, you know. Since the war, almost anyone can get in the service."

"Yes, I know what you mean."

"Riff raff, undesirables. Times have changed."

"Have they?" I said.

I placed my coveralls and fresh clothes in a neat bundle high in a depression in the stone wall and submerged to my neck. My muscles relaxed in the warm water. There was no hurry, it was only 1400. It

129

would take forty-five minutes to drive to Constantine, and the driver was signed out until 1800.

I scrubbed and rescrubbed my body, then scrubbed again dissolving the last bit of green Palmolive soap I had brought from the states. I had been in North Africa two and a half months and it had been a month since my last bath. Rumors were our base was to be relocated, so every improvement, including a shower, had come to a halt. I was glad the cave was dark and I couldn't see the dirty water. The last time I had come to the pool I was sure I felt a piece of feces float by. Now I just wanted to lie in the water in the quiet darkness.

Ten minutes later, two English officers dropped in. I got out, dried myself, and dressed in fresh pinks and blouse while the driver waited. Feeling like a V.I.P., I had him drive me the thirty kilometers to Constantine.

The city looked old and dreary under overcast skies; the streets were crowded with people, dogs, and donkeys. The only vehicles were U.S. military. The driver took me to the center of town and stopped in front of a large warehouse with an American flag, the U.S.O. We arranged that he'd check back in three hours. If I wasn't there when he returned, he'd figure I was staying overnight, and I could get a ride back to the base in the morning.

I opened the door and was assaulted by a Victrola's scratchy and broken refrain, "Don't Fence Me In." There wasn't a familiar face. The room was furnished haphazardly with drab and worn couches where lounging G.I.'s read or wrote letters. On a tripod near the door was a cork board with a sign, "Check here for messages and special events." Just below, printed on an index card was written, "The first Seder is tonight. Check with Esther Rosen in the office."

I hadn't realized it was spring already. Time was disjointed for me being so far away from home. I felt a pang of homesickness and went to find the office.

The U.S.O. office was in a tiny room crammed with papers, disorganization, and Esther Rosen. She was about twenty-eight and chubby. I waited in the doorway while she gave what I imagined were instructions to a young Arab boy. She spoke French rapidly, not taking time to breathe. When the boy left, I squeezed in between tables littered with magazines, V-mail blanks, dirty dishes,

and ashtrays overflowing with cigarette butts. She smiled warmly
and extended a hand like we were old friends.

"Hi, Esther, they keep you busy, huh?"

She shook a fist full of forms and said, "I can't imagine what they
do with all these reports. I have so much to do and I end up
spending most of my time shuffling papers." She studied my
uniform, and my medals. "Flyboy, huh? Don't see many of you
fellows around. Bombers?"

"Fighters."

"Looks like you've seen some action. How many missions have
you flown?"

"Thirteen."

Her shoulders twitched involuntarily. "That's a lucky number.
Where's your base? No, scratch that. I'm not supposed to ask things
like that. It's just that we'd like to see more of you fellows when you
come to town. Where do you guys go for fun?"

"I thought the U.S.O. was for enlisted men only. It's my first time
in town."

"Well, it's great you're here, we're organizing a dance for tonight.
As you can hear, the victrola is broken, only newscasts on the radio,
so we may have to hum a lot. Please stay," she added, running her
sentences together. "I finally got cooperation from the local church
to let the girls and their chaperones stay until ten o'clock. The girls
love to practice English. We're setting up card tables, checkers, we
have V-mail blanks and some old books. We're really in business
and things are going to get better. Please stop by everytime you're
in town, O.K.?"

"What about the Seder?" I asked.

"Seder? *Landsman*? Fantastic! You don't look Jewish."

She took both my hands in hers and we laughed. I felt like I had
discovered a favorite cousin I didn't see very often.

"Where are you from?"

"Chicago."

"So am I! What part?"

"Northside."

"I went to Senn," she squealed.

"Lakeview."

"We must know the same people. The Shapiros? The Goldbergs,
Manny and Ethel? What's your name? This is too good to be true!"

"Kohn."

"So what's a nice Jewish boy doing flying around in an airplane?" she laughed. She had beautiful white teeth.

"You really want to go to a Seder?"

"Sure. Where's it being held?"

"There are a few in town. Jewish families are opening their homes to Jewish servicemen for the holidays. You'd be a prize. An officer and a flyer! There's a young girl sitting in the hall, maybe you noticed when you came in, about thirteen, dark little thing, only speaks French. Her name is Yvonne Sebbah, comes from a nice family. She's been waiting all morning to bring a Jewish American soldier home for the Seder tonight.

"Father's a butcher, very old family, been here for generations. They're so grateful to be liberated from the Vichy French, her father brings us little gifts ever since we occupied Constantine. You know, a little piece chicken, some meat cakes, see the box in the corner? Full of *matzoh*, just for me. Here have a piece. You speak French? Well, it doesn't matter, if you want to go to a Seder, it'll be a *mitzvah*, you'll make them very proud. They've had a bad time since France fell, well, you'll see for yourself. Wait! Don't move, I'll get Yvonne." She barely managed to squeeze past the desk.

I extracted a piece of *matzoh* from the box. It was shaped like a thick round plate. The shape was different from the flat, thin squares I was used to, but it tasted like the Passover *matzoh* of my grandmother's Seders.

Esther's non-stop French bounced off the doorframe. She came back into the room leading a slender young girl, very dark, barefoot, her thin arms hanging from a faded sleeveless dress, her long brown hair in two tight braids tied neatly with string. Her eyes avoided mine when Esther made the introduction. She fidgeted uneasily. Esther told me I was to go with Yvonne to her home and explained that the little girl was uncomfortable because she didn't believe I was Jewish. Jews couldn't become officers, the little girl thought.

"Can you say something in Hebrew? Anything?" Esther pleaded. I laughed. *"Sholom alechem; Boruch ahtoh. . ."*

Yvonne smiled. Her black eyes softened, and she looked at me with affection. We were three people with a common bond, the trust and tenderness of one Jew for another in an alien place. She kissed the back of my hand, squeezed my fingers, and chattering in French pulled me out of the office. I turned and said goodbye to

Esther, telling her I'd see her again. She waved and blew a kiss.

Yvonne walked several paces ahead of me. I lengthened my stride, but she quickened her pace keeping the same distance between us, hugging the sidewalk closest to the shop doorways and entrances to dilapidated tenements. The muscles in my jaw tensed at the sight of a *Mogen David* splashed in yellow paint on the window of a dry goods store. Vichy bastards! I thought. Inside the dark interior I saw a bearded man examining bolts of fabric. He glanced up as we passed, then turned his back. I sucked in deep breaths. Yvonne tugged at my sleeve. She had been watching me.

We walked through a neighborhood of narrow streets, spiced with unfamiliar odors, small shops, and haggling merchants. Two American soldiers came out of a shop and snapped to attention, holding their hands to their caps until I returned their salutes. Yvonne watched the exchange, questioningly at first, then slowly smiled. Across the street, another yellow star painted on the back of a bench. Further on, several soldiers walking in our direction, saluted. Yvonne dropped back and walked close beside me, tentatively holding my sleeve between two fingers.

We appeared to be crisscrossing streets we had walked a minute earlier, streets frequented by American soldiers. Soon I understood Yvonne was showing me off. I enjoyed the attention. Allied sailors and soldiers saluted, even Algerian policemen. When we passed two G.I.'s with their backs to us, Yvonne called, "Hey JOE!" and giggled when they turned and saluted.

The Sebbah home was two stories of wood and stucco, clean but in desperate need of repair. A young girl in her early teens stood in the front yard throwing grain to a flurry of chickens. When she saw us she ran to the door calling in French, and a middle-aged woman emerged from the house. She cupped a flour-caked hand to her mouth and called toward an open second-story window. People came running from all directions—Yvonne's father and mother, a very old grandmother, two sisters, a ten-year-old brother, and the husband of her eldest sister. Yvonne's father called a loud *"Bonsoir"* to neighbors half a block away so he could display his special guest. When in the deepening darkness my uniform was no longer visible, we went inside to begin the Passover ritual.

Yvonne reappeared in a fresh dress at dinner, a flowered print bleached almost white from countless washings, standing stiffly

away from her thin and undeveloped figure. She smiled shyly at me
when I said how pretty she looked. We all sat at the table laid with
platters of food and glasses of wine. Everyone had dressed specially,
the children in freshly ironed clothes, the adults in the outfits they
saved for occasions.

*   *   *   *

It was always exciting for Bob and me, preparing to go to my
grandparent's house for the holiday. For weeks, grapes fermented
in a large cloth bag hung in my grandmother's kitchen, dripping
sweet wine into a pail. My grandfather chopped different kinds of
fish and patted them in balls in preparation for the feast. And, for
the men, he rolled special tobacco leaves into handmade cigars. The
Seder service stretched long hours with passages we all read aloud
in Hebrew. Then Bob and I played games with my cousins. After
dinner my father would talk with his parents in Yiddish and trim his
father's beard and fingernails.

"Look papa, see how big the children have grown? Freddy,
Bobby, talk to grandpa, tell him about school. He will understand
you."

*   *   *   *

My memory of those days sharpened with the aroma of chicken
soup coming from the kitchen.

Mr. Sebbah prayed aloud and, as I had done when I was the
youngest male at the Seder table, his little boy was given the honor
of asking the traditional four questions of the Passover service in
Hebrew. The ancient ritual was repeated, as it had been for four
thousand years. The *matzoh* was hidden, we sipped sweet red wine,
tasted bitter herbs to remind us of the days of slavery in Egypt, and
reclined on cushions and pillows.

When the time came to eat, the men were served first. Mrs.
Sebbah stood at the head of the table and ladled individual portions
from bowls in front of her—generous helpings of fish, hard-boiled
eggs, soup, peas, carrots, chicken, hard fragments of *matzoh*
broken from thick-baked discs, and honey cake.

When the Seder ended, the family sang in Hebrew and danced

until midnight. Then they said goodnight, embraced and kissed one another on both cheeks, and filed past me politely squeezing my hand. I approached the old grandmother and Mrs. Sebbah and kissed their cheeks, much to the pleasure of the whole family. This called for an encore of kissing, and when I came to Yvonne, her olive complexion turned beet red. She held her chin high, her arms pressed to her side, and her fists clenched. Everyone laughed gently and said good night.

In pigeon-English, Mr. Sebbah insisted I stay with them, saying he would be insulted if I refused his hospitality, and he led me to a bedroom. I was too tired to refuse. It was the best night's sleep I had since I joined the squadron. It seemed impossible that, only hours before, my mind was full of death and destruction.

In the morning, we ate soft-boiled eggs, *matzoh*, and thick demi-tasse for breakfast. Yvonne made me understand that when her mother was ready, we would walk to the synagogue for services. Quickly Yvonne and Mrs. Sebbah cleared the dishes. Cleaned plates disappeared behind the mahogany doors of the sideboard, the tablecloth was neatly folded, and a copper bowl enamelled with Hebrew letters was placed in the center of the table. Jacob Sebbah opened a shallow drawer, tenderly removed four silk prayer shawls and several skull caps, and slipped them inside a blue velvet pouch embroidered with the Star of David. He pointed to the fine stitching, *"Eh? Magnifique, oui? C'est Yvonne qui l'a fait."* He beamed at his daughter, then stood for a moment while Mrs. Sebbah made a few final adjustments, her eyes examining the rest of the room. Satisfied, she walked to the front door. We followed.

Outside we were greeted by an assortment of neatly dressed men and women and their families. I was warmly admired, my uniform receiving their careful inspection. After much mutual hand shaking, we formed an orderly group, Jacob and I in the lead, and walked quietly down the dusty, deserted street into the congested part of the *mellah*, the Jewish quarter of Constantine.

The street was dirty and poor, dried mud caked in crevices of the unmortared cobblestones. The sidewalks narrowed, forcing our group into columns of two, our heels on the pavement creating a pleasant rhythm. Moslem women hurried past wrapped in plain white fabric, white veils stretched taut beneath their eyes. Outside one shop, barechested workmen in knotted briefs, their bare legs dyestained crimson, stirred vats of blues, oranges, greens and reds with wooden paddles. Dripping fabrics hung from poles to dry. Two blocks further, we entered a courtyard, and at the far end, behind one of many store fronts, was a poor and very old synagogue.

Services were in progress. Shawl-wrapped bodies swayed to mumbled prayers. When we entered, there was a hush and heads turned. Men whispered and pointed. The rabbi looked up from the Torah; the cantor slowed his chant. At the far side of the crowded room, my eyes spotted another American serviceman. He winked and pulled aside a black and white *tallas* to expose a 12th Air Force shoulder patch and corporal's stripes. I winked back. The corporal tucked his prayer book under his arm, sidestepped his way between benches, and when he got close enough held out his hand.

"Hi, *landsman!*" He handed me a *yarmulke* to exchange for my cap. Jacob Sebbah slipped a *tallas* over my shoulders.

"Name's Gabor, sir," he whispered, "with the 321st headquarters. I come here every Saturday. You're the first Jewish officer this bunch has seen. Nice to meet you. A pilot, huh? Boy, the sight of an officer's uniform sure shakes 'em up." The corporal turned and spoke rapidly to Jacob in French, then said, "They didn't think you were Jewish. There are no blond, blue-eyed Jews in Algeria." Gabor laughed.

The cantor's tones rose and fell demanding that the whispering stop. We were escorted to a front-row bench and soon everyone's attention returned to the prayers. I wondered where Mrs. Sebbah and Yvonne had gone. Suddenly, I remembered women didn't participate in the services at an orthodox synagogue. Above our heads was a balcony shielded by a lattice of carved wood. Although I couldn't see past the tiny openings, I suspected the women were there.

The rabbi moved forward and, using eye contact, called upon four men to read in Hebrew from the Torah. I felt his eyes on me. Gabor pressed my arm with his elbow. "You have the honors, Lieutenant."

Not a chance," I whispered, "I can't read Hebrew." I looked past the rabbi, ignoring his attempt to get my attention.

"Relax, Lieutenant. I'm asked up there every week. They get a kick out of hearing Hebrew with a Brooklyn accent. I'll take your place and tell them it was an order."

Gabor's Hebrew was familiar, like the prayers I had heard as a child. The congregation mumbled to one another and leaned forward, smiling and nodding approval. When he finished, Gabor was handed the Torah and was joined by another man who carried a second set of scrolls. They stepped down from the pulpit. The congregation rose, intoning their prayers, straining for a glimpse as the young American advanced with his precious burden.

The two men approached Jacob and me, the stranger transferring his scrolls into my arms. Warmth spread through my body, and my hands tingled at the touch of the holy scrolls. Gabor and I walked side by side down the center aisle, old men reaching toward us to touch the Torah with the corner of their *tallases,* the long fringes twined about their fingers, returning the fabric to their lips in respect for their heritage.

When the services ended, the Rabbi spoke in Hebrew and what he said brought sobs and cries from the congregation. Gabor repeated, "My, oh my...my, oh my." Horror spread across his face and tears came to his eyes.

I didn't understand. "What is it?" I asked.

"Later. I'll explain later," he said.

A saddened congregation crowded around us as we pressed our way through the narrow double doors at the entrance, blending with the women and children as they came down the cramped stairway. All of them touching, patting us, speaking in French and Hebrew, we spilled into the already crowded narrow street behind the synagogue.

"They're thanking us, Lieutenant, you know what I mean. They say we saved them from the Vichy French and maybe being shipped off to Germany."

"What happened inside?"

"The Rabbi said Jews are being shipped to concentration camps to be exterminated." Gabor looked me in the eyes.

"You don't believe that do you?" I asked, fervently hoping he had made some mistake.

"He said Jews are being gathered from every country Germany occupies. Thousands are being shot, gassed, buried alive, and there's no one to stop it." Gabor hesitated. "It's true, Lieutenant."

"It can't be true," I said. "Why haven't we heard anything about it?"

"Two families in the congregation escaped from one of those camps in Poland. They saw it. They swore on the Torah and the lives of their children. It is true."

Gabor introduced a bent and elderly man as the president of the temple. I followed Gabor's lead, bowed my head, and leaned forward. The old man draped his *tallas* over our shoulders and gave us his blessing. I felt honored. We stood, swaying with the crowd to the rhythm of his prayers. Gabor translated. "He asks God to be merciful, to stop the slaughter of our people. . . ."

A horn blasted. An Army jeep skidded to a stop in front of us. Falzone, Smith, and Elkhorn were in the back seat. Foster was in the front with the driver. The horn blew again.

Foster's lower jaw dropped as recognition registered. "Jesus H. Christ, that's Nose in that costume consorting with the natives!"

"Back that jeep out of here," I said to the driver. "Street's closed."

The driver looked at Foster.

"How come you didn't invite us to your block party?" Foster asked.

Falzone tapped the driver's shoulder. "Do as the man says. See you later, Kohn."

The old man finished his prayers and introduced a younger man, who had waited impatiently, shifting from foot to foot. Gabor introduced him as the old man's son, Joseph Barkatz. The younger Barkatz spoke in rapid-fire French, ignoring Gabor's thanks-but-no-thanks gestures.

"What does he want?" I asked.

"It's this fellow's new baby, old man Barkatz's first grandson. There's going to be a *bris* this afternoon. They want us to come, you know, an honor, a *mitzvah* for the baby. I told him we couldn't go with him, lieutenant." He glanced at his watch. "I have to report to the O.D. within the hour. Guess you've had enough."

"A *bris*? You mean a circumcision?" I asked.

"Yeah. Ever been to one?"

"Sure," I said. "When I was seven days old."

The young father must have misinterpreted our laughter for assent, because the old man kissed my cheeks and held my hands. Gabor shrugged.

"Sorry Lieutenant, looks like you're on your way to your second *bris*. If you want, I could still get you out of it."

"No, I'd like to go."

"The whole thing shouldn't take more than a couple hours. I gotta go now or I'll get chewed out real good."

Gabor touched as many hands around as he could, then took one step back, snapped to attention, tapped his right brow in a sharp salute, and barked, "SIR!" I returned the salute, Gabor did an about-face, and sprinted down the center of the street.

"Excuse, please. I speak little English. My name is Gaston Melki." A well dressed man in modern clothes, about ten years my senior, explained he was a relative of the Barkatz family and would escort me to their home. I wished the Sebbah family goodbye and pressed Yvonne's hand, determined I would visit them and bring them gifts when I visited Constantine.

For a moment, untouched by the war, our proud group padded its way through narrow shop-lined streets, greeting Arabs and Jews at their daily routines. The hot late-morning sun spawned a steady flow of perspiration inside my cap, around my collar, dripping down my sides and the small of my back. The formfit heavy gabardine blouse pulled on my shoulders. Off base, American soldiers were required to maintain proper dress. I hesitated to loosen my tie or open my collar, though a queaziness had begun to radiate from my stomach. As we walked, I pressed close to the walls, searching for shade.

We continued for perhaps thirty minutes, until we came to a vacant lot, piled high with refuse and garbage, with an old apartment building in the background. Small, dark-skinned, barefoot boys played in mountains of decay, throwing handfuls of rubbish at one another.

"We are here!" Gaston pointed to an open window through which I could see a party in progress. "There are many family Barkatz and many friends. They will be happy you came."

I was perspiring heavily, holding my breath against the waves of unpleasant odors rising from the mounds of waste, blurred in the shimmering heat by swarms of blue flies. I unconsciously moved my hand to push it away. Embarrassed that Gaston noticed my sensitivity, I lit a cigarette and inhaled deeply, anxious to disguise the foul taste in my mouth. The tobacco tasted like the odors. Bile rose in my throat. I flicked the burning cigarette at a pile of garbage. Quickly, two little Arab boys raced up the mound, sinking ankle-deep in the filth. One scooped the cigarette, crammed it in his mouth, and warded off the other with a hail of garbage.

We climbed three flights of stairs in a passageway so narrow my shoulders touched the walls. The apartment was on the third floor.

The heat and odor from the dump below followed us up the stairs. Gaston and I entered a livingroom packed with noisy, perspiring, excited men wearing *yarmulkes*. The women occupied one of the smaller rooms in the back. Gaston's lips moved, his voice lost in the loud conversation. The noise and the pressure of shoulders and bodies held me captive. In the distance I heard a baby's cry. More people pressed into the already crowded room.

"Gaston, please. I must go."

"Yes. The *mohil* is coming now."

"No. I cannot stay."

"Yes, yes, we are happy you are here."

I held my wrist in front of Gaston's face and tapped my watch. "I must go! I must meet Jacob Sebbah." Any excuse, I thought, to get out of here.

"Oh," Gaston smiled, pointing to the far corner. *"Voilà, Monsieur Sebbah."* Jacob was huddled in conversation with two old men. Oh hell, I'm stuck, I thought uneasily.

A tiny glass appeared in my hand. My arm was jostled, some of the liquid spilled. Gaston and the men around me raised their glasses, *"Santé a l'enfant!"* I sipped the clear white liquid. It seared a path to the pit of my stomach. *"A la victoire!"* All glasses raised to me. Impaled by their twinkling eyes, I drained my glass. Again it was filled. A damp hand grasped my wrist, a platter of anchovies on little rounds of matzoh was pressed under my nose. I drew back. Eager fingers removed all except one, waiting expectantly until I took it from the tray. I watched mouths move and bits of cracker and fish disappear. I was going to be sick. I pulled Gaston close, *"La salle de bain?"* I shouted in his ear. No, that wasn't right. *"La toilette?"* Damn it! That was wrong too.

"Ah!" Gaston exclaimed, *"Je comprends.* The W.C. But of course!"

I held onto his shoulder as we channeled our way toward the door. I slipped the glass onto a table as we turned into the hall. The white letters "W.C." were painted on a door. Gaston gave me an encouraging slap. It felt like a finger was in my throat. I clenched my teeth and hooked a thumb in my belt, applying pressure against a cramp.

Inside the W.C., a small dirty pane of glass allowed enough light to display a sloping floor with a pair of raised concrete impressions of feet straddling an open four-inch hole. Many past users had missed their target. I heaved a shot of burning liquid, then dry-heaved for a couple of minutes longer. Slightly relieved, I backed out into the hallway. It was empty. I leaned against the wall, closed my eyes, and held my breath. I could leave, I thought, run down the stairs and find a ride back to the base. No, I shook the idea away. I had promised them. I must return and take part in the celebration. I wiped the perspiration off my face with my bare hands, dried them on the seat of my trousers, and walked back to the living room, my knees trembling.

"Monsieur l'officier!" Gaston called, swallowing a drink. He pointed to an empty chair, stuffed his mouth with hors d'oeuvres, and handed me another glass of wine and a napkin bulging with food. Nearby, I noticed a handsome man with dark brown features, a finely trimmed beard, and wearing a red fez, who nodded and smiled pleasantly. I raised my glass to him in a toast. He tipped his head in acknowledgment.

Suddenly, a happy commotion announced the arrival of the *Mohil,* a tall man dressed in white cap and surgical gown stretched tight across his barrel chest. Displayed on the gown were two rows of colored ribbons and tiny medals. He moved slowly, deliberately, with unsmiling importance, chin slightly elevated, head straight and body proudly erect. The room became quiet. A path cleared quickly, men backing away and bowing in deference. He nodded to those he knew, and when the Barkatz family proudly presented me, he shook my hand with an air of distraction, indicating that it was my honor to meet him.

The *Mohil* directed me to stand next to a closed French window which bathed my back in waves of heat. Young Barkatz, the father of the baby, stood on one side of me, Gaston on the other. Several men formed a half circle around a large overstuffed armchair. Gaston, sobered under the responsiblity, explained I had been placed in a position of honor normally occupied by a close friend of the family. "The bris is our covenant with God," he said. "Our commitment, our promise never to forget we are Jews."

My stomach had settled. I must not get sick again. It would be over soon. But I could only feel I didn't belong. I thought of circumcision as a health measure to be performed in a hospital. Was I so assimilated I couldn't respond to one of the most ancient Jewish traditions?

A fragile little man, his feet barely touching the floor, was seated in the armchair. The *Mohil* placed a pillow on the man's lap and covered it with a large piece of stained oilcloth. He himself wore an apron made of the same discolored material. He handed a third man a box of instruments. Gaston whispered to me that everything was "hygienic," the results would be superior and there would be no infection.

The *Mohil* spent what seemed like endless minutes fussing over the pillow and the placement of the oil cloth. When would it end? A shaft of sunlight bore down on the back of my neck. I breathed deeply, ignoring the trail of perspiration that ran down my forearm, over my hand, and dripped from the tips of my fingers.

The *Mohil* signaled. All heads turned to the back of the room. There were words in French, and the bedroom door opened. A robust middle-aged woman entered, a sleeping infant covered with a pale blue blanket cradled in her arms. The woman kissed the baby's forehead and handed the infant to the *Mohil*, then hurried out of the room dabbing at her eyes with a handkerchief. The blanket was removed and the *Mohil* opened the instrument box and removed a silver razor with an intricately engraved handle. He began to chant in Hebrew, eyes closed, swaying back and forth. The men mumbled and swayed in unison. Then, from his closed fist, the *Mohil* poured dried seeds and green leaves into our palms.

"Bonne chance, bonne chance," everyone said. I put the seeds in my breast pocket. He handed Gaston a bottle of alcohol. "You see," Gaston whispered, nudging me with his elbow, *"Hygienic."* The *Mohil* placed a small plate in my hands, and from a leather pouch carefully metered out a few ounces of dirt into the center. "Ah!" Gaston beamed, *"Terre de Jerusalem."* A new series of chants began.

The baby awakened, looking around wide-eyed. The *Mohil* grasped the baby's penis, working the tip between his index finger and thumb, pressing and drawing in an outward movement. The baby began to cry, trying to move his legs against the viselike grip of the old uncle. The *Mohil* continued to squeeze and pull until the foreskin moved freely away from the penis. Then he slipped a tiny clamp over the foreskin to prevent the loose flesh from sliding back in place. The baby was quiet. The *Mohil* held the bit of foreskin between his fingers and with his free hand pressed the silver razor against the clamp. He spoke a few words of Hebrew, made an almost imperceptible motion, and the foreskin was severed.

The *Mohil* removed the clamp and smoothed the skin back to its original position, exposing the head of the penis. Blood flowed over the baby's legs, the penis rose and a fountain of urine splashed in the air. Everyone laughed. The baby was calm and silent.

The *Mohil* dropped the tiny piece of severed foreskin on the dish of soil in my hand. I had forgotten I held the plate and stared at the bloody bit of flesh. An odd numbness descended through my legs. I dropped one hand to my thigh, pinched my leg, but felt nothing. I turned my head and looked out the window. I needed fresh air.

The *Mohil* took the bottle of clear liquid from Gaston, filled his mouth, and with bulging cheeks sprayed a fine mist between the baby's legs. Then the baby screamed, loud and long, so hard he lost his breath and no sounds came at all. The men cheered. Red and pink rivulets dripped into a puddle on the oilcloth. Blood from the *Mohil*'s hands transferred to his apron.

He dipped his fingers in the puddle of blood, reached out and touched the forehead of everyone around him. I pressed back harder against the window. The fingers touched my forehead. Warm blood trickled down between my eyebrows and around the bridge of my nose. My vision dimmed. I saw things as though through a grey curtain. I pressed hard on my stomach muscles, forcing the circulation up into my head in an attempt to regain my sight. I reached up to wipe the blood away, but Gaston held my arm. "But no!" he admonished, *"Bonne chance! Bonne chance!* Wear it proudly. Let all who see you know you are a Jew."

The man wearing the fez approached. "Are you not well?" The voice was quiet and cultured, the words distinct and refined.

"I'm O.K., thank you."

The *Mohil* sprinkled powder between the baby's legs and wrapped the penis with gauze. I was barely able to see. I pinched my leg again. No feeling. I turned my head and stared with open eyes into the bright sunlight. I saw nothing. The quiet voice asked, "May I suggest we go into another room?" The dish was removed from my hands and I looked in the direction of the voice, trying to understand the words.

"Your color is not good. Do you understand me?"

"I can hear you," I said, forcibly keeping my voice calm, "but I cannot see you." Strong hands gripped my arms, voices and background sounds slowly faded. Then it was silent.

My first awareness was of my head between my knees, and cool air sweeping across the back of my neck. Gaston, making reassuring sounds, pressed curious people out of the room and closed the door. The man in the red fez gave me a glass of water.

"It is natural, from a bottle," he smiled. "I am Mohammed Sharif. I explained to the family you received a vaccine and it had a temporary effect. But now you are feeling better, yes?"

"Yes. How can I thank you?"

"Promise when next you visit Constantine you will be my guest."

That night, I gave Mohammed, our laundry boy, a sketch for his sister to embroider on the forehead of my leather flying helmet. It was the outline of a Jewish star. When he gave it back, I painted the center yellow.

15

Six O'Clock High

THE NEXT MORNING BROOKS SAUNTERED to the platform, the flaps of his helmet knotted above his head, both hands dug deep in the pockets of his coveralls, a stub of a burning cigarette clenched in his front teeth between open lips. I wondered if he remembered what Sadler looked like. He kept his back to us while he studied the map of Sicily and, when he spoke, it was as if he were talking to the charts. "It'll be high altitude, B-17 escort. The target is Trapani.

"Keep in mind we're out here for one reason: that's to knock the shit out of the fucking Eyeties and Germans. Keep your mind on your work. I'm leading, so I call the shots. Any of those guys who got it had their heads stuck up their ass. They fucked up. You got to be ahead of your plane every minute.

He turned and faced us.

"Shorty says they beefed up the defenses around Trapani and they'll know we're coming long before we get there. So stay on the ball! And better be damn sure everything's working right before you go charging down that runway, 'cause with full fuel and ammo, ain't a man in this room can recover if you lose an engine on takeoff. The power of the good one'll flip you like a flap jack."

Brooks glanced at his watch. "You've got 45 minutes to takeoff. Here's the line-up for the flights." Brooks chalked in my name as Element Leader, but I was disappointed. I was in Cominski's flight. I had my own wingman, but I wanted more. I wanted Tex to make me a Flight Leader. I had flown with Cominski once before. It was bad. He would lag, then boost throttle to catch up. I was better than

Cominski, even though he had three missions more than I had. I knew I was qualified to lead. Tex had never flown Cominski's wing. He couldn't know his deficiencies.

One day I had waited until we were alone in the tent and told Cominski he made it rough for me and my wingman to stay with him. I suggested he improve his technique. He went back to polishing his shoes. Sitting on his cot, a shoe pressed between his knees, pumping away with a polishing cloth, pausing now and then to dab on a precise amount of shoe polish, he buffed and shined and caressed that leather. G.I. oxfords never looked so good.

There's no easy way to tell a guy he's a lousy pilot. It's like saying he's no good in bed. After that, it was never the same with Cominski. But I wasn't interested in being well-liked, nor least of all, dead.

*   *   *   *

In less than a 360 degree turn after takeoff, our twelve planes were in correct formation. I stuck close to Cominski as we came around the village of Khalifa. Arabs working in the fields paused and looked up in unison. We headed for the area where we could test our guns before starting the long climb to meet the bombers.

Our laundry boy lived in a village like Khalifa, close to our base. He was a small, skinny little fellow, dressed in shabby clothes with bare feet who looked about ten, but claimed to be fourteen. He bowed, pressed his hands together, and told us his sisters, his mother and his father blessed us every night. We were messengers of Allah. Proudly he showed us their beautiful laundry work. We paid him more than he asked, gave him cigarettes, shirts with frayed collars, socks with holes, and odd bits of surplus military insignia. He became a proud composite of discarded military attire and imitated our ways. When I asked for the bit of embroidery on my helmet, he rushed it back to me before lights out and wouldn't accept payment. He smiled with pride, "My father said your star is the sign of Moses. Go with Allah and my father's blessings."

Generally, we were disliked by the Arabs of the surrounding villages. What appeared to be uninhabited terrain below was dotted with small houses. Shorty had received reports of accidental killings of livestock and people, shot by our stray bullets. The army compensated families $150.00 for each burro killed and $100.00 for each male Arab. An order was posted assigning an uninhabited restricted area near the foothills for test firing. I didn't believe the Arab population could read the notice. Thereafter, I cleared my guns only over water.

Just before we crossed the coast, my wingman pumped his stick, giving the landing signal, and turned back. I had a profound sense of foreboding sitting alone in third position, waiting to be chopped off. But I'd had that feeling before. It would last a few minutes and then everything would be all right. Everything's fine Dad, I said out loud. I can take care of myself. High-flying escort's a piece of cake. And only twelve more missions to go.

The climb to meet the B-17's was uneventful. It would take an hour to reach Northern Sicily. I kept a steady conversation going inside my oxygen mask. That's the boy, Cominski, nothing fancy, stick close to the others, you're doing fine. Isn't that right, Dad? Cominski's going real good. We're going to cruise over the big water, the 17's will drop their load, and we'll be back in time for dinner. Weather's crummy to the west, but the forecast says it'll remain clear.

This plane wasn't so bad. Mine was down for repairs. I'd been assigned a new H model—the same plane made with identical parts, but oddly not the same. I missed the familiarity of my own cockpit, the worn knobs, its special odor, the makeshift ashtray Chad had fabricated and installed behind the flap handle. Still, it was a good plane, strong, reliable. Same creaks and groans over the sound of the engines, the constant pounding, throbbing roar of pistons that beat a comforting rhythm against the sides of my head. It isn't LMA, but it sounds the same. The cockpit formed a shell of security around me. But were there a change in the beat, should the tempo alter, a misfire, an unexpected surge of rpm, an unfamiliar sound, or worse yet, no sound at all, that would send a scream for attention through the exposed nerves that triggered my reflexes.

Soon we were in sight of the target. No enemy fighters. We were home free. The bombers started their run through a piece of sky mined with flak while we circled at 22,000 feet, waiting to cover them on the return home. It was stinging cold in the cockpit. Thousands of feet below in warmer air lay a dark grey blanket of cloud which stretched from the coast to the horizon. Our three flights circled impatiently in a continuous turn.

"Blue Flight! Fighters at six o'clock high!" It sounded like Falzone. I looked back quickly and saw four ME-109's spiralling down behind us. They were flying slightly faster than we, as though they were late and had caught up to join us. Ahead, Cominski and his wingman remained in a shallow turn. Goddamn it, turn into the attack, you asshole, or we're going to get it! I hissed into my mask.

The radio was flooded with frantic calls reporting enemy attacks. The Germans were up in force. I'm going to get killed! I thought. Adrenalin pumped through my body. They were behind me. Four 109's converging on my tail. At last, Cominski banked hard. I jammed the throttles, prop, and mixture controls to the fire wall. Still I pushed harder and harder, praying for yet another ounce of power. Trying to stay with Cominski and his wingman put me at the end of a whip, going faster and faster, hanging on for my life. I crowded him, pressing him on, hoping he would swing around, close the distance, and get on the tail of the German fighters.

The Messerschmidt's took their time, coming around deliberately, no excess speed, blending into position behind me. The seven of us were locked in a vertical turn; the tip of my right wing pivoted on an imaginary point in the clouds below. I yanked the control wheel toward me with all my strength, screaming and squeezing to keep my stomach muscles tight and the blood circulating in my head, my body compressed under five times the force of gravity. I felt the calluses split and the moist, warm flow of blood on my buttocks. The plane shook and rattled under the stress.

I jerked my head back to glance at my attackers. It was an eerie sight. They were skillfully following my arc, but they couldn't get a shot at me unless they turned tighter and aimed their guns ahead of me, like a hunter leading a moving target.

Come on, Cominski, let's shake 'em! The 109's were starting to have trouble staying in the turn, stalling and losing altitude, their noses pointed far behind me. Soon we'd all drop into the cloud deck and they'd run for home, or we'd get a shot at them. Who says they're better fliers? Then Cominski pulled too tight and stalled. His right wing pulled down, almost flipping him on his back. We lost speed. The 109's moved in like greedy sharks and opened fire, their tracers coming within yards of my tail.

My controls were heavy, as if I were flying through mollasses. I kept stalling, vibrating, buffeting in the turn. I squeezed tighter on my stomach muscles to prevent blacking out. Again and again I dared to look back, snapping my head quickly to see the attackers and jerking back to check Cominski's position, less than a plane's length away. A moment's lapse and I would run into him.

The closest Messerschmidt was in good position and in range. Little bright flashes twinkled on the leading edge of his wings. All his guns were firing. I was scared. I must get out of there. We're going to get killed! I pulled harder on the controls, turning inside Cominski. The blood drained out of my head, my vision started to go. I hit hard right rudder and down I skidded, then top rudder, cross controlled, anything to shake those bastards off my tail. Cominski and his wingman disappeared above me with two 109's after them.

Now I was alone. The other two on my ass refusing to break the coupling. They turned, rolled, and dropped with me, duplicating every maneuver. My head and body swiveled to the rear, watching them fire. I stared at their silhouettes. Should I zig, zag, climb, or dive? If they were bad shots, I might turn into a torrent of gunfire.

The radio transmitted hysterical cries. The sky was peppered with individual dogfights. In front of me a plane blew apart, its forward motion disintegrating into hundreds of falling pieces. I screamed in anger, swearing at the 109's. The sons-of-bitches were trying to kill me! I had to shake them. Please, somebody! Kill the sons-of-bitches!

A violent snap slammed my head against the plexiglas canopy. The plane flipped on its back and went into a spin. The control wheel pressed into my lap. Outside, everything was a blur. My body pressed hard against the left side of the cockpit. The altimeter spun down past 19,000 feet. Power surged intermittently, then died. The right engine had quit.

The airplane continued to spin, falling into a rhythmic oscillation. Bright sunlight disappeared as I plunged into dark, dense cloud. I laughed wildly, tears blurring my vision. The spin was my salvation! I was free from the attack, safe, hidden in the clouds.

I jockeyed with the right engine controls, pushed and pulled on the throttle, the prop and mixture levers, flipped switches on and off, checked the fuel flow in an attempt to restart the engine. Nothing happened. Then I saw billowing black smoke blending with the surrounding cloud and, what I dreaded most, fire. A red line appeared on the side of the engine nacelle, green paint blackened, blistered, then melted. The line widened and, like a blowtorch,

Independence Public Library

flame shot through the metal cowling.

Quickly, my hands snapped off switches. The instant I cut the fuel supply to the damaged engine, the flames went out. I set the right propellor switch to feather. Slowly the giant three-bladed prop flattened into the airstream and reluctantly stopped turning.

At 15,000 feet I dropped out the bottom of the cloud deck, surrounded by long tails of grey drizzle. Then, reducing power on my good engine and pushing opposite rudder I slowed the spin, curving out of the dive at 8,000 feet. Just like Tex said, pulling this baby out of a spin was as easy as possum shit sliding off a pine cone.

A lone 109 broke out far above, circling, sniffing, searching, eager to confirm the destruction of a P-38. In a minute he disappeared into the moisture laden ceiling. My body began to tremble.

"You bastard!" I screamed through my mask. I shook my fist, "Up yours!"

16

Apparitions in the Desert

I FLEW BETWEEN GLOOMY CLOUD LAYERS in the darkening late afternoon. Come on, baby. I leaned forward as if to increase the speed. My fears of bad weather ahead were confirmed. Anxious calls from scattered remnants of Doorknob Squadron reported overcast conditions with fleeting holes in the cloud cover. Then silence. I wanted to believe they had made it. Come on baby, a little faster. You can do it.

I called Washboard. I was on course. It was comforting to hear a voice. He relayed three pilot reports, all bad, adding that maybe I'd find a hole over home base. And if I didn't? I wouldn't let down in the blind. Wagner and Lynch tried that in Morocco and got killed.

Twenty minutes later I circled above a solid cloud deck that topped three thousand feet. My base lay below. Jagged mountain peaks poked through the overcast. Doorknob advised they were socked in. This mustn't happen to me. It would be dark soon. I had to get down.

I called Washboard for a vector to good weather.

"Doorknob Five Two. A bomber squadron was diverted to Malta. They're clear. Sunset 1930. Authorization for a night landing required. Over."

"Negative, Washboard. Too far. I have one hour fuel. Over."

"Pilot reports fair weather over Tunisia."

I didn't answer. Tunisia was occupied by the Germans. He continued. "Weather clear at Biskra, south of the Hodna Mountains, 85 miles, 195 degrees."

"I can do that in thirty-five minutes."

"Be advised. Communications unreliable beyond the mountains. Do you read?"

"Roger, I read."

"Doorknob. Vectors to the abandoned field at Biskra are approximate."

"What do you mean 'abandoned,' Washboard?"

"Biskra is deactivated but can be used for emergency. What are your intentions? Over."

"Stand-by." What was there to decide? The longer I waited, the less chance I'd have of reaching the desert before dark.

"Doorknob Five Two. If able, climb to 10,000. I'll spot you over your home base and you can bail out. Over."

I didn't answer. I was thinking.

"Doorknob Five Two. What are your intentions?"

"Washboard, Doorknob Five Two. Vectors to Biskra." I surprised myself.

"Take a heading of 195 degrees. Expect Biskra in thirty-five minutes. Field southeast of the town, five miles. Winds westerly, velocity unknown. Stay high and give me a call before you start down. Over."

"Roger. Out."

Orange and yellow reflections bounced off the mountains. Tops of the cloud deck broke into blotches of light and dark patches. I passed one hole, then another. At the next, I dove through for a glimpse of terrain. I found myself boxed in and pulled up. Dusk was falling quickly. Minutes later the clouds dissipated, and I dropped to a thousand feet above desolation—torturous cragged rock formations spotting a bleak, barren wasteland. Next time I called Washboard, he didn't answer. I was either out of range or blocked by mountains. A landing field was nowhere in sight. Soon I wouldn't be able to see the ground. I had only one engine. I was beginning to panic.

On the chance I could be heard, I maintained a steady broadcast of flight details. Time was running out. I began broad sweeps 30 degrees left, then back to centerline, searching for a village or a sign of life. Forty-five minutes had elapsed. I've gone too far. A wheels-up belly landing in that *mischegoss* of a wasteland would be insane! Then I saw the field. I banked sharply. The plane responded easily, as if it were as anxious as I to be safely on the ground.

As I came around, I saw that it was neither a city nor a village, but only three buildings that may have been used for base operations. I raced for it, passing over hostile uncleared ground. At the last moment, secure I could make it, I switched on the landing light, dropped the landing gear and flaps, chopped power, and held the nose high.

The powerful finger of light exposed a surface strewn with rocks the size of melons. That's no runway, I'm going to crash! I thought crazily. The instant the wheels hit the ground, I stomped on the brakes, the plane skidded and lurched, I heard the tires blow as the right gear dug in, and the plane swerved to the right, shaking to a stop.

In the quiet that followed, I tried to calm my trembling. It was dark and cold. The landing light illuminated a panorama of sand, gravel, and boulders. To conserve the battery, I switched off the light and everything electrical except the radio. I tried Washboard again and again. No response. Still hoping they might hear me, I transmitted in the blind, giving my location and saying I was down at Biskra and I would broadcast again after sunrise.

With the landing light off, the landscape plunged into darkness. There was no moon yet, and no sounds except for an occasional creaking or groaning from a remote part of the plane. My feet were cold and cramped. But I wasn't frightened. I was safely down and alive.

The first priority was to relieve myself. I got out and stood on the wing. The force of the wind whipped the urine into a fine spray. I never heard it hit the ground. The cold wind raised goose flesh. I returned quickly to the protection of the cockpit and cranked the windows shut.

In the last remaining light I inventoried the contents of my pockets. Eleven cigarettes. I immediately rewarded myself by lighting one. Four Tootsie Roll segments and two Chuckles, one lemon and the licorice one I always saved for last. I ate a piece of Tootsie Roll and put the rest back in my pocket. I had a .45 automatic pistol in my shoulder holster and a canteen of water hooked on my belt.

It was difficult unzipping the backpack from the parachute harness. Once I had laid it out on my lap I needed to switch on the tiny cockpit spotlight to take stock of the contents of the survival kit. It held a combination fishing/sewing kit, a machete with a ten-inch blade, ten yards of bandage impregnated with sulfa powder, one waterproof matchbox with compass and twenty matches inside, a magnifying glass to start a fire, a whistle, a waterproof cover for my pistol, twenty .45 calibre cartridges, a first aid kit, two tins of K-rations in waterproof wrappers, two five-minute flares, mosquito netting, and assorted Italian, French, and German currency wrapped in waxed paper. I put the packet of money in the pocket below my knee.

I was in good shape. I had water, candy, and cigarettes. I turned the light out. I had landed safely, the plane could be seen from the air, and I would be found. Still the question nagged: had I made a serious navigational error? Never mind, I would think about it in the morning. Washboard mentioned only one abandoned airfield in the northern desert, and I had found it. I had shelter. I would pop my parachute in the daylight and drape it over the wing as a signal for a rescue party.

Within an hour, the temperature inside the cockpit dropped below forty, transforming my sweat saturated coveralls into an icy wrapper. I slapped my arms, pounded my feet on the metal floor, and rubbed my hands together. Then I must have fallen asleep, because I woke with a start. The wind had lessened and the dark, hostile landscape was clearly defined against a bright night sky. My coveralls held my body warmth and I curled my legs beneath me, hugging myself inside the tiny plastic and metal capsule, waiting for sleep.

It could have been worse. Mom used to say "count your blessings," and I counted them. Dad used to say "this too shall pass," and I was sure it would. Again I woke with a start. Or was I still dreaming? I considered whether I had crashed and was dead. I touched the plane's cold metal interior. Reality. It was midnight. I lit a cigarette and jumped at the bright flare of the match, the light magnified a thousand times by the faceted surfaces of the cockpit interior. Nine cigarettes left. I'll save the rest.

I woke in three hours, alert, impatient for morning. The smallest markings on the instrument panel were visible in the moonlight. The stars were holes in a grey cloth. The overcast in the north formed a smooth blanket over the mountains. Beyond the plane's shadow on the rough ground, I could see huge boulders and knew the plane could never take off. It would have to be abandoned.

I warmed the radio and tried another transmission. Still no

response. My words echoed through the cockpit. I yielded to the temptation to have one more cigarette. I deserved it. I couldn't sleep and hours remained before sunrise. The reflection of the lighted match danced inside the canopy like fireflies. I thought the horizon moved! My eyes were playing tricks. I cupped my hand over the glowing end of the cigarette and focused in the direction I thought I had seen movement.

To my right were mounds and outcroppings of rock defined against the night sky. I sucked in my breath, startled to see several mounds disengage themselves and slowly stand. I struck another match and watched as more figures stood. Then five, ten, maybe twenty human forms began to move, slowly encircling the plane at a distance of a couple of hundred feet. Several carried what looked like long-barrelled rifles. They made no move to approach. I made no move to open the canopy.

I struck another match. They were on their feet. When the match went out, I puffed on the cigarette so they could see the glow. I opened both windows a crack to be sure I would hear them if they came nearer. But no one moved. They waited and I waited.

As the sky lightened, I could see them easily. They were draped and hooded in enormous robes, sitting or squatting, shapeless white mounds blending with the terrain. I made another attempt to contact Washboard to add new information: I had company. Then I lowered both windows and threw back the canopy. I stood on the seat and all of them stood. I waved both hands in a friendly salute. They didn't wave back. I cupped my hands and shouted, *"SAL-LAAM ALAY-CUM! SAL-LAAM ALAY-CUM!"* But they remained silent.

They moved away from the front of the plane, keeping their distance, and regrouped toward the rear. Four machine guns and a cannon sticking out of the nose were a forbidding sight. I dropped my .45 on the seat and slid off the wing to the ground. Both main tires had blown. The torn remains of the right tire were partially buried in the stony ground, but the plane stood braced on its three legs. I had been lucky.

I waved and waited. "SAL-LAAM ALAY-CUM!" They conferred quietly. I understood nothing they said. My mouth felt dry. Four men with rifles broke from the others and walked toward me, stopping about ten feet away. They were bearded, darkskinned, and unfriendly. I forced a smile. Look fellows, I'm a good guy. See?

Nothing in my hands, nothing up my sleeve. The tallest man shouted something, speaking rapidly, waving his hands. The others joined in the confusion. One shook a clenched fist at me. I kept a frozen smile on my face, shrugged, and opened my palms to indicate I didn't understand, all the while repeating a few Arabic phrases I had learned.

"Salaam alaycum, fellows. Peace be with you. *Salaam, salaam.* America! The United! States...I'm your friend. *Hamm'dallah, Bismillah."*

The tall one unfolded an arm from beneath his robes, pointed a black finger at the horizon to the south, then drew a line across the sky to the north. His face was hidden deep within the folds of his hood, but as he looked up to the sky I saw his nose, a sharp narrow beak, and squinting eyes beneath heavy eyebrows. His face and beard were jet black. He shouted at me.

"O.K.! That's enough!" I began talking loud and fast, "I don't understand Arabic or whatever it is you're talking. I'm not here to give you any trouble. Look at me! Do I look like I could hurt anybody? I was born in Chicago. I'm an artist. My plane can't fly. I need help. I'm hungry. How about a sandwich?" I pointed north. "See? That's where I came from. I'm an American, the United States, damn it . . . ." They stopped talking and listened, their mouths agape. They shrugged, and when I stopped talking, we stared at one another.

I withdrew a wrinkled package from my breast pocket and thrust it toward them. "Cigarette?" I disguised the tremble in my hand by shaking the package until a few broken cigarettes stuck out. Quickly four hands appeared and four cigarettes disappeared beneath the folds of their robes. "O.K.? No thanks? No smiles? That's O.K. We're friends now." I pointed to the yellow and brown package, "Look! Camel!" I tapped my chest and made undulating motions with my hand suggesting a ride across the desert. "See! Camel!" One came close and squinted at the picture. *"Ah! Jamal!"* he smiled. I smiled.

I pointed to the plane, flapped my arms, and frantically shook my head in exaggerated display of sadness. They shouted again in a furious four-way discussion. What did they want? If they knew I had money they might kill me. The inside of my mouth felt like cardboard. I thought of the security of my cockpit and the gun on the seat.

I reached inside my knee pocket. They watched. Maybe they

think I have a gift for them? Carefully avoiding the packet of paper money, I removed the Blood Chit with a flourish and held it out for their approval. The Chit was an official military document made of cardboard, the size of a folded greeting card. It was considered a guarantee of safe passage in North Africa. Did they know this? On the cover was printed an American flag. It contained a message in English, French, and Arabic, endorsed with official U.S. government rubber stamps.

> To all Arab peoples: Greetings and peace be upon you. The bearer of this letter is a soldier of the United States Government and friend of all Arabs. Treat him well, guard him from harm, give him food and drink, help him return to the nearest American or British soldiers and you will be liberally rewarded. Peace and the mercy of God be upon you.
>
> Franklin D. Roosevelt
> President of the
> United States of America.

On the back on the Chit were seven useful words and phrases with their phonetic Arab equivalent. "Sal-lom alay-koom." I had pronounced it right, "a salutation of one stranger meeting another." I tried another Arabic expression, "Take me to the Americans or English and you will be rewarded." I failed to capture their interest. Perhaps there was something missing in the inflection? There were words for "American," "friend," "water," "food," "money." I tapped my chest and said the word for friend, "Sadeek, sadeek." They laughed, pointed at me, and said, "Sadeek!" I was relieved to see them laugh. I held up the card and pointed to the flag. They watched. I opened the Chit to the Arabic message and handed it to the tallest man.

He received it respectfully and studied the writing slowly, turning the card sideways, then upside down, rotating it again and again in careful examination. Oh god, I thought, he can't read! The others crowded, looking over his shoulder. He passed the card to them and each in turn handled it without much enthusiasm. One man tugged at another's sleeve, they turned and walked away. It scared the hell out of me to think they would leave me there. I didn't even know where I was. I'll give them the money! I thought. Everyone understood money. They could have it all.

I reached for the packet in my knee pocket and fumbled with the tight wrapper. Then the tall one stepped very close and spoke harshly. The others fell silent. His arms were folded across his chest within his coarse robe. He looked down at me. The first rays of the morning sun disclosed the brownish black texture of his face, creased and crackled inside the hood of his burnoose like the parched surface of a dried river bed. I couldn't see his eyes. Beneath the sacklike cloth was a blouse of fine quality with a delicately embroidered collar studded with glass and ivory beads and brass chains. He repeated some words, at the same time tapping my goggles with his middle finger.

"Ah!" I said, "Goggles! Flying goggles! Sun glasses! See?" I pulled them over my eyes, pointed and looked into the sun. "They're great! You'll love them! Take 'em, add 'em to your collection!"

Hanging from his neckchain something caught my eye, an angry brass eagle clutching the world in its claws and emblazoned across the globe, a swastika. It hung alongside a gold Turkish moon and star, a French enamelled flag, and several other tokens and amulets. Who was he? Did he profit by bringing stranded pilots to the Germans?

He touched my helmet and again uttered the same words. I unsnapped the elastic band, motioned for him to bend a little, and nervously slipped the goggles over his hood, adjusting the dark green lenses over his eyes. With a slight pressure on his shoulder, I turned him to face the sun. Slowly his eyelids opened, he stared, his lips parted. A minute passed. I waited, my heart pounding. Maybe that's all he wants. Maybe trinkets for the local natives are more valuable than money. Then he removed the goggles, reverently rubbed his fingers over the glass and handed them back to me. Again he reached toward my helmet, placing an index finger on my forehead, *"Yis-rail-eet?"*

I ran the syllables through my head and mouthed them. Then they came together, crashing like cymbals.

"Israelite! Oui, oui! Sholom Alechum! Salaam alaikum! Israelite!" He smiled and touched my hand lightly, then kissed his fingertips and called to the others. He had recognized the Star of David. Jews were his brothers! In moments I was surrounded by the grinning friendly faces of all those men who had waited through the night. I kept blinking to keep tears from flooding my eyes.

I pointed to the ripped tires and motioned for them to wait while I returned to the cockpit for one last futile attempt to raise Washboard. There wasn't an area of clear ground in sight. Even if the tires could be replaced the plane could never takeoff. I simultaneously pressed two buttons to destroy the secretly coded identification radio to prevent it from falling into enemy hands. I slipped the .45 in my leather jacket and closed the canopy. They gestured for me to follow and I eagerly joined their procession. I'll go anywhere with you guys. I'll join your tribe. I've had all the combat I need.

We walked away from that place that had never been an airfield, over quiet desolation and difficult terrain, retracing the way they had come during the night to see the strange object that fell from the sky. When we approached their camp, women ran for cover or pulled black kaftans across their faces. Bashful children played near makeshift tents. Dogs barked and nipped at my coveralls. Camels, tethered and disinterested, rested alongside large, bulging canvas-covered baskets. An air about the camp suggested they had recently arrived or were preparing to leave.

As if by signal, the men formed a circle and sat folded in their robes looking like soft pyramids and ant hills. I joined them on the ground and we smoked. When they spoke, each in turn, all listened. At my chance to speak I said, "Biskra?" several times. They merely smiled and nodded in amusement. I pointed to the miniature French flag that hung from the tall man's neckchain. He spoke and a young man separated himself from the circle, harnessed a bored camel, and with a crack across its knees, persuaded the beast to stand and lope off toward the northwest.

At midday we dipped hard crackers in warm cereal from a common bowl and sipped thick, black, bitter coffee. I caught occasional furtive glances from the women and children. And if I looked at them they scurried away. I slept that night in my clothes, warm and happy within one of the shelters alongside four men. The odor of human excrement was everywhere and strong, but I didn't mind. It was distinctive. It smelled good to me. I felt secure.

We ate grains, hardtack and dried scraps of meat for breakfast. Afterward, the men moved several paces away from the camp and squatted, relieving themselves on the ground. Then they rubbed themselves with dirt. I did the same. There was no water for washing.

Late in the afternoon, the children jumped and ran toward sounds of backfiring. I wanted to run with them to see what was coming but I remained with the men and joined them in hand-clapping while we watched and waited. An ancient automobile following the young man and his camel, wheezed into the camp. The vehicle was a strange collection of mismatched parts with two enormous tanks strapped to the roof. I thanked the men next to me, repeating over and over again. *"Shocron, shocron."*

The auto stopped in front of us and when the engine died in a final gasp of clatter and belching fumes, the men approached and greeted the driver, a Frenchman in his mid-fifties. Even the women ventured out and waved. The Frenchman was neatly dressed, but strangely, I thought, for the climate. He wore a black suit, white shirt, and small bow tie. Squarely perched on his head was a panama hat, apparently as new as the day it was made. The effect was friendly and somewhat comical.

"Eh bien? Un pilote!" He shook my hand. *"C'est magnifique! Mon générale. Un Américain aussi!!"* He turned to the others, speaking in their language, all the while patting my back.

"I am Monsieur Robar, the magistrate of Mahaff Ekbob."

"Is that near Biskra?"

"It is the same."

We spent the hours until sunset talking, all the males of the tribe sitting in a great circle on the ground. Their tall leader was casual and warm, hardly the same man who the day before had seemed so formidable. Monsieur Robar interpreted for us all. We laughed a great deal. It was wonderful. The mission, my plane, and the war seemed a dim recollection. These were my new friends. I could stay with them forever. I was grateful to be around people who cared and out of the oppressive presence of Foster.

Monsieur Robar slapped his hands, threw his head back, and cackled, "You said *'Jamal'* and they thought you wanted to trade your *avion* for a camel!" He convulsed with laughter and tears came to his eyes, "Oh this is *extraordinaire!* They say it wasn't until you examined the undercarriage that they understood your problem. *C'est fantastique! Non?"*

"I have to admit I was frightened. They seemed so angry."

"Ah, but yes. It is not the custom when you trade to display big guns from your machine. They were offended. They are a peaceful people. I met *le Chef's* father eighteen years ago, and I have seen them only three times since. But, you see? They are my friends. You are very fortunate they made camp so close to the old quarry, young man, and to be found by them."

"Who are they, Monsieur Robar? Are they Arabs? They didn't seem to understand the request for safe passage from my government."

"They speak a dialect and do not read. They're called Tuaregs, nomads descended from Arab traders who married with women of Timbuktu. They consider Jews and Moslems their brother, though they are neither. They do not keep a permanent camp but always move between the southern Sahara and the northern Hodna mountains, a journey of over a year. It was pure chance they stop on these salt flats we call Chott Melrir. Probably because of the strong winds."

I knew it. I must have drifted from my original vector to Biskra. "Where is Biskra?" I asked.

"West. Sixty-three kilometers. A half day by machine or camel. Every year, caravans of Tuaregs come to Mahaff Ekbob to trade with the Germans, Arabs, Hebrews, French. They barter. They use no money."

He puffed on a pipe. We talked. He told me more about my hosts and about the French in North Africa. I smoked half of my remaining cigarettes and the tribesmen chewed black berries, spitting in concert with the camels. I nibbled on small pieces of dried meat from a wooden bowl that passed from hand to hand around the circle. Monsieur Robar ate food from tightly wrapped waxpaper packets, drank from his own green bottle, then belched and coughed loudly, causing every head to turn while he tapped his abdomen and popped a white pill in his mouth.

"Digestif!" he said. "The Tuaregs understand I have stomach difficulties that prevent me from sharing their food. I could not retain their friendship if I refused their hospitality.

The bowl of dried meat reached my hands again. "That is *chien,* how do you say? cat? dog? A rare treat by their standards, preserved in a special way to withstand the desert heat, available only when the poor animal died by accident or old age. I find it disagreeable."

I found it very agreeable. I smiled at the others as I savored a morsel. So, it's not kosher. I'd eat camel dung with them. They saved my ass.

The following day I bounced across the long rocky trail to Biskra with the magistrate. Monsieur Robar spoke French words of encouragement to his strange vehicle. Before we left, I asked him to tell my friends, in compensation for their kindness, they could strip the P-38 at the quarry and take what they could carry. I thought it was a good trade. I said goodbye to the chief and gave him a Tootside Roll segment and my flying goggles.

I saw him last staring up into the midday sun.

17

Eye of the Storm

"WHEW! YOU STINK" FOSTER MADE an exaggerated gesture of grabbing at his nose. Foster and Falzone were alone in the tent. It had been a four hour back-wracking ride from the Tuareg's camp to an Army motor pool in Biskra, and then another jolting seven and a half hours by military truck to my base. I dropped on my cot, exhausted.

"Did you shit in your pants again?"

"You got back just in time," Falzone said. "I was having a hell of a time keeping the guys from dividing up your stuff. We heard you landed near Biskra."

"How did you know?"

"A high flying transport said they heard your transmissions. I didn't know they had an airbase down there."

"They don't."

"Jesus! Why doesn't he go outside? He's stinking up the whole tent."

"It won't help, Foster. He needs to be fumigated."

I pointed a finger at Cominski's empty cot. "Where's Cominski. I have to see him."

"If he had known you were coming back he'd probably have been here to greet you," Foster sneered.

"I'm not flying with that joker anymore. He led our flight like we were flying through molasses," I said.

"He really needs your advice on how to fly."

Falzone shook his head. "Cominski's dead."

I shook my head in disbelief.

"They got it two days ago. Both him and the wingman. Same day you went down."

I gasped. Waves of remorse crowded my thoughts. Oh shit, both of them. I had to believe it couldn't have been bad luck. One of them had to have screwed up. Stay on the fucking ball, and you had a chance. I looked at Cominski's empty cot. It wasn't fair. It should have been Foster.

"Yeah," Foster muttered. "And you were no help."

Falzone threw a canteen cup at Foster. "Knock it off, you lard ass. You never quit. Get some shut eye, Kohn. The weather's been piss poor. If it breaks, we're on for tomorrow."

I took an army bath with a cloth, a little soap, and a few ladles of water and lay down again, intending only to take a quick nap. I woke up near morning with the sweats, shivering in the cold air. The stove had gone out and I cuddled in the sheepskin jacket trying to keep warm. I recalled bits of a dream. Strange that while I dreamed, I knew it was a dream. I saw myself hanging onto the control column of the plane with nothing behind me, my back cold and exposed to attacking enemy aircraft. I kept thinking, this is impossible, wake up.

I heard the others' breathing. Garrett will probably remove Cominski's cot today, I thought. No one's interested in my near miss. You either make it or you don't. From the distance came the sounds of rodents scurrying to the safety of their holes. A dog barked. I was glad at least they had made it through one more night. Comforted, I fell asleep.

I heard the thudding of heavy shoes outside the tent long before the corporal stuck his head through the opening. His voice was quiet.

"Falzone, Foster, Kohn . . . up and at 'em."

Foster turned and moaned in protest. Falzone remained buried in his bunk.

I dressed quickly, brushed my teeth without water, and, still shivering, headed for the briefing tent, a few paces behind Foster and Falzone. The jeeps were already waiting, motors running, to take us to our planes after the briefing. The tent was crowded. On the map, a string stretched from our base across the blue

Mediterranean to northwestern Sicily. The target, Palermo. Not bad. High-altitude escort on the coast. B-25's don't screw around like 17's. They get in and get out fast. Good, we'll stay out of the flak, I thought.

Tobacco smoke hung like dense fog. Light from bare bulbs was diffused in the cloud. Everyone smoked. I lit my second Raleigh. No conversation, only gutteral throat clearing and hacking coughs. A few sipped thick black coffee from aluminum cups. We were hardly like the glorified recruitment posters showing the American fighter pilot. The folks back home should see us now. I patted my knee pocket, glad to feel the Tootsie Rolls. I had traded Curtiss one pack of cigarettes for them, a small price for breakfast and lunch.

Cominski's name had been taken off the board. Chalked in big white letters: FOSTER, FALZONE, and KOHN, FLIGHT LEADERS TO PALERMO. Good I thought. I lead with Huston on my wing; Barnett, element leader; Hailey, tail-end-Charlie. Two planes down for repairs, Cominski's and his wingman's planes gone, and the new "H" wiped out in the desert. That meant there were no spares. I didn't like that. If one plane turned back, there would be no one to fill in.

Shorty ambled in holding a file folder bulging with maps, charts, and weather graphs. Here it comes, I thought, watching him shuffle his notes, a few papers floating to the dirt floor. He's going to tell us how easy it's going to be, light flak, very few enemy fighters, a real gravy run.

Shorty adjusted his heavy bifocals, squinted through the top half, and then grinned like a preacher nodding to his congregation.

"Gentlemen, the American and British armies have captured every German airfield in Tunisia. We now have air superiority in North Africa." There was no reaction among the pilots. Just silence. Our war was in the skies over Sicily and Italy. This didn't concern us. We knew little about the greater war, and cared less. He added, "Mission's been scratched."

No one asked why. Crane, a new pilot, looked disappointed. The others filed out.

"How about it, you guys," hollered Curtiss. "Let's make the mess sergeant break out some rations. Come on, Foster. You can always eat."

"I don't know how you guys eat that slop," I said.

"We don't have a choice," Curtiss said. "You've cornered the

Tootsie Roll market. If you ate something besides candy, you wouldn't have to carry that hunk of sheep's wool to cushion your ass. You know, Kohn, you've lost weight everywhere except your nose."

"Thanks, anyway, but I'll pass. Why not come to our tent for breakfast. What do you say, Falzone? Let's show these country boys how to live? Curtiss, bring your ration of powdered eggs and we'll show you how to make it fit to eat."

Twenty minutes later, Curtiss, Elkhorn and Anderson came to our tent. I was chopping onions and green peppers with my hunting knife. Smith was peeling potatoes, and Falzone was heating a large frying pan on our pot belly stove. The aroma of garlic hung in the air.

"Smells like a westside tenement," Elkhorn said.

"Ambrosia for the Gods." Falzone kissed his fingers.

"Where the hell did you get this stuff?" asked Anderson.

"Our laundry boy smuggles it in," said Smith. "Hey, Foster. Where you going?"

"You jerks are crazy. That local stuff is fertilized with Arab shit. I wouldn't touch it," said Foster.

"Better than that army *chozzerai* you guys eat," I said.

"What's that?" Curtiss asked.

"Food for pigs."

"Kohn's right," said Falzone, "You know that brown dust that blows up from the road and settles on the pots and pans and your food? Our laundry boy says that trail's been used by shepherds for thousands of years and our trucks have pulverized it. Everytime you guys eat outside the mess tent, and a wind blows, you're eating shit. Sheep shit."

"It's still better than I got at home," said Curtiss.

"Come on, old lard ass. Kohn's heating it so hot it'll kill anything that's moving."

"Gotta share the same tent with him but I don't have to eat his food." Foster started for the entrance.

"Wait a minute, Foster," Falzone held up a burlap bag. "I was going to keep this for myself, but since the mission was cancelled, let's celebrate. There are seven of us and I've got eight fresh eggs. Cost me an old pair of trousers. How do you fellows want 'em?" Everyone screamed with delight.

Anderson ran back to his tent for spices. Falzone heaped our mess kits with large portions of potatoes, onions, green peppers, one egg, and whole cloves of garlic.

"Enjoy it while you can. It may be weeks before we'll get any more. O.K., who wants the last egg?"

"Why don't we leave it?" Smith said. "For Cominski. He would have liked that."

*   *   *   *

Later, while we were outside the tent wiping our mess kits, Tex came by in his jeep.

"Kohn! Foster! I want you up there today on a practice flight. From now on you'll be leadin' flights so practice every chance y'get. Keep switchin' positions so's y'can polish your technique."

Ten minutes later Garrett picked us up. I slid into the front seat. Foster vaulted into the back. Garrett let out the clutch, and we headed for the planes.

"Practice, huh, Lieutenant?" Garrett asked. "Even when there's no mission scheduled the C.O. likes to keep you busy."

"I don't mind. Need all the practice I can get."

"Kinda late to be learning, Nose."

I shrugged. You stupid bastard, I thought. You *shtick flaysh mid oygin.* Can't you ever lay off?

"This ought to be very interesting. Have anything special in mind?"

"Not really."

"Why don't you take the lead first? We'll switch around later."

"I don't mind," I lied, thinking it would take more energy than it was worth to shake him.

Foster and I had never flown wing to wing before. We had moved ahead in the squadron at the same pace, and as flight leaders we led less experienced pilots. I instantly regretted having to fly with him, to subject myself to his evaluation and his critical mouth. I had heard him grumble about bad wingmen and complain that replacement pilots were poorly trained. What's more, I wanted to think he was clumsy. I took pleasure in believing he was a bad pilot. Now if I discovered he wasn't, I would be disappointed.

Takeoff was easy and Foster trailed, remaining a good distance behind even in the climb. Once airborne it became obvious why the mission had been cancelled. An overcast extended out over the

Mediterranean. Without an instrument landing system or ground radar guidance at our base, the squadron couldn't be guaranteed a safe return.

I remained low, a few hundred feet off the ground, following dirt roads, curving around small hills, sliding into lazy turns, and making a pass at imaginary targets; then hauling back hard into an abrupt climb and practicing cross-controlling to point the nose one way while the plane skidded in the opposite direction, an evasive manuever to avoid gunfire which was sure to follow. Foster remained ten lengths behind. I knew he was evaluating my flying. Screw him.

We had been gone an hour. I broke the silence, "Foster. How do you read?"

"Loud and clear."

"Had enough? What do you say we go back?"

"I'm moving up."

On a turn to the right, Foster closed the distance and I saw him in his cockpit. He looked good, just another fighter pilot, man and machine. He didn't look like Foster anymore.

Near the coast the clouds darkened and lowered to two thousand feet. There would be no missions until this weather cleared. I hoped it would stay bad for the rest of the war.

We passed over Sidi Khalifa. A few Arabs stood by the roadside, looked up, and watched us cruise by. They didn't wave. The weather to the east looked threatening, black between the hilltops and the overcast, the horizon punctuated by scattered rainshowers. It was cool inside the cockpit, a pleasant change from the oppressive heat usual at low altitudes.

Like a crop duster returning to a familiar farm, I headed for a stretch of wheatfields, isolated and remote, where I had practiced before, perfecting vertical banks a few feet above the grain. The bent yellow tassels showed a strong easterly wind, the undulating waves transforming normally placid farmland into a turbulent sea. Foster closed in tight behind me. I dropped to a few feet above the land and stayed low for a mile or two until the plains butted the foothills of the Constantine mountains. Then I climbed gently, staying cautiously below the overcast. It was a bad day to practice. I turned for home.

Foster slid ahead of me taking the lead. Without a word, he banked sharply down for another pass at the field. I stayed close as he levelled a few feet above the grain, going lower until the tips of his propellers cut into the gold waves, harvesting a giant cloud in his wake. He was good. Very good. I held my position two plane lengths behind him in loose formation.

With the weather deteriorating, I expected Foster would quickly head back to base. Instead, he flew straight ahead, and in minutes we crossed the coast. The ceiling was lower and the horizon disappeared in a haze between sea and clouds. Soon we were dodging dark columns of rain. Why didn't he head back? Consumed by the awesome beauty of the surrounding elements, I blindly tagged along.

We plunged into a vast cathedral, a menacing whitecapped floor with billowing, surging clouds forming an angry ceiling above. Foster had challenged the elements as a civilian pilot before the war; it was a new experience for me. We hurtled through space, flying without fear of enemy planes, twisting through narrow cotton tunnels, piercing through the roof into blinding sunlight, then plunging down to a few feet above a choppy sea.

I followed as Foster shot up through a small hole into a pulsing cavity, only room enough to hold a continuous turn scraping the boiling cumulus walls, then descending quickly before the hole closed. My plane shuddered in the turbulence. Even in the clear, the air was rough and unstable. Foster felt it too. He banked and I knew we were going home. Traces of light rain splattered and dissolved on the windshield. The force of the wind cut the tops off whitecaps, forming a blanket of fine mist. There could be no missions in such weather. I'd have at least three days in Constantine.

I was startled by Foster's voice piercing my earphones. "Target! Twelve o'clock!" He stopped the turn and levelled his wings.

In the limited area between sea and sky, less than a hundred feet above the water, I saw the plane a few miles ahead, heading north, large, perhaps a bomber or transport.

"I have him, Foster. He must be lost."

"Let's show him the way to go home."

It looked like a B-24, or a B-25, but as we came closer, I was surprised to see three engines. My God! I thought, that's an enemy plane! At the same instant, Foster's voice boomed, "That's not one of ours!"

I studied the design of the bomber. It was definitely not American. Nor did it have the British or German functional boxlike appearance. This plane had smooth lines; the fuselage and wings were clean and uncluttered, blending naturally into a tail assembly—all of it a beautiful, simple expression of the designer's love of flight. But there was something glaringly wrong, something missing in the picture. There was no insignia; all markings had been painted out.

A few miles ahead of the bomber, a jagged bolt of lightning cut down through a black column of rain and struck the sea. The crew made no change in their course nor movement to indicate they were aware of our presence. They grazed along, oblivious that they were prey being measured for the kill.

The pleasure of flying was suddenly gone. Now I was doing a job. I pressed the mike button, "Foster, let's take another look...the British have three-engined bombers." But I knew it wasn't British. Its delicate silhouette matched the one-second images flashed on a screen: Italian bomber, Canterre 1007, stored like an index card in my memory ever since training. It was on a heading straight for Sardinia. Probably V.I.P.'s leaving Africa ahead of Montgomery's army, using bad weather for safety, gambling none of our planes would be airborne in weather like this.

We crossed over the bomber a second time. Still no sign we had been seen.

"What do you think?" Foster demanded. "What is it?"

"I'm not sure."

Damn! What's it going to be, Freddy boy? Is that a friend or an enemy? You shot down two fighters to defend our bombers. You called that self-defense. What do you call this? That beautiful baby skimming the waves below is no threat. Think about the eight men inside maybe with eight Italian families waiting for them. This guy's not dangerous, he's running away.

"I'm leading this flight, Nose, and that looks like the enemy to me. What are you afraid of?"

"Let's make sure. It could be a terrible mistake."

"You coming down with me or aren't you? Make up your mind cause I'm going after it!"

O.K., knock it off! I'm programmed to perform certain functions. I shook myself back to the moment. My voice bounced inside the earphones, "It's Italian, Foster, I'm sure of it!"

"Hot damn!" Foster called back. "She's mine! Give me room. Make your pass after I finish."

I choked with hatred for Foster. How could he enjoy this? They don't have a prayer. God, I hope they don't see it coming. I reduced power, letting him move well ahead as he peeled off into an attack. Still no sign we had been seen. The bomber continued on course.

I fell in trail a few hundred yards behind Foster. Too soon, much too soon, Foster opened fire. I watched expended shell casings pour from beneath his plane. Tracers made bright dots and dashes, missing the target by a wide margin. Then the bomber came alive. Its left wing dropped and a gunner began firing from a large opening in the side.

Foster, anticipating a turn to the left, banked sharply, but the bomber pilot flipped right. Good boy, I thought. Come around tight now and he can't touch you. The turn caught Foster by surprise, forcing him to follow, firing wildly and skidding from side to side, tracers spewing harmlessly left and right beyond the bomber. The side gunner continued to fire as Foster whipped past.

No longer was the bomber heading for the safety of the storm. Spotting me, he reached for the clouds overhead, climbing desperately as I closed to within a few hundred yards. Slowly he came around, fishtailing in an agonizing turn. You still have a chance! I thought. Don't just hang there. Come on, fella, dump your fucking nose and there's no way I can get you! The gunner swung toward me, guns pumping, like a man with an unruly garden hose, unable to compensate for the frantic maneuvers of his pilot.

Damn you! I said out loud. You blew it! Dump your nose! Turn into me! But he was stuck on my windshield next to the illuminated gunsight, like a fly in a web. I recognized the warmth that spread over my body, the dry throat, the familiar pounding of my heart, the rivulets of sweat that ran down my face. Mixture full rich, rpm's 3000, gunsight and gun switches ON. My plane strained to perform its real purpose and only reason for existence. I fired a two-second burst. The bomber's left engine erupted in an orange and red ball. The gunner kept firing as the plane slowly rolled over on its back, hit the water nose first, and exploded.

I caught up with Foster and we threaded our way toward the coast. Rain showers and squalls crowded our path and flashes of lightning punctuated every quadrant. How easy it is, I thought. Time your turn, slide in like a skater behind his partner, point your cock, come up his ass, and press the trigger. I killed them. In three seconds I killed all of them, and they saw it coming. *Schmucks!*

What the hell were they doing there? I was a killer. I felt tears well in my eyes.

*   *   *   *

We never owned a gun in my family. My father was a gentle man. I had never known him to raise his voice in anger. It was disturbing the one time I saw him use violence.

Bob and I were in our early teens. One night we returned home past our ten o'clock curfew. Mom was in the dining room crying.

"Bob, do you realize how late it is?" my father said. "Once more and you won't be allowed out after dinner."

Bob used a nasty tone with Dad he often used with me. "I'm too old for curfew! Fred can come home at nine o'clock, not me! And if that brat tags along, I'll break his head, goddamn it!"

I hated those winter nights, stamping my feet to keep warm while Bob and his friends pressed and squirmed their bodies against girls in dark passageways beneath the apartment buildings. Dad had said we were responsible for each other. He told us we had to stay together.

"I'm fed up being treated like a kid, damn it."

"Don't talk like that, Bob."

"All the guys stay out 'til eleven or even twelve! Ten o'clock is stupid," Bob shouted.

Mom inhaled sharply.

Dad shook his head, looked at his beautifully manicured fingernails, and said quietly, "That's enough! That kind of talk will not be tolerated in this house." He looked very sad.

I grabbed Bob's arm. "Cut it out, Bob," I whispered. He shoved me backward. "Get lost, you little punk!"

Mom was sobbing.

"From now on I'm staying out 'til eleven o'clock."

"Lower your voice. We'll talk in the morning. Now go to bed," Dad said, his voice still low and even.

"No! I want it settled now!"

"Bob, stop this or I'll make you stop."

"Stop me? That's a laugh, what'll you do, hit me?"

"If I must," Dad said, almost in a whisper.

"Go ahead," Bob goaded, sticking out his chin and pointing to it, "I dare you! Hit me. Go ahead, hit me!"

Dad rose from the couch, swung and hit Bob on the chin. Bob lost his balance, stumbled against the wall, and slid to the floor. Dad sat on the sofa and began to sob while Mom put her arms around him. I ran to help Bob. Soon, we were all crying.

Later, Dad came into our bedroom to say good night. He sat on the edge of Bob's bed and stroked his head. He was no fighter, he told us. It pained him to have hit Bob. He said he was sorry. "Never raise your hand to anyone," he said. "Take care of one another. Never fight, it's senseless."

"Even if someone wants to kill you?" Bob asked.

"That's not the same. Talk yourself out of danger. If you can't, do what your grandfather did in Russia, run away. If that's not possible, fight until the threat is gone. Do what you must."

*   *   *   *

I swept the picture of the bomber's explosive plunge and the death of its crew from my mind and concentrated on flying.

The number of storms increased, the downpour became constant. We lost forward visibility and turned in whatever direction seemed the clearest. The clouds pressed us down to a few hundred feet above wildly churning water. For several minutes we burst in and out the ragged ceilings, then abruptly I was swallowed in dense cloud and torrential rain. I was being punished for killing those people! Flying blind, I had to rely on my instruments to maintain control.

"Lost you, Foster, I'm climbing out of here!"

"Me too!" he shouted, "Don't crowd me. See ya on top."

I held a steady climb a few degrees left to avoid overtaking and colliding with Foster, waiting anxiously to reach clear skies above the cloud.

Foster called out new altitudes, increasing our separation and safety.

"I'm heading 185 degrees, 200 miles per hour," I called.

"Good, I'm higher and faster...whoa, getting a little bumpy up here...I'm going..."

"Say again. You were cut out...Foster, say again."

I could barely see the faint outline of my wingtips inside the dark cloud. Suddenly, a dazzling white flash dissolved the colors of the cockpit. Lightning! We were inside a thunderstorm! Again and again it had been hammered into our heads not to come within ten miles of a thunderstorm. The turbulence could shatter a plane.

Foster's transmission was badly broken, ". . . passing eight thou. . ."

At seven thousand, my plane slowed under the weight of the water. I was submerged, tossed like a cork, fighting each violent movement with a sweaty death grip of the control wheel. I jammed the nose down while the vertical climb instrument indicated a climb of 2,000 feet per minute. The next instant, I was in a screaming descent. A bolt of lightening, then oddly a moment of calm, followed by an impact as if I had smashed into a solid wall. I jerked hard against the shoulder harness, every joint of the plane shuddering with the jolt.

The dials a blur, water smashing against the windshield, streaming through seams of the canopy and gun cowlings, splashing over my ankles, the sound magnified a thousandfold by the plane's speed, I felt trapped inside a metal drum, pelted by a volley of steel balls. This was punishment for killing the men inside the Italian bomber. I was close to panic. I must maintain control, I ordered myself. I hadn't heard from Foster. G forces had pulled my throat mike too low to use and I didn't dare spare a hand to hold it. He's on his own, I thought. I must not think about him. Save yourself. Do what you must, I urged.

There was a brightness on the left, then it was gone. Was it my imagination, a hole in the clouds or more lightning? Again it was bright. I risked a turn, nature gave up the fight, I spat out the hook and slipped from her grip into the clear, bathed in brilliant sunlight. I was free and heading west. Behind and high above, I saw the churning wall of imbedded thunderstorms, towering cumulonimbus reaching 40,000 feet, a curtain stretching north and south to the horizon. I could never have reached the top!

"Foster! I'm in the clear! Turn to 270 degrees and you'll bust out."

". . . trying!" he answered, his voice higher pitched than usual.

"What's your altitude?"

"Fifteen thou. . . sometimes."

Over my right shoulder I saw him pop out of that billowing white wall, the sun glinting off his canopy, coming down in a steep dive. I never thought I would be glad to see his fat ass again.

"Yeeowwweeee!" he screamed. "Let me out of there! Where are you?"

"Keep your heading and I'll join you." I switched to channel "A." "Washboard! Washboard! Doorknob Five Two, over!"

The reply came fast. "Go ahead, Doorknob."

"Can you contact my base and get their weather?"

"Standby."

Ahead was the coast of Africa, beyond the hills, the dry Lake Fetzara.

"Your base is reporting a ceiling of two thousand," Washboard called. We would have a low but clear flight back. Foster attached himself to my wing as we scooted under that great wall of weather. Images of the bomber's dive into the Mediterranean crowded my thoughts.

"Take the lead, Foster."

"O.K., but stay close. Let's show them how tight it can be."

God, is that all you can think about? As his plane moved alongside to pass, I tapped his wingtip twice with the tip of mine. Close enough, you *schmuck?*

"Jesus!" he yelled, "You did that on purpose!"

My throat tightened. I'm going to be sick. I'm not a flyer, Dad, I'm a killer. Tears rolled down my cheeks.

We made a low pass and landed in formation.

Garrett was alone in the debriefing tent when Foster and I walked in. He typed out our report and told us we were free until the twenty-second of April. Flight operations were suspended for four days due to weather. Most of the pilots had already taken passes and gone to town. In a way, he said, it was a celebration. The British 8th and American 2nd Armies had broken through the Mareth Line in southern Tunisia, and Rommel was on the run. Most of the North African coast was in Allied hands. If we wished, the motor pool would arrange transportation to Constantine. "Looks like you guys had quite a day," he said, pulling the paper out of the typewriter.

Garrett tossed the report in a box labelled John Wallace, Captain, C.O., shook Foster's hand, and said, "Congratulations, Lieutenant, your first confirm and a big one!" Foster laughed and punched a fist into the palm of his other hand. "Not bad, huh Sarg? Wow! Those Eye-ties never knew what hit 'em."

I walked back to the tent feeling dazed. Foster's account of the incident was different from the way I remembered it. He claimed his bullets struck and disabled the rudders, causing the plane to go out of control and crash. I thought his gunfire had missed. But I was relieved. I hadn't killed them. If he'd hit the rudders, all I had done was pump more steel into a dead body. It was Foster's confirm and I didn't want to contradict his report.

When Foster had finished, Garrett looked at me. I added that I made a pass after Foster, hit the left engine, and confirmed the plane was destroyed with no survivors. Yet it bothered me I could have been so wrong. I remembered the well-timed evasive maneuver the pilot had made during Foster's pass. It would have been that maneuver that had lost him airspeed and control. On the other hand, I was a good distance behind and wouldn't have seen the damage inflicted by Foster. I shuddered with the memory of the incident. Leave it alone. A Yiddish expression of my father came back to me, "Never walk on another man's grave."

18

Cocheem

I WAS DISTURBED BY THE destruction of the bomber, unable to find a comfortable place for it in my mind, confused that it had upset me so. I asked Tex for a pass to Constantine.

"Boy, you deserve it."

*　　*　　*　　*

"Tell Cocheem when the temperature is to your liking. Say *'Achot,'* it is the word for 'good.' It means, 'it is satisfactory.' "

The girl was barefoot, brass bangles hung from her ears and wrists.

"Monsieur Sharif, you're too kind."

He held up his hand indicating that I should not object and opened the door to the bath. "See, everything is being prepared for you. There is soap and a razor."

Sharif spoke in Arabic. The girl, about twenty, moved swiftly to the bath, picked up a tall copper vessel, and poured steaming water into the enormous tub. Her robe was coarse, hanging loosely from her shoulders to the floor. She made no move to cover her face. She handled the heavy copper jug with ease. Steam from the hot water formed a fine mist on her face, accenting amber and almond highlights on her nose and cheeks. Loose strands of licorice hair curled down over her eyes, the rest bundled hurriedly at her back and skewered by random tortoise pins. Quickly, she moved to the next vessel of hot water. I was captivated.

"Monsieur Sharif, how can I thank you?"

"It is I who must thank you. You honor me with your visit. We have much in common. Allah is the same God as the Jewish Jehovah, and in the Koran it is written that Moses is our prophet. So, we are brothers. But, forgive me, I talk too much and I think you must rest."

"I am looking forward to that bath."

"You will have complete privacy. After your bath, you have the afternoon to rest. This evening, many of my family will come to visit. Join us for supper. My sons speak English. They know you are my guest and are eager to meet you."

He went to the far side of the room, and pulled back a drape covering French doors. Light flooded the room. Floors and walls were covered with ornate Persian rugs, a low bed was piled high with colored pillows.

"Whenever you visit Constantine, think of this as your home. I must excuse myself now. It is time for evening prayers."

I grasped his extended hand, but it was limp, delicate, only to be touched, not squeezed. Embarrassed, I gently held it between both of mine and said, "You're very kind."

"Enjoy your bath and have a good rest. Cocheem will tell me when you are ready to come downstairs."

The bathroom was beautiful. Ceramic tiles covered the floors, walls, and ceiling. A gracefully curved porcelain tub stood on clawed feet. I reached in to touch the water. It was lukewarm. I pointed to the two remaining vessels of hot water and motioned that I wished both of them poured into the tub. Cocheem understood and silently emptied the vessels. Water splashed on the tiled floor. Quickly she wiped it dry and left the room, quietly closing the door.

On a chair, next to the tub, was a towel and a bar of soap. I undressed and draped my clothes over the chair. I felt good. I stepped into the tub, sliding down into clear, warm, water. I lathered my head again and again, then ducked below the surface. When I opened my eyes, I saw Cocheem adding another jug of water at my feet. Without thinking, I covered my groin with my hands. But the girl was like the models I had sketched at the Art Institute, seemingly unaware of my presence, preoccupied with her duties. She picked up the empty jugs and turned to the door, her robe moving with the motion of her swinging hips. She would make a good subject, I thought. I would like to paint her. Someday, I 'll be a fine artist. That is, if there is a "someday." The Italian bomber intruded into my thoughts again. I didn't want to think about that now. I lathered my head once more and snuggled down in the hot water.

The door opened. Cocheem came in carrying two more jugs, one on her hip, the other on her shoulder. She deftly hooked a bare foot around the door, flipping it shut behind her. She began to pour both jugs at once.

"Enough!" I yelled. The water was scalding. "That's great. Thank you. Thank you." She smiled and kept pouring. "*Achot, achot*, very good, very good," I repeated. She poured until the jugs were empty. Her face was alive, her teeth brilliant ivory against brown lips and skin. She placed the empty jugs next to the wall, pulled the sleeves of her kaftan up to her shoulders, exposing bare arms, leaned over me, and thrust her strong fingers into my soapy scalp. I groaned with pleasure. Next she took a firm grip on my right wrist and soaped my neck and arms with a rough cloth. The wide sleeves of her kaftan exposed her body, naked to her hips.

As she reached over me to scrub my left arm, I could see her lovely breasts jiggling with every movement. I became big and hard. I wanted to touch her, to run my hands down her body. I was afraid my penis would come up through the lather on the surface of the water and betray my thoughts. But I couldn't look away. She was beautiful, graceful, her body exquisite.

She took my right leg in her hands, turned her back on me, and concentrated on scrubbing. Her garment molded to her narrow waist and showed every contour of her buttocks, as though she wore nothing. I gripped the sides of the tub until my knuckles went white. It had been months since I had touched a woman. But I didn't want to think of the past. My mind reeled with ways of touching Cocheem by accident. How would she react? Enough! I was a guest in this house, and I would leave this girl alone.

When at last she had finished washing me, she reached through a slit at the waist of her robe and drew out a thin matching rope, which she looped between her legs and around her waist, making bloomers out of the loose fabric and exposing her bare legs. She dropped to her knees, swirling a towel across the tiles in great arcs. There was a pixie quality about her movements, something childlike, despite her woman's body. With these thoughts I went limp and lost my sexual appetite.

I stepped out of the bath and wrapped myself in a dry towel. Cocheem took a fresh towel and, kneeling, began drying my legs. I couldn't resist touching her. I stroked her hair, and when she looked up at me I caressed her face. The tortoise pins came out easily, and her hair tumbled over her shoulders. She was lovely, her skin velvet smooth to my touch. I trembled. I was becoming hard again. I must stop teasing myself. I patted her head, thanked her in Arabic, and walked to the bedroom. I climbed into the bed and covered myself with a single sheet. Cocheem followed, drew the drapes, leaving just a trace of light, pulled her kaftan over her head, stood for a moment next to the bed, and then quietly slid in alongside me.

I awakened in darkness to voices filtering through the French windows, echoes of conversation bouncing off the cobblestoned courtyard below. The voices merged with sounds of splashing water. Cocheem was preparing another bath.

*   *   *   *

Bobbie and I were fifteen. She was tender, young, and beautiful. I had been commissioned to paint her portrait by the publicity committee of our high school. That year she was homecoming queen. We talked and laughed for hours during the countless sittings. She was soft-spoken and lively, and even after the portrait was finished I kept asking her to come back, making believe I was still working, just so I could look at her and feel her presence. I was in love.

Bobbie and I met often after that. We went dancing, we spent long afternoons walking in the park, and we helped each other with our homework. One day after school, we stopped by her house so she could change her clothes. Her mother wasn't home.

I heard water filling the bathtub. A few minutes later, she called, "Fred, do me a favor, please."

I came to the bathroom door. "What do you need?"

"Scrub my back."

I didn't know what to say.

"Fred, come on. You're an artist. Seeing me without clothes shouldn't bother you."

The door to the bathroom was ajar. Her back was toward me. She held out a washcloth and a bar of soap. I scrubbed her neck, her back, her arms. Her body was exquisite. Bobbie and I became lovers. Sex was natural and uninhibited. It was the first time for both of us.

Seven months later, I received a letter from Bobbie. She was vacationing in Indiana with her parents.

"It's been two months and "Granny" hasn't come."

She was pregnant. We were sixteen years old. After the third month, we were frantic. She didn't want to have the baby, but neither of us knew where to turn for help. Our grades began to drop. We were afraid of failing school. We discussed leaving Chicago, getting married, having the baby. In the end we agreed the best solution was for her to have an abortion.

I asked my brother for help. He was seventeen. He would know what to do.

"You're a real *putz,* Fred. Leave me out of it. I don't know what the hell you should do. What makes you so sure you're the father? If she spread her legs for you, she'll do it for anyone. Boy, if the folks hear about this!"

I went to see Dr. Goldman, and told him I knew a girl in school who was pregnant and needed to find a doctor.

"How does your friend know she is pregnant?" he asked.

"A test was done with rabbits."

"Go to your father, Freddy. He will help you."

"No, it's not for me. It's for this girl I know."

"I know, I know. I can see in your face you're in trouble."

"Can you help?"

"Even if I knew where to send you, I couldn't. It's a serious matter. There are laws that must be obeyed. It is not a medical problem. I cannot help you. Please, go to your father. He will help you."

"I can't. He'll be ashamed of me."

"And the girl's parents?"

The next day Bobbie and I took a bus to a neighborhood across town. She wore a suit and looked older with her hair pulled back. I wore a tie and my best suit with a vest. She had found an old wedding band of her mother's. We stopped at the first sign that said "M.D." The receptionist asked who the patient was.

"My wife."

She looked at us for a long time before speaking.

"You'll have to make an appointment."

"It's very important. We'd like to see the doctor."

After a moment, she said, "Have a seat."

In the doctor's office, I stuttered and stumbled through an explanation that my wife's pregnancy made her very sick and we wanted to have an abortion.

"Who referred you to me?"

I didn't know how to answer. I looked to Bobbie for help. She was so lovely, so afraid. How could I have done this to her? The doctor didn't wait for an answer.

"Get out!"

"Could you . . ."

"Get out of here!"

When I got home, I lay on my bed and cried. That night, my mother asked what was wrong with me.

"Are you sick? Dave, look. He hasn't eaten a thing. It's that *shiksa* he's been seeing. I know it. I told you no good would come of it. What, Jewish girls aren't good enough for you?"

"Now, now, Idele. Leave the boy alone. Freddy, are you all right?" my father asked.

"I'm just not hungry," I said.

Bob remained silent.

After dinner, I stood at the door of my parents' bedroom and asked if I could speak to my father alone. Without a word my mother got out of bed, slipped on a robe, and left the room.

"*Nu?* So what's so terrible?" my father asked.

"Everything!" I blurted out, "It's so awful!" I put my arms around him and sobbed, my body convulsing, distorting the sound of my cries. He hugged me, "Now, now, nothing can be so terrible, everything will be all right."

"Bobbie's pregnant!"

Over my sobs I heard his consoling words, "It'll be all right . . . it'll be all right. Don't worry anymore." And with a tenderness that caused me to sob even harder, he asked, "And Bobbie? How is she?"

I was barely able to answer, "She's so frightened."

"Do you want me to talk to her parents?"

"On no! We can't tell them!"

"I won't do anything you don't want me to do."

"What can we do?"

"I don't know, but trust me. As hopeless as it seems, this too shall pass." He patted my head. "Tomorrow we'll see Sam Shapiro."

Sam Shapiro's office was down the hall from my father's. He was the attorney for Uncle Al's manufacturing company, a pleasant older man. On those occasions when I visited Dad at his office and we met Mr. Shapiro in the hall, Dad would say with pride, "Sam, you remember my son, don't you? Freddy, say hello to Mr. Shapiro."

Sam listened to my father's story, his face without emotion. Then he asked me, "Have you had any correspondence with the young lady?"

"Yes. We wrote often while she was away," I answered.

"Do you have all the letters she wrote you?"

"Yes, sir."

"Can you get them?"

I turned to my father. He said, "Tell Mr. Shapiro what he wants to know."

"Yes, Mr. Shapiro, I can. But why?"

"I would like to read them."

"I don't understand."

"It could have a bearing on whether or not you have any responsiblity in the matter."

"I *am* responsible."

Sam looked at my father.

"Sam, if he says he's responsible, he's responsible. The question is, what can be done? They want to . . ." Dad hesitated, "ah . . . terminate the situation."

Sam looked at me. "Would you marry this girl?"

"Yes."

"You see what you're dealing with, Dave? Marriage between children . . . abortion. And have you considered what will happen if the girl's parents find out? You could get yourselves in serious trouble. It's the girl's parents' responsibility. Let them make the decisions. It's possible she's taking advantage of Fred."

"I know the girl, Sam, and I know my son. It's not like that. Can you help us?"

"I can review the letters to see if they are incriminating. After that, it's her word against his. Beyond that . . . ," he shook his head.

"Dave, among our friends...in our community, do you know anyone who does these things?"

When we left Mr. Shapiro's office, Dad put his arm around my shoulder. "Don't worry. Everything will be all right. I will take care of it."

The next day, My father handed me an envelope. "Here. An appointment has been made for Bobbie in the name of Mary Parker. The address is in the envelope with two hundred dollars. Give it to the doctor." The money in the envelope was more than my father made in a month. I took it and kissed his cheek.

The doctor's office was located in an office building on Diversy Street. The receptionist asked, "Do you have an appointment?"

"Yes, Mary Parker."

"And you?" the woman asked looking at me.

"We're together."

"I'm sorry, you can't wait here. You'll have to leave."

I kissed Bobbie and gave her the envelope. "Don't worry. I'll be downstairs."

"I don't know how long it will take," she said.

"It doesn't matter. I'll wait."

In a few minutes Bobbie found me in the lobby. She was crying. "They're terrible people! I couldn't do it. What are we going to do?"

I hugged her tightly. "We'll have the baby. I'll quit school. If I work full time, I can make more money. And that's not all. I've been asked to make portraits of the motion picture executives along film row. A restaurant where they have lunch will pay $25.00 for each one. We'll do fine."

"We're sixteen years old! My mother and father won't let me get married."

That night, I phoned Bobbie and told her my father would find another doctor. We agreed to meet at her aunt's house the following evening. Bobbie had a key. It was our secret meeting place. I was surprised when her aunt opened the door. Her tone was crisp and cold. Bobbie was in bed in the next room. She reached her arms out to me.

"It's all over," she cried. "My aunt arranged for a woman to come here. I gave her the money. That was all right, wasn't it?"

In the spring, her family moved to another city. I didn't see Bobbie again for five years.

*   *   *   *

Cocheem took my hand and led me to the bath. Our shadows, cast by several candles, danced on the walls. My uniform and underclothes were neatly laid out on the bed, freshly laundered and pressed, shoes cleaned and polished. The war was a million miles away.

During the last afternoon of my two-day pass, I sipped coffee at a sidewalk cafe with Habeeb, Mohammed Sharif's son. I was to meet the transportation truck across the street. We talked and I sketched. He had given me several sheets of coarse white paper. I drew the shops around the square in which we sat. He offered me a Turkish cigarette.

"No thanks," I said, offering him one of mine.

"*Avec plaiser,*" he answered.

"Next time I'll give you the whole package."

"Good. We'll do business. Since the Americans have come, the people of Algeria have acquired a taste for chocolate, chewing gum, and American tobacco. Our friendship will be greater if we profit from each other. I have beautiful things—brass trays, daggers, handmade linen. Whatever you bring I will pay a fair price."

"I'm not a merchant, my friend, and I have nothing to sell."

He laughed. "Nothing? From what Americans throw away I can became wealthy. Three days ago on the road to Wadi el Chamire an Army truck and its cargo were abandoned. The driver reported the vehicle stolen. In less than three hours, nothing remained larger than a tire, and within two days every part had been resold many times over. Our people are ingenious. We are poor so we must improvise."

"I don't understand. Was the truck stolen?"

"Algeria is dotted with vehicles that ran out of fuel, deserted camps picked clean by Berbers who bring me broken cots, stoves, pots, and torn canvas tents. I am unable to import from Europe since the war began. This is not my war. We do business where we can. Even old battle fields are a source of supply."

He shrugged. "You think that's so terrible? There is no dishonor in survival. A poor family does not ask a pair of boots if its owner was German or American.

An hour later, the transportation truck arrived and I climbed aboard. There were blue holes in the overcast sky and I wondered if a mission was scheduled for the morning.

19

Can't Remember Everything

TEX HELD GARRETT'S REPORT IN one hand and drummed on the desk with the other. He looked irritated. I had a sinking feeling in the pit of my stomach. Foster stared at his feet.

"Somethin' doesn't jibe here," he said impatiently. "Says here you flew over a couple of times to identify the plane, right?" Tex turned to me.

"Don't tell me that plane was British!" I glanced at Foster.

"No, she was Italian all right," Tex said. "The question is, Ko-han, were you flyin' Foster's wing at the time the plane was destroyed?"

"Sure. He was in the lead."

"I told you I was leading," Foster said.

"That's not the question. Were you his wingman?"

"I suppose so. We traded the lead a few times, like you told us to. What difference does it make?"

"Be specific. Exactly where were you in relation to one another? Foster was out front so he wouldn't know."

"The truth, Nose. Didn't we go down on that plane together?"

"No, I followed after you started your pass."

"But you were my wingman, right?"

"Yes, that's right."

Foster slapped his hands together. "That's what you want to know, isn't it Tex?"

"Kohn, try to remember. Were you within a few plane lengths of Foster?"

"No, more like a city block. Let me show you." I rubbed a clear space on the blackboard and rapidly sketched a sequence of scenes from my memory of those few seconds. When I finished, Tex asked, "Why did you hold back?"

"Hold back?"

"Yeah. How come you didn't dive with Foster?"

"I don't know. Took me longer to make up my mind, I guess."

"Well, we got the film back from your gun cameras yesterday. Foster's shells passed to the left of the bomber. Yours hit the engine just like in your drawing. Even so, if you had been flying his wing at the time your pictures could have been recording the damage done by Foster's guns. No doubt about it, it's your confirmation. Congratulations, Ko-han. Too bad, Foster."

I was overwhelmed with shame, not pride. Why must it be like this?

After Foster left, I went to find Garrett.

"You didn't forget, I don't want this published back home."

"Don't worry," he said, "After the last time, I tagged your file. A deal's a deal, Lieutenant."

"Thanks, Sergeant. There's something else you can do for me, though. Check my log. I flew four combat missions when I was at Marrakech. Add those to your tally and I only have a few more to go."

"I'll ask Captain Wallace about that. There's a letter here for you, Lieutenant. And sir, congratulations!"

The envelope was addressed in an unfamiliar hand but the return address was my parents'. I slit it open carefully. There were several sheets of paper inside.

May 2, 1943

"Dear Lieutenant Kohn,

Remember me? Ginny Lilienthal, Al's younger sister? We haven't heard anything more from the government, but I just know Al's alright and he'll come back to us.

Everyday after school, your father writes with his finger on my hand, like he did with you, and I write it down. It takes a long time, but I'm getting the knack, and it makes me very happy to do it. Now he can write to his sons. He's a wonderful man and very proud of you.

My mother and father took me to a movie last night all about flyers in the war. So, like they said,

Happy landings, Ginny

P.S. All the words are his.

Letter No. 1

Dear Fred,

We have been receiving your letters. Some times one at a time, then days later we'll get six or seven at once. I will number my letters like you do so that we can tell if one fails to arrive.

Your sketches add so much, a flavor of your surroundings, I almost feel I've walked the streets of Marrakech with you and seen the exciting things you have. Thank God you are far from Tunisia where the war is.

My heart goes out to those men who risk their lives to defend our country, and I pray Al will come home to his family. However, I am unashamed and grateful that you and Bob have been spared from having to bear arms.

Bob is now a Staff Sergeant. A radio operator in the Air Transport Command. They ferry aircraft all over the world. And, my son, you are blessed. To teach others, share what you have learned, is the highest calling of Judaism.

Your mother is well, but it saddens me to have become such a burden to her. And now, with thanks to dear Ginny for making it possible to speak to my son, I close,

Your loving father.

Ginnie didn't have to translate Dad's irregular pen marks at the end. Reading his words choked me up. I knew the painstaking effort it took for him to communicate his words to Ginnie. I read it all again.

The idea of my parents' learning I was in combat haunted me. Each time I wrote, I made up more stories about training pilots in flying technique. But it wasn't such a big lie telling them I was an instructor. Within a few months of our arrival in North Africa, the

four of us in tent number eight had been made flight leaders, and
with that position came the responsibility of evaluating new pilots
before they went on their first mission.

The next morning, I had a particularly frustrating practice flight
with a new captain. After we landed, I watched him stroll into the
debriefing tent. I'd been waiting for him for five minutes.

"What happened to you up there? Sorta got lost, didn't you?" I
asked accusingly, not really interested in his response. I could never
have been an instructor. I had no patience.

"What do you mean?" Captain Fleming asked, avoiding my eyes.

Garrett looked up when he heard the tone of my voice, then
busied himself with the day's intelligence reports.

"After my first turn," I continued, rubbing the furrow on my
forehead made by the tight-fitting helmet, "you fell behind four
plane lengths..." I looked hard at him trying to capture his
attention. "Then I made a wide turn so you could catch up. After
the second break, you got lost again and never regained position."

Captain Fleming dipped in his breast pocket for a package of
cigarettes. I measured my words slowly, "Captain, I know you don't
have many hours in a 38, but formation flying's no different in this
crate than any other plane..."

Fleming turned and looked me squarely on. He was half a head
taller, his baggy coveralls inconsistent with his erect military
bearing. Two creases separated his platinum eyebrows; he
squinted as though he were looking into the sun.

"O.K., Lieutenant, what do you suggest?" He poked a cigarette in
his mouth.

"You have to anticipate a turn...."

"Sergeant, got a match?"

"Garrett patted his pockets, "I think so, sir."

"You have to pull in fast when I start to turn away from you.
That's where you got into trouble, you weren't on top of it. I
think...."

Garrett held a light while Fleming scanned the papers on his desk,
"Got me down for tomorrow, Sergeant?"

"....it's something you might want to work on." I finished
through clenched teeth. I knew he wasn't listening. Fuck you, I
thought, you stuck up West Point prick. It's your ass. I'd known the
Flemings of the world at the Illinois Athletic Club and in Chicago's

restricted suburban communities. They had a way of talking past you. Especially if your name was Kohn.

" 'Scuse me, Captain," Garrett whispered, "Lieutenant Kohn's flown almost twenty missions and he knows what he's talking about."

"I asked for a match, Sergeant, not your advice."

"Yes, sir!"

It had been a scorcher, and I was glad when the sun went down. The camp lights hadn't come on yet and it was getting dark in the tent. A field rat raced across the fiber floor mat and disappeared. I tucked the mosquito netting in tighter around my sleeping bag and wondered why crickets didn't make their special sound in the daytime.

"In the pad so early?" Falzone came into the tent with a couple of letters in his hand.

"I saw our little friend making one of his mad dashes," I said.

"Was it Leppy?" Falzone asked.

"How can you tell one rat from another?" I asked thinking of Foster and Fleming.

"Hey, something eating you?" Falzone asked.

"No, nothing."

I lay on my cot gazing at the ceiling. Heavy footsteps brought me back to the present.

"Anybody home?"

"Won't cost anything to take a look," Falzone answered.

A head and broad shoulders squeezed through the narrow opening. Neatly stacked boxes of letters, mess kits, and other paraphernalia crashed to the floor.

"Christ, it's dark in here! You in here, Ko-han? What's wrong with the light?"

"Yes, sir, I'm here." I was startled at the sound of Tex's voice. It was the first time he had come to our tent. I sat up in bed, keeping the mosquito netting pulled around me. "Sit down on Foster's bunk, he won't mind," I said.

"I'll just spread my carcass here on the floor, where I won't be in anybody's way." With his face in shadow, Tex looked older than his twenty-six years.

"How'd y'all make out with Fleming?"

"Not too good."

"Good enough?"

"Nope."

"He don't have to win no prizes, just mosey out and back."

"If he can fly formation, he's keeping it a secret," I said.

"Captain Fleming asked to go along on tomorrow's mission," Tex said.

I slapped at a mosquito and missed. "Real eager, isn't he?"

"He's only goin' to be with us for two weeks."

"Two weeks!" Falzone whistled, "That's what I call temporary duty! How come?"

"He's on special assignment from the Academy, gettin' firsthand experience."

"What can he learn in two weeks?" Falzone asked.

"Just exposure, learn about the Air Corps, get a better understandin' of the role we play."

"Flying a fighter in combat is a tough way to learn," I said. "How come he doesn't take a ride in a bomber instead?"

"Some are doing that. Fleming's part of an experiment. Regular Army, specialists in strategic warfare. He's one of a dozen or so West Pointers selected to learn about the Air Force. They had to learn to fly, and Fleming's checked out in fighters. When the war's over he won't be takin' his uniform off, like y'all. One day he'll be callin' the shots. We want to cooperate, right?"

Tex's respect for Fleming irritated me. As an experienced Commanding Officer, Tex's promotion to Major was assured. He'd probably stay in the Air Corps after the war. But he sounded a little jealous. I guess even his status wasn't the same as coming from the Point. The rest of us pilots took the war seriously, but not the service. After it was over, Falzone would return to teaching, Smith had a family business waiting for him, and Foster already had a career in commercial aviation. None of us looked to the military as a way of life. Maybe Tex even resented that about us.

A mosquito, heavy with blood, swung past my ear on final approach. I slapped hard against my neck. The exploded remains left a bloody pattern in my palm. Greedy little bastard went over gross, lost speed and maneuverability.

"Fleming says ya gave him a hard time."

"I'm flattered he remembered my name."

"Says ya tried to make a fool of him."

"He didn't need any help."

"I want him to fly."

"Give him a plane and let him practice."

"Hey, simmer down, boy. You used to be so nice and polite when you first came here, a real gentleman. Now you sound like you got a hair up your ass. What's with you?"

"It's his attitude. He's a bad man," I said.

"What y'all talkin' 'bout? He's bright as hell and he's on a serious assignment."

"I can smell him. Guys like him spend most of their time under rocks."

"Ko-han, y'all got a problem. Loosen up, y'hear? If the work is getting to you, go see the doc."

"What for, cocktails?"

"Well now, don't seem like there's nobody in this outfit meets your standards. Fleming will be flyin' my wing tomorrow, so you won't have anythin' more to do with him. Now do y'self a favor and relax. Listen here, we got a special assignment for tomorrow."

Tex explained that Montgomery's Eighth Army was advancing on Tunis from the south, the British First Army was pressing from the west, and the U.S. Second Corps was coming up the middle, squeezing Rommel into a corner of Tunisia with his back against the sea. Our job was to keep the German troops demoralized and moving, harrass, terrorize, and strafe their flanks to prevent them from digging in.

"Do you want my opinion?" I asked.

"Not really, but you're going to tell me anyway."

"Strafing in a combat zone is a waste of time. If we're too high, they all look alike. We kill our own. If we stay low, we pass 'em before we can see 'em."

"O.K., ya had your say. Now we'll do what Wing wants. We're gonna split the squadron. Each of us will take a flight, stay together until we're over enemy territory, then pick our own targets. We're gonna hit and run, and give 'em hell."

I shook my head in disbelief.

"You see something wrong, boy?"

"And you're going to take Fleming as your wingman?"

"That's what the man's here for. No better way he can see it like it is."

"Lot's o' luck."

"All he's got to do is follow the leader. I'll keep it loose and I don't care if he doesn't fire a shot."

"You're the boss," I said. "You want to take responsiblity for that West Point *putz*, that's your problem. As for me, I'm going to look out for my own ass."

Tex shrugged and said, "By the way, boys, I've got good news for y'all. Wing has stretched the tour to fifty missions."

"I'll be goddamned," said Falzone.

I whipped the netting away, "Another twenty-five? Who asked for a second tour?"

"It's the same tour, Ko-han, only now it's fifty."

"The deal was twenty-five." I said, suddenly flushing with anger and frustration. They weren't sticking to their bargain. I felt betrayed.

"Yep, it was, when the average life span of a fighter pilot was three months," Tex said. "Now we've got air superiority, so Wing figures our chances have improved a hundred percent. We got a good team now. Shucks, the second half will be a breeze. Besides, the extra missions ought to make Foster happy. Give him more time to get a confirm. He hasn't smiled since you got credit for that Italian bomber, Ko-han."

"You win some, you lose some," said Falzone.

"Tex, what about those combat missions I flew out of Marrakech?" I asked.

"Don't worry about those Ko-han. I can't see that they count."

"Could we get an opinion from Wing?"

Tex squinted, "Don't push me, boy."

All I could think about were those bastards at Wing Command. I had only five more missions to go. Now it's thirty. It was worse than starting over.

It was just getting light when the jeep dropped me in front of my plane. I put some finishing touches to my last drawing, then wrapped the sketchbook in paper to protect it from Chad's greasy fingers and handed it to him. He'd give it back when I landed.

"Take a look at my artwork, Lootenant. Pretty, huh?" He pointed at an Italian symbol painted next to the two German swastikas. "Wasn't easy. You're the first one in the outfit to shoot down an Italian plane. We don't have a stencil for that fancy 'fascista.' I painted it by hand. How do you like it, Lootenant?"

"Great, Chad." Let him take credit, I thought. I don't want it.

"Take care of the book, will you?"

Twelve planes took off in soft morning light, Tex leading the squadron with Fleming on his wing, and Falzone leading the third flight. We stayed together until we reached Medjez el Bab in Tunisia. Then we peeled off, each flight going its own way. I took my three men and snooped low, sniffing for the enemy. The radio was quiet. For forty minutes we couldn't find anything that looked like a target. Then, frightened voices broke the silence.

"I'm hit! I'm hit!"

"Doorknob White flight! Let's get the hell out of here!"

"Split up, goddamn it! Those assholes are firing at us!"

I held my breath, listening to the calls, hoping whoever it was would be all right. The three planes in my flight moved close to me. I started weaving, looking for the others. The sky was clear and the ground looked peaceful.

I called, "White Leader, this is Doorknob Five Two. You O.K.?"

No answer.

"How about it Tex, you O.K.?"

A new voice called, "Don't know where Tex is. This is White Three. I'm looking for my wingman. We ran into ground fire. The whole fucking sky blew up. White Two and Four, check in! Over."

"White Four here. I'm hit but O.K."

"Roger, this is White Two, I'm O.K." I knew that was Fleming.

"Fleming," I called. "Where's Tex?"

"Don't know. Lost him in a turn."

"Can you find your way back?"

"I can make it."

I tried Tex again. No answer.

"Falzone, you O.K.?"

"Yeah, Nose, we're fine. What happened?"

"Don't know. Where are you?"

"At the south end of our sector. We're going back."

"Roger. Out."

I tracked back to Medjez el Bab, anxious that Tex hadn't called in. That it could happen to an experienced and skillful pilot rattled me. Tex was my guarantee that if you were good and kept your head on a swivel, you'd make it. I'd been counting on skill, technique, and conditioned reflexes to do the right thing. If I stayed alert, I'd be all right. Now I wasn't so sure.

I kept my flight low, skidding, turning, trying not to stay on one track long enough to let anti-aircraft gunners get their sights on us. But what about bad luck? I knew that somewhere below they were cranking their guns around, computing the angle. If I zig or zag, maybe I'll run into the shot that would have missed. It wouldn't take much—a hunk of metal ripping through the bottom of the seat, an incendiary in a fuel tank, hit the main spar or delicate tail boom—and it was over.

"Doorknob Blue Flight! Aircraft at two o'clock high!"

Almost out of enemy territory, there he was, a single plane, high and diving straight at us.

"O.K., I've got him," I yelled. "Let's go!"

We swung around into a head-on attack, adrenalin coursing through my system. Kill the fucker, kill the fucker! My fingers were on the buttons, waiting for the right moment.

"WAIT!" some one screamed. "That's a P-38! Maybe one of ours!"

"So what? If he's pointing his nose at us he's the enemy."

Wing tip to wing tip he was inside my gunsight, his nose sprouting guns and cannon. A P-38, no mistake.

"Doorknob Five Two, it's me, Fleming, White Two, let me in!"

I yelled, "I don't care who you are. Break off, you asshole, or you're dead! BREAK OFF NOW!" Less than a second and we would be within firing range. Now, I thought, now I've got him.

The nose of the 38 yanked to the sky, its belly exposed.

You *putz*! You West Point *putz*! I hissed, my heart pounding in my head.

"O.K., Fleming. Hold that heading." I flew by him, he tacked on in fifth position, and I turned for home base.

My flight, with Fleming bringing up the rear, was the first to land, Falzone came in next. The jeep picked me up, then Falzone. We parked at the end of the runway and watched White Three and Four land five minutes apart. More jeeps and an ambulance arrived, ground personnel came by foot, and we waited.

Fleming walked over and stood alongside. I scannned the eastern sky for a sign of Tex's plane.

"You think I screwed up, don't you, Lieutenant?"

"We all make mistakes, Captain."

"There was a lot of confusion. One minute my flight was there, the next, they were gone . . ."

"You shouldn't have been out there in the first place."

"I was so glad to see you guys, I forgot how to rejoin the flight." Fleming seemed sobered by the experience.

"We don't get medals for shooting down P-38's," I said.

"Would you really have shot me down?" Fleming asked hesitantly.

"Guess we'll never know, Captain."

Falzone called on the jeep radio every few minutes, but Tex didn't answer. No one spoke. I checked the time as though to slow the minutes remaining, calculating Tex's fuel supply to the point of exhaustion.

"There he is! There he is, goddamn it!" screamed a corporal.

"I see him! Real low, about a quarter mile east!" shouted Chad.

"Oh shit!" said Falzone. "He has a prop feathered! C'mon baby, you can do it."

"Holy Christ! He's going to be short!"

Captain Willard stood on the front seat of his jeep. "Everyone, get your asses in gear! Let's get him out if she blows!" Every vehicle leaped forward, accelerating parallel to the runway.

"He's got it! Look at that ol' son of a bitch fly!" I said. "He's going to make it!"

The plane held steady, nose level, gear and flaps up, clearing fifty feet above the end of the runway and settling gently until the props and belly of the gondola touched the steel mesh and skidded in a shower of sparks. We raced alongside.

Falzone and I were the first ones out of the jeep. We ran across the wing, Falzone yanked the canopy open. Tex's bulky frame filled the cockpit, the control wheel nestling in his lap.

"You O.K.?" I asked.

"Yep."

"Then let's get the hell away from here."

"Don't go gettin' your water hot, boy. Switches are off."

"What happened?" I asked.

"Lost the left engine and my radios."

"And your hydraulics?"

"No, they're O.K."

"Then how come you didn't lower your landing gear?"

Tex looked up at me and shrugged. "Can't remember everything."

Late that afternoon, five of us rode back from the sulphur baths.

Not far from the base, a three-axled supply truck overtook us and signalled for us to pull over. Smith was driving, Tex sat next to him, Falzone, Foster, and me crowded in the back.

A stocky corporal jumped to the ground and called, "Your right rear's almost flat. Glad to fix it for you. Only take a minute," he said, removing a toolbox from the back of his truck. "You're pilots, aren't you?"

"Fighter pilots," Smith corrected. "Where you going so late?"

"Tebessa." He turned to Tex. "But I got a late start, Captain. Can I spend the night at your field? Not safe after dark without a convoy."

"Glad to have ya."

The corporal set a jack under the rear axle and Foster kneeled next to him, handing him tools as he needed them.

Falzone and I wandered over to the supply truck.

"Well, well, well. What do we have here? Hey, Nose. A little something for our kitchen." Falzone pulled the curtain aside and pointed to boxes stencilled: "M-2568/US-3 12/32 OZ. JUICE. TYPE-GRAPEFRUIT, UNSWEETENED. WEST TEXAS PRODUCE COMPANY, USA."

"Where did this come from?" Falzone yelled.

"The US Navy," the driver laughed. "The fleet's in Algiers. They live good. Fresh meat, real eggs, and beer. My C.O. paid off a Navy Commander to get those boxes."

"Who's your C.O.?" Tex asked.

"Colonel Grey, 447th Ordinance and Supply, sir."

"Those lucky bastards," said Falzone. "We should have joined the Navy."

"It's a *mechaieh*," I said under my breath.

"What do you say, Nose? Do we fuck the colonel?"

"I say, the colonel is a kind and generous man."

Accomodations were arranged. The corporal took an extra bunk in Chad's tent. And while he slept, with the help of both our ground crews, Falzone and I emptied the truck and distributed boxes of grapefruit juice to each pilot of the 71st. At breakfast, we called the corporal to our table. In the center of every table in the mess hall was a can of grapfruit juice.

"Corporal," Tex said, handing the man an envelope addressed to his commanding officer. "We thank you for your assistance last night and request you convey our respects to Colonel Grey. We are indebted to him for his generous gift to the fighter pilots of the 71st Fighter Squadron."

20

Unknown Heroes

"JUST THE GUY I'M LOOKING for," Elkhorn said.

"What's up?" I was sitting outside the chow tent sipping some freshly brewed tea, and sketching the ground crews playing ball. It was early in the morning and we had been informed the entire Squadron was to be non operational for the next two days.

"Guess you heard Anderson didn't come back," Elkhorn sprawled on the ground next to me.

I nodded. "But I don't know the details." I watched the drawing flow out of the tip of my pencil. If I concentrate on drawing the rippling muscles of the men, I don't have to remember what Anderson looked like, or that by next week Elkhorn might be dead, or that I might.

"I wasn't on the mission. Curtiss said two guys didn't make it. One of them was old Andy. Curtiss didn't see it happen but he's real shook up. He and Andy started out together like you and Foster. Real close, you know. It's tough. The way I figure it, there are only eight of us left out of the original seventeen."

"We're lucky," I said. "My father taught me a glass is half full, not half empty. The percentages are on our side."

He tapped out a cigarette and gave me one. "I hear you're an Ace, Kohn. Got the big number five yesterday, huh? Congratulations."

"Thanks," I said.

"What was it?"

"Focke Wolfe 190."

"I was adding it up . . ."

"Our losses?" I asked. Elkhorn was making me nervous.

"No, the Squadron confirms. Our bunch has accounted for eleven of them, not counting if J.B. and Layton got any. I guess that more than evens the score.

"The reason I was looking for you is Tex has us posted for a practice flight this morning, you, me, and Foster. Since we have to fly anyway I asked if it would be O.K. if we paid a call on our old buddies. I thought it'd be neat to see old J.B. and Layton."

"How do you know where they are?"

"Last week I ran into a guy in Constantine and learned where the 14th is based. It's only a hundred miles from here. I'm sure I can find it."

"I haven't heard much about the 14th," I said.

"I hear they've had heavy losses."

"What would you call ours, chopped liver?"

"Come on, it'll be fun to see them again." He paused. "Goddamn it, Nose, I don't know if they're still alive and there ain't no way to communicate with them. What do you say? I've already told Foster. Come on, we have to have the planes back before noon. We'll have a few laughs."

I agreed to meet them at the end of the runway at 0900. Elkhorn was on time and we waited five minutes for Foster, our engines idling. Finally, he taxied up in a new "H" model.

"Boy!" he cooed over the radio, "This is class! Maybe they'll take my old bird in trade for this sweetheart."

We waited while he checked his engines and rammed full throttle, his props churned a boiling cloud of dust. "That's what I call POWER!" Foster gloated. "Let's go you guys, and give me ROOM!"

Elkhorn took the lead, remaining low and we headed northeast. About fifteen minutes later he pulled up in a steep bank to the right. "I think this is it!" he called. We swept around a small group of hills. "There, off to the left. That's the base."

I searched the terrain and then suddenly I saw the camp. The tents blended nicely with the landscape. But the runway and taxi paths confirmed it was an airbase. Considering the elapsed time and speed, we had gone considerably less than 100 miles. We lined up and prepared for landing.

"You going to request permission to land?" I asked.

"Don't know their code name or what channel they're on," Elkhorn said. "They must have seen us by now."

We passed low over the runway. It looked different from our mesh and a lot shorter. Foster saw it too. "Guess they ran out of money when they built this pea patch. Let's make it look good. Ol' J.B.'s probably watching. Christ, it's short! It ain't gonna be easy."

"Maybe you should have come by jeep," Elkhorn said.

"Up yours," said Foster.

We slowed, dropped gear and flaps, and landed. Elkhorn was at the far end of the runway by the time my wheels touched. He braked to a stop without room to spare. I hit the brakes, bounding over patches of steel mesh and deeply furrowed earth. My right main hit a hole, metal struck metal, sending a shudder through the airframe. I careened down the last half, slowing whenever the tires grabbed the mesh and skidding in the areas that were dirt. I was still rolling when I came to the end and turned abruptly to make room for Foster.

Two men waved us forward about fifty feet, stopping us in front of a small shed. We lined up wingtip to wingtip and cut the engines. The men waited for us to slide off our wings. I ducked under my wing and found the right gear strut almost flat, noticing out of the corner of my eye that both men were Negroes.

"Hi," Elkhorn called. "This the 14th Fighter Group?"

The heavier of the two smiled slowly. His eyes darted to each of us, then to our planes. "No, suh," he drawled. "We're not the 14th but we're mighty glad y'all are all right. Never saw landings like that." He put his hands on his hips, threw his head back, and laughed.

"You say this isn't the 14th?" Elkhorn asked again.

"No, suh," the large man shook his head with a friendly smile.

"Jesus! Damn you, Elk!" Foster glared. "Thought you knew where the 14th was. What the hell we going to do now? Where are we, anyway? I thought : was landing on someone's driveway. How in the hell we going to get outta here?" Then turning to the heavy man, Foster asked, "You guys flying Piper Cubs outta here?"

"No, suh!"

"Sure fooled me," Foster said irritably. "Looked like an air base from the air."

"It is," said the man.

"It is what?"

"An air base."

"An 'air base' what, mister?" Foster spit the words through

clenched teeth. The man stiffened, his smile traced a hard line.

"An air base, SUH!"

"What outfit, boy?"

"99th Fighter Squadron! SUH!" He had assumed an attitude of semi-attention, but he retained a smile.

"The 99th," I said. "Remember, Foster, we covered them at Sousse. They called themselves Peachtree." I counted the stripes on the big man's sleeve. "P-40's, right Sergeant?" He nodded with pride, less tense.

"Oh yeah," said Foster. "I remember. That southern bunch, talked like Georgia Crackers, fresh from the hills."

"The British didn't know the difference," Elkhorn soothed. "They called 'em 'Yankees' too."

Foster lowered his voice. "Even brought some darky cotton pickers."

"Gotta admit," said Elkhorn, "Those southerners were good. We were late once. By the time we caught up they were on the deck. I mean right down in the trees going after tanks. They really flew those clunkers. One of those Confederate gents said, 'Sho glad y'all come to the party,' and above us a British Spitfire on the tail of a Jerry yells 'Tally ho!'. Didn't know if we were after foxes or raccoons."

Foster laughed like it was the funniest joke he ever heard. Elkhorn turned to the sergeant. "Where are all the planes?" The sergeant waved his hand in a wide circle, "They's all around, leastways those not flyin'. They's tucked away outta sight. Shucks, that ain't hard considerin' they's half the size of y'alls ay-row-plane, suh."

Foster shook his head. "P-40's. Holy Christ. The Flying Tigers used them in China when the war started. What I'd give to fly one of those buggers!" Then he spoke to the sergeant. "Tell me, boy. You know where the 14th is?"

"No, suh. Ah spect mah C.O. knows where they is and he'll be back soon."

"Sergeant," I said. "I'd like to check my right gear. Could you locate a mechanic?" He wiped his hands on his coveralls. "I'm a mechanic, suh. Be glad to look at it."

"You familiar with this type aircraft?"

"I can tell if y'have a problem. I'll get my tool box. Back in a minute." He walked away in the direction of a small shed. I called after him. "I'll be waiting at my plane." Elkhorn and Foster and I sat in the shade under the right wing.

"You going to let that monkey fool with your plane?" Foster asked.

"Why not? He says he's a mechanic."

"If he said he was Jesus it wouldn't mean he could walk on water. He's an uppity son-of-a-bitch, that one, I can tell." Foster lit a cigarette. "Mechanic, shit! Probably works on toasters. You got a lot to learn." He looked up inside the wheel well.

"Relax, Foster. I don't think I broke anything, and it won't hurt if he takes a look."

"The only thing he could recognize is the ass end of a mule. None of 'em are any fuggin' good." He kicked the tire with the heel of his shoe. "I wouldn't let no jigaboo touch my plane. They don't have what it takes. You wouldn't think southerners would use niggers. Never seen one assigned to an air base. Whew, it's getting hot. Boy, did you see that black son-of-a-bitch sweat?"

Elkhorn propped his head against the wheel, fanning at a few persistent flies. The sergeant returned with a small tool box. He knelt on the ground and studied the part of the landing gear strut that joined the retraction mechanism. I crouched next to him. His large fingers caressed the casting, slowing checking the linkage and pivot points. He touched the plane the way Chad did, a private communication. He compared the left gear to the right, murmuring to the plane, "Ummm, mmm! So they calls you a Lightnin'. Yo sho is a fine lookin' flyin' machine.

"Don't seem like anything serious, Lieutenant. I 'spect these here castings hit with a big bang. Must have sounded worse 'en it was. Should have maybe five inches in this strut and you've got less 'en an inch. What does she weigh?"

"Over nine tons fully loaded."

"That's a lot of aye-row-plane! And that runway is only half as long as it oughta be and as pock full o' holes as a piece o' Swiss cheese. I'll get some air, and if the seals hold, y'all be as good as new."

He caught the sound of aircraft engines before I did and looked up at the sky. "That'll be our planes comin' back. 'Scuse me, Lieutenant, suh, I'll see to them and be back with an air tank soon's I can."

Elkhorn, Foster, and I watched the approaching planes. A half dozen single engine Curtis Warhawks streaked across the camp, rearranging their positions in trail behind the leader, then pulled up in a graceful curve, extended their gears, and one by one descended. They reached down until their wheels lightly touched the runway within ten feet of the boundary. Foster slapped his hands. "That's what I call a landing!"

"They know where the holes are," I said, defensively.

Each of the planes followed the lead plane off at midfield, then taxied away in different directions. The leader followed the sergeant's hand signals and rolled to a stop down the line. The P-40 looked small next to Elkhorn's plane, a tail-dragger just like a Spit on a 109 except it's dull-green color came out of the same paint bucket as ours.

The pilot unbuckled his chute, and with a little help from the sergeant, he stepped down.

"Here we go," said Elkhorn. "He'll be curious to know what brings us here."

We walked toward his plane. "Shape up fellows, that's a Captain," I said reading the stencilled white letters against the green: Charles O. Williams, Captain, U.S. Army Air Corps. Like Tex, he seemed too tall for a fighter pilot, half a head taller than any of us. His worn leather jacket hung loosely on his lanky frame, and his weathered face was framed by a sweat stained cloth helmet and green goggles.

Foster stopped in his tracks and groaned, "Holy Mother of God. I don't believe it!"

He grabbed us both by the arms. "Look at that pilot." His voice was low. "Bet your ass, that's a nigger!"

A jeep pulled up with two more pilots. Both the driver and his passenger were Negroes.

Foster hissed, "I didn't think they let niggers in the army."

"C'mon, Foster," said Elkhorn. "Knock it off. A minute ago we were saying what great pilots these guys are. This must be a whole colored outfit."

"I suppose you wouldn't mind that black buck flying your wing, huh?"

The same old shit, I thought—nigger, kike. I forgot my normally cautious attitude around him and said, "Foster, you're an asshole and everything that comes out of your mouth stinks!" I spit out the words. His neck swelled and a vein in his temple throbbed. "Watch your mouth, Kohn. I never took no crap from you before and I'm not going to start now."

The captain was less than twenty-five feet away. He removed his helmet, watched us and waited.

"How about it, Elk?" I asked. "What do you say we check in with our superior officer?"

Elkhorn turned to Foster. "Come on, Foster. Cool off. One of these days, that goddamn temper of yours is going to get you killed."

We walked up to the captain, Foster a few paces behind, snapped to attention, and saluted.

"Lieutenant Elkhorn, sir!"

"Lieutenant Kohn, sir!"

Foster mumbled his name. The captain returned the salutes and said, "My name's Williams. Welcome to the 99th, gentlemen. Sergeant Jackson told me y'all come looking for the 14th."

"Yes, SIR!" said Elkhorn. The snappy address was his answer to Foster. The captain reached into his breast pocket. "Cigarette?" Elkhorn and I accepted a cigarette. Foster took one of his own and we all smoked. The captain spoke slowly, in an easy cadence.

"The 14th was based here 'til a couple of months ago. We moved in at the beginning of the month." He had a strong southern drawl. His speech and manner were cultured and authoritative. I was sure I'd had heard his voice over the radio during combat missions.

"Where'd they go, Captain?" Foster said.

The captain hesitated, then he said, "Don't know. Any special reason y'all lookin' for them?"

Elkhorn laughed. "Nothing official. Wanted to say hello to a couple of old buddies."

"They had their share of bad luck."

"We heard."

"They were having trouble the last month they were here. Most of the time they couldn't get a full squadron off the ground."

The sergeant interrupted. "If y'all 'scuse me, suh, I'll be takin' care of the strut for the lieutenant. If they's no tank ready, ah'll have to fill one from the compressor." He walked off in the direction of the shed.

The captain continued, "Toward the end they weren't able to put up a squadron. They missed rendezvous with us twice."

Elkhorn shook his head. "Come to think of it, some time ago they were supposed to go on a run with us to Naples. The last minute the 82nd substituted."

"So, where are they now?" Foster pressed.

"I'll check if your friends are MIA."

"Would your C.O. know where they moved to?" Foster persisted.

"Was it poor maintenance," I interrupted. "Or were they short of pilots?" The captain looked at me but didn't answer. "Was that it, Captain?" Suddenly it was important for me to know.

"No, it wasn't poor maintenance. Any of you others have any trouble landing?" The captain parried my question with a smile. "In the short time between when the 14th left and we arrived, the locals made off with half the steel mesh runway. It can get a little hairy landing."

"The engineers patched ours in nothing flat," I suggested.

The captain laughed. "Guess P-40's are low priority."

"Captain," said Foster. "If you can find out where the 14th is, there's still time for us to pay them a visit. They gotta be stationed somewhere close."

"They're not." The captain wasn't smiling now.

"You mean they're regrouping?"

"No. They've been deactivated."

I looked at the others. None of us seemed to understand what he meant.

"Gentlemen, as of the moment, the 14th doesn't exist. Their ground personnel have been reassigned. I don't know what's going to happen to their pilots, but we could sure use their equipment." He patted his plane, "P-40's are great if you don't have to fly higher than a barn door."

Elkhorn frowned. "I don't get it."

"Let me put it another way, Lieutenant. It was a question of morale. They couldn't make it anymore."

Foster pushed past me and snorted, "You saying they quit?"

"Let's say they wouldn't fly anymore."

"You mean they were yellow? No guts? You don't know any of this for sure." Foster sounded mean. The captain didn't answer. Foster turned to Elkhorn. "You don't believe any of this shit, do you?"

"Easy, Lieutenant," the captain said.

"I was telling my friend here it wouldn't be right to believe just any old thing 'til it's checked out with a *reliable* source," Foster added.

The captain glanced at his watch. "Chow time. I suggest you take off to the west regardless of wind direction. Keep well to the left.

The worst section is down the center. Soon as you run out of steel, yank her off the ground. Stall her off if you have to. The ground past the mesh is soft. Your nose wheel could dig in."

"Thank you, Captain. We'll manage." Foster saluted. "How about it, Elk? Ready to go?"

"What about you, Kohn?" Elkhorn asked.

I'm going to wait to pump up my gear. Go ahead, I'll see you back at the base."

The roar of the four engines attracted everyone's attention. Two of the ground crew turned their heads in unison, the captain stopped in mid-sentence, and the driver leaned out of his cab for a better look. Elkhorn and Foster banked, circled the field in formation, and seconds later were gone. The P-38 was an awkward praying mantis on the ground, airborne it was as natural as the wind.

"That's a *good looking* airplane," the Captain said. "Mind if I look inside?" He sat in the cockpit and we spent a few minutes discussing flying technique and the limitations of our aircraft.

"Were you always interested in flying?" he asked.

"My mother always said, 'If God meant us to fly, he would have given us wings.' I guess I agreed with her for a long time. Now it's a part of me. How about you?"

"I wanted to fly from the time I was a little kid. But even with a college degree, the Army wouldn't let Negroes become cadets until a bunch of us took flight training at Tuskeegee Institute. Then they had to let us in. They formed the 99th just for us," he laughed. Then he said, "I'd invite you to lunch, but we don't have an area set aside for whites."

"Do you have one for Jews?" I asked.

"You're a funny man. So that's why you wear that yellow star. I don't have that problem. I've got all the color I need."

Sergeant Jackson came out of the shed pulling two air tanks. The captain shook my hand. "Tell your friend, the one with the short fuse, what happened to the 14th is no crime. None of us is flyin' these machines 'cause they put a gun to our heads. No tellin' when anyone of us will wake up one mornin' and say, 'I just can't do it anymore.'"

Pilot and Crew Chief, ages 21 and 23.

The cockpit and instrument panel of the P-38.

A P-38 with two 150-gallon disposable belly tanks.

Flight Leader and his Wingman.

Direct hit on munitions dump, Palermo, Sicily. March 22, 1943.

The railroad marshalling yards, Caltagirone, Sicily July 11, 1943.

A P-38 leaves formation with deadly results.

Harbor of Porto Torres, Sardinia. May 19, 1943.

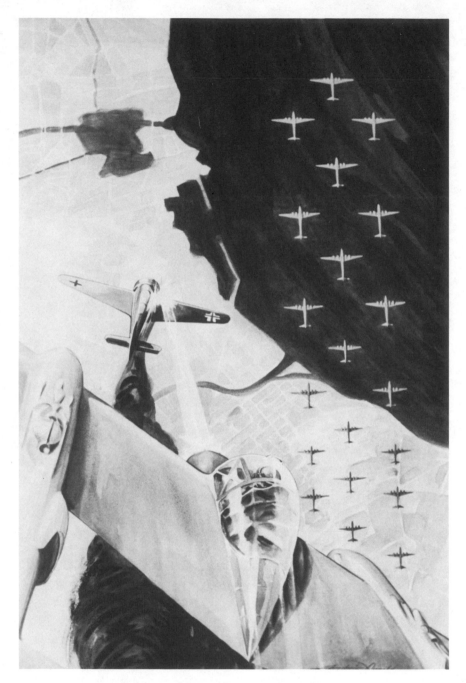

Unsuccessful attack against B-17s by FW 190.

Head up and locked.

Squadron showers made from belly tanks.

Never a long wait.

21

A String of Pearls

A SPECIAL MISSION IS LIKE A necklace of pearls, perfectly sized and color matched, carefully strung and knotted, crafted with precision, something to be admired. That is, if the string doesn't break.

I had been in combat three months and coming up on my thirty-ninth mission when, late one afternoon, all flight and element leaders were asked to report to the briefing tent. A briefing the day before an early morning mission was a harbinger of something unusual or complicated about the assignment.

A series of black and white glossy enlargements—aerial views of a coastline and harbor and multicolored terrain maps—were tacked to the large plotting chart. A table of antiaircraft gun emplacements, enemy fighter strength, and locations of air bases was meticulously lettered on a blackboard. Captain Tex Wallace and two higher-ranking officers watched the ten flight and element leaders drift in. We knew that six of us were to be named for tomorrow's mission. We didn't know who, and we didn't know what the mission was to be.

"Hey, Shorty!" Foster yelled, "Scratch one P-38. Smitty's plane will never fly after that landing this morning."

Smith feigned surprise, "What's Lardbutt doing here? I thought only pilots were invited to this briefing."

Foster laughed, "You guys should have seen it! After the third bounce I thought we'd have to shoot him down."

Falzone and Smith settled down crosslegged in the front row. I sat on a bench behind them. Tex rocked on his heels, his arms folded across his chest, looking like he was about to give each of us a million dollars. He pointed to the display. "We've got ourselves a prize! A big, fat, juicy target waitin' to be . . . are you ready for this men? . . . we're gonna dive bomb it!"

There was a ripple of excitement. "Hot damn!" Foster said. Falzone slapped his thigh.

Tex tapped one of the photos. "It'll be the first time a P-38 will be used as a dive bomber. There are two transports docked in the harbor of Porto Torres at the northern tip of Sardinia. Intelligence says from the way they lie in the water, they're loaded to the limit. They docked early this mornin' and there's no way they can off-load until noon tomorrow. Y'all are goin' to blow 'em out of the water."

He glanced my way. I felt myself flush. I knew Tex would choose me to lead one of the flights. Ironic how eager I was to strap a bomb under my wing. It had been three continuous weeks of escort duty—nursing bombers, watching them drop their loads, waiting for 109's to take pot shots at us. Now I was eager to perform, go my limits, test my skills.

"The set-up is perfect," Tex continued. "Shorty says there are gun emplacements along the coast and around the city. If y'all do it right, they won't be a factor 'cause they'll never know you're comin'. I convinced Wing we're the outfit that can do it. I've asked Major Pillard here to explain what they want accomplished by the mission and to answer questions. Then, I want each of you to study these photos and maps."

The Major wore command pilot's wings and a double row of ribbons, topped by the Distinguished Flying Cross and Air Medal with oak leaf clusters. He was the most heavily decorated pilot I'd ever seen. He silently examined each of us before he began.

"I don't know you men personally, but your C.O. believes you're the best bunch of fighter pilots in this theater." He paused and lowered his voice. "Gentlemen, this is a first. Twelve P-38's, each carrying a one thousand pound bomb will dive bomb that target. Twelve planes, that's 12,000 pounds, the total bomb capacity of three B-17's. No one says the 38 was designed to be a dive bomber, least of all the engineers back at Lockheed. But the ones who are going to be most surprised are the guys in those ships at Porto Torres.

"We need pinpoint bombing on this one so we can't use bombers.

Besides you're all we got."

There was laughter. Then he strung the first pearl and knotted it in place.

"They'll never know you're coming. It's minimum risk, with the possibility of inflicting great damage on the enemy. With surprise, you can hurt them real bad. *Surprise.* That's the key. And that's what I want to talk about. This isn't the wild west where you wait for the other guy to draw first. The Japs understood that at Pearl Harbor. 'Sneak attack?' Bullshit! They were smart: they didn't send a telegram they were coming. No one's fighting this war according to the rules of Queensbury. No ten second count. Knock 'em down, wipe 'em out. Those are the only rules."

Curious, I thought. It had never occurred to me that surprise might be unethical. I had always thought it was essential. He seemed to be trying to defend it.

"We're going after them hard. They'll remember this mission for a long time to come. First you're going to take out those ships, and before they get a chance to recover, you're going to hit 'em again, and again. And while the whole island is shaking and their mouths are stuffed with spaghetti, you're going to hit 'em again!"

I knew that speech by heart. All I was interested in was who was going to lead it. Tex talked like he wasn't going. Falzone's O.K., but I would prefer Brooks. It could be a quicky, in and out, and credit for one more mission. Then, eleven more to make fifty.

The Major took a piece of paper from Tex, glanced at it and scanned the group. "Which one's Kohn?"

I raised my hand.

"You're leading the squadron."

Another pearl on the string. This one was better than I had hoped. I was always relieved not to depend on someone else's judgement. No crapping around. I'll get 'em in and get 'em out. I liked having the men put their trust in me and this mission was special. Tex had chosen me to pull it off.

The Major angled his body toward me. I leaned forward to hear him better. He pounded a fist into the palm of his hand, "You gotta surprise 'em, Kohn! Stay low. Low as you can all the way. Don't go higher than thirty feet above the water or you'll be picked up by radar. And the rest of you, track on him, drift lower and you could hit the water. It'll be a good two hours so stay awake! When you're within a quarter mile of the coast, haul it up a thousand feet."

He pointed at me, speaking in time to an inner metronome, and slid more pearls on the string. "You better be lined up on that harbor, ships in sight, so you can come down on them before they blow the whistle. Turn inland too soon, or too late, and you've got troubles. You can't hang around looking for the target, 'cause enemy fighters will be jumping all over you within five minutes after you're sighted.

"Remember, it's the ships we're after. If you're attacked before you reach the target, you'll have to jettison your bombs, and there goes the ball game. And if you don't find the target in a reasonable amount of time, you won't have enough fuel to go looking for a secondary one. Bombers can return with an unused load. You can't.

"By the way, don't come back here with those goddamn bombs! No way you can land with those explosives. Remember that. They're armed and if you screw up a landing, you'll take the whole base with you.

"Now, I'm sorry I can't send a navigator with you, so study those maps good, figure your time and distance, airspeed and drift, and most of all get a handle on what you can expect that piece of land to look like from the direction you'll be coming. Shadows can play tricks. I know navigation's not a fighter pilot's strong point."

That was a giveaway. Major Pillard was from Bomber Command. Tex stiffened. "It's true, major, two hours of dead reckoning over water can put you off a mite. But once Ko-han here has seen a map, he'll recognize the terrain. Look through that pile of his drawings. He shows it the way we see it, not like those photos taken by high-altitude recon."

I raised my hand, "Sir, seems like a perfect target for B-17's."

The major's answer came fast. "There's a town attached to that pier. Wouldn't look good if our bombers blew up a whole Italian fishing village, and with their aim it could happen."

Tex shot me a glance. I squelched the crack I was about to add. We knew too well how often the bombers missed their mark. The major went on stringing pearls.

"O.K., this is what we expect. Your leader will dictate dive-bombing technique. If you have any doubts, follow him. Whoever's bringing up the rear, don't straggle. The bombs will be set to explode fifteen seconds after they hit, so you'll have to be in and gone within ten seconds after the first flight drops their bombs. Fire your guns and cannon in the dive to distract the gun emplacements on the ground, but make it count. Try to set fire to cargo and equipment stacked along the docks. If nothing else, it'll scare the shit out of them.

"Stay low over the town to discourage following fire. Continue south hugging the valleys and roads, hitting targets of opportunity until you reach Alghero airfield." He pointed to another photo. "You'll recognize it, looks like a parking lot for 109's, Machies and Regiannies. Destroy as many planes on the ground as you can on your first pass, then strafe the hell out of the place.

"But don't hang around too long. Captain Wallace says some of your wingmen are inexperienced. We don't want to plant any of them on those hills, do we? All hell's going to break loose back at the harbor, so everyone at the airfield will be wide awake by the time you get there. They probably won't be able to get any planes up in time. You should have yourselves a field day. Then come home. O.K.?"

The necklace was strung. The men were strangely quiet. In a confidential tone, the major added, "This mission is very important. Done right, it'll get you dive bombing assignments for the invasion of France and Italy. It could even earn your squadron a Presidential Citation.

"And remember, if things get screwed up, get rid of those bombs Find something, anything, another target—trains, trucks, camps, emplacements, guns, troops, anything is fair game—and drop on it. I don't care what it is. Better to drop those bombs than bring them back here. We're not trying to save money, it's all expendable. Don't worry about saving those bombs; we have a lot more where they came from.

"One last thing. I want those people over there shook, so shook they'll never come out of their holes again. There's no romance in this. Get that out of your heads. If it's not his ass, it's going to be yours. If I had a bomb big enough to wipe out the whole Italian peninsula, I'd kill every mother-fucking son-of-a-bitch over there. I'd end this fast! Isn't that what we want to do? End this frigging war? This little nipping away, a hit here and a hit there. That's not going to do it. And if negotiations could have done it, this war would have ended years ago. So we may have to annihilate every frigging man, woman, and child before it's over. Any questions?"

Tex stepped forward. "Foster will lead the squadron if Kohn makes an early return. Elkhorn will lead the third flight. Fellows, we

want those ships. Everyone, be on time at the morning briefin',
0500. Anythin' else, Major?"

Major Pillard held both hands high with thumbs up. "Kohn, good
luck."

"Major. Sir, I have a question."

"Yes, Lieutenant."

"The distance between Porto Torres and the airport is thirty
kilometers. That will take three minutes ,and if its our intention to
get their before enemy fighters get airborne..."

"Hell, they can't scramble eggs in three minutes much less get
high enough to give you a problem." He laughed.

"And you want us to hit 'targets of opportunity' during that time?"

"Yes."

"That could cause a delay."

"No. Just strafe anything in your line of fire."

"There are only country roads."

"That's it Lieutenant. Fire at anything that moves." Major Pillard
grinned as though we shared a private joke.

"Donkeys move..."

"That's right. Anything that moves."

"Farmers in the field move."...

"Knock it off, Nose." Foster growled. "You know fucking well
what he means!"

"Women washing clothes along the riverbank move..."

"You got the idea, Lieutenant."

"You said blowing up the town wasn't a good idea..."

"That's not what I said." He glared into my eyes. "You a Phil-
adelphia lawyer? What I said was, it wouldn't *look* good. We got to
hit 'em where they live. When the Italian G.I.'s get the word, there
may be no one left at home to go back to, maybe they'll drop their
fucking guns and quit!"

For months we had debated the meaning of "unconditional
surrender." I guess this was it.

"Well?"

"Sir?"

"Do you understand?"

"Yes, sir."

Tex walked me back to my tent. "Ko-han, I got a radio message
for you and it ain't good. Here, Garrett wrote it down."

The message read: "Peterson and Layton listed MIA two weeks before deactivation. Signed, Williams, Capt. USAC."

Thank God, I thought. It's not my father.

"Buddies of yours?"

"Yeah, the glass is one-third full and there's a hole in the bottom."

"What's that?"

"How many missions have you flown, Tex?"

"Oh, I stretch 'em out. Have to be on combat status to keep my command."

"This isn't what I had in mind for a career. If I had the Marrakech four, I'd have only eight to go."

"Can't give you those."

"I never turned one down, Tex. But I can't handle the one tomorrow. I don't talk the Major's language."

"You sure are somethin', Ko-han. You know that major only carries orders, he don't write 'em. Don't make waves."

"How do you feel about this "targets of opportunity'?"

"Doesn't bother me. It's simple. Wing figures Italy's ready to surrender. Everytime we see an Italian plane, it's runnin' for the hills. They just don't have their heart in it. They're demoralized. So, with a little push from us, they'll pack it in sooner rather than later."

"I'm not killing any civilians."

"Come on, boy, don't go gettin' your water hot. You're missin' the overall picture."

"Get yourself another 'boy.'"

"You sayin' you won't take this mission?"

"I'm saying I can't."

"Now you listen here. I had a hunch you were goin' to act like this. Why, hell, jus' ignore that 'targets of opportunity' shit. Nobody can make you do somethin' you don't want to do. He was just lettin' the boys know they could have some fun if they wanted. You're squadron leader. It's your show, you call the shots. Once you're off the ground, there ain't no one can tell you what to do. Just you get me those ships and planes and we'll get dive bombin' assignments. That's a hell of a lot better than freezin' our asses off playin' nurse-maid to those fuckin' bombers."

"I think it stinks."

"Come on, Ko-han. There ain't another guy in the squadron who would lose any sleep over it. Do it your own way. Durin' practice, you found the hole in the doughnut more times than anyone else. Take the squadron tomorrow and our twelve peashooters will sink more tonnage than the U.S. Navy."

"I still think it stinks."

Thirty minutes after the morning briefing we were on our way. I held mental images of the maps and photos, blue and purple depicting elevations, green and yellow showing valleys and low-lands. I conjured a picture of the coastline, a silhouette of hills, the blue expanse of water separating Sardinia from Corsica. I branded the picture into my brain.

For the first hour, I kept the squadron a few hundred feet off the water. It relieved the strain. Low flying took its toll. That's how Anderson got it. He'd let his wing drop, the tip dug in the water, and the plane cartwheeled like a stone bouncing across the surface of a lake.

Within fifty miles of Sardinia I dropped to twenty feet. The others followed in trail. At that height, the curvature of the earth blocked the enemy radar from taking a line-of-sight fix on us until we were within eight miles. I settled on a rigid course, like a streetcar on tracks. The sea was calm and the prop wash of the squadron left a rippling wake.

I had set the clock to turn inland precisely one hour forty-two and one-half minutes after crossing a predetermined checkpoint on the African coast.

The morning briefing had gone well. As squadron leader, I set the rules while everyone listened. "We'll stay low. Keep off the air unless we're jumped. When we get near the target and I start to climb, spread out and be prepared to drop tanks."

Two weeks earlier, armament and bombing technicians had arrived with steel cradles, hydraulic lifts, fuses, time devices, and racks of big black bombs. They had outfitted our squadron as the first American dive-bombing fighters of the war. Chad and Ted tested and retested my release mechanisms, dropping 1000 pound dummy bombs onto a pile of sand beneath the wing.

"For you new men, when we reach the target, if your belly tank hangs up, don't stick around. Those tanks will have a few gallons sloshing around inside. That's a highly explosive mixture of fuel and gas fumes. Get hit with a stray shell or hot flak and you'll disappear and maybe take someone with you. If a tank hangs up, turn back. That's an order. No exceptions."

"Where do we go if a bomb hangs up?"

"Land on the dry lake, very softly, and you'll be picked up."

"Yeah, with a blotter," Foster added.

"A word about the dive. I don't use the gunsight. It's unreliable for bombing. The bombs will fall short or long. I put the tip of my nose on the target with the gunsight above, and hit the button an instant *before* I pull out.

Foster slapped his leg. "Hear that? He puts the tip of his nose on the target."

I raised my voice to be heard over the laughter. "Even in a steep dive, the bomb falls in a curve as soon as it's released. I'll line up with the length of the ships so there'll be room for error. They're docked parallel. Flight leaders and their wingmen go for the one on the left, element leaders and their wingmen go for the right. Aim ahead to the ship's bow and your bomb'll probably go down the stack. Stay tight and we'll make the pass in less than five seconds, in case any fuses are running fast."

I drew a new pilot named Hartman for my wing, Barney flying element leader for the first time and Sheppard as tail-end-Charlie. Barney asked, "Do we remain in pairs after the bombing?"

"No, re-form and all flights stay together."

"All the way to the airport?"

"All the way."

"While we strafe?"

"We'll strafe only at the airport."

"The major said . . ."

"He said I'm responsible for the mission and our asses."

Several pairs of eyes turned to Tex. He tapped his wristwatch, "Come on Ko-han, get this show on the road."

I dipped my wing in the direction of land. In five minutes the tops of the three hills rose on the horizon. On the left a clear expanse of water appeared, and beyond, a thin shoreline that fit my mental map of Corsica. Two minutes more and we faced jagged cliffs rising out of white surf. We climbed parallel to the sharp angle of a hill, a twenty-foot air cushion separating us from the barren stone face, and the squadron shot above the peak, one by one, like pulsating fragments from a roman candle. The quiet harbor of Porto Torres lay a thousand feet below.

I pressed the radio button. "DROP TANKS!" Seconds later I heard, "Doorknob Leader! Your tank is hung up!"

Both indicator lights glowed in confirmation. I punched the button, pressed it, wiggled it, and jabbed at it. Nothing. I pumped the control wheel hoping to jar the tank loose. Still it hung on.

"Doorknob Leader, what are your intentions?"

Ahead lay the ships stradling the pier like the pontoons of a catamaran, the roar of our engines still inaudible to those on the ground.

"Stay with me!" I called.

I was committed, incapable of letting them go it alone. I pushed the control column forward, sighting down the plane's nose, the bow of the ship between the barrels of my guns. My grip tightened as the speed increased, my arms rigid against the mounting pressure. My plane screamed in protest like a body bent on self-destruction, hurtling from a cliff. Several figures on the ship froze at the sight of the diving planes. The surprise was complete. The angle was perfect. I felt no danger as the bomb parted from my plane. Below, tiny, helpless, stumbling figures scrambled for safety.

I came out of the dive several feet above red-tiled roofs. Behind me, consecutive explosions lifted great chunks of Porto Torres and ships' fragments in slow motion. A belching column of black and red burning oil formed a mushroom that dwarfed the surrounding hills and blotted out the sun. First Hartman, then Barnett and his wingman whipped past. Slowed by the drag of my trapped tank, I couldn't keep up.

"Barney, this is Doorknob Leader. Take my flight. Foster, take Doorknob to the airfield. I'll meet you there."

I arrived at the outskirts of Alghero one minute past the scheduled time. The squadron was nowhere in sight. Troop carriers were fanning trailing plumes of dust. The props of several 109's churned the earth preparing for takeoff, like threshing machines pumping grain. I had heard no sound over my roaring engines, but those on the ground had heard the explosions and were springing into action. Doorknob should have wiped out the airfield by now. With growing anxiety, I called, "Foster! Where are you?"

Two 109's broke ground and started climbing toward me. I heard Foster yell, "There it is, Elk, on the left. Let's go!"

A flight of P-38's swept in from the opposite side of the field. Another flight of four banked and dove. The radio emitted shrieks, static, and the squealing of a stuck transmitter button. The remnants of my flight approached high, three planes in perfect alignment with the runway and a string of parked planes. A battery of guns at the foot of the runway opened fire. The three P-38's of my flight, so intent on their first strafing attack, were unaware they themselves had become the target of murderous short-range antiaircraft fire. That *shmuck*, Foster. Where had he been? What took him so long?

The lead 109 was turning toward me. I was trapped, cruising across the Messerschmidt's sights like a target in a shooting gallery. My testicles drew up into my body as though to deny their relationship to me. Run! Run, screamed my instincts. Turn and run! No, you can't outrun him hung up with the goddamn tank, argued my indoctrinated brain. There's no choice but to turn into him, attack head-on

Even as I turned, his hungry tracers nipped at my wing tip. I screamed and squeezed both triggers in protest. Machine gun and cannon shells pumped out, describing the arc of my turn, wasting themselves helter-skelter across the field toward the gunners at the foot of the runway. They swung their barrels toward me but I was too low to turn. With three P-38's a dozen feet above them, the 109 pressing on my left side, my options were gone. I was helpless to change course.

A black Messerschmidt twisting and straining in a frantic effort to destroy me; frenzied men clawing at munitions boxes; others bent over smoking gun barrels incessantly pumping shells and tracers; the ever-expanding letters on the side of the closest P-38—these will be the last impressions my brain will record. The 109 passed within yards to my left. I gripped the wheel as though it were a lifeline, squeezing both gun buttons, bringing my sights to bear on the gun emplacement, my shells exploding in the midst of metal and flesh, and I flew between them, inches below the belly of Barney's plane while the tips of my propellers nicked the silenced gun barrels below.

We regrouped at the coast, all planes accounted for, and took a heading toward Africa. The men, no longer constrained by radio silence, talked over one another, each recounting what he had seen. The return flight provided them ample time to rethink the experience. The result was a disjointed barrage of heroic deeds masking, as far as I could tell, what had really happened.

When the jeep swung into my parking space, Barney, Elkhorn, and Foster were already crowded in the rear seat. Barney was talking as I climbed into the front seat. "My bomb dropped right down the funnel of that fucker. Blow! Did you see it blow? Took half the town with it."

"And at the airport, I got me three on the ground and one in the air!"

"I got one just taking off."

"Me too! Blew the ass end off one sucker before he got his wheels up. And that counts. I saw you get yours, Elk. You'll confirm mine, won't you?" Foster said.

"It was a breeze. Caught 'em with their pants down and didn't lose a single plane."

"Sorry you missed it, Kohn," Barney said.

"I was at the airport. I saw what you did."

"So that was you, came sliding under my flight. Close call."

"Barney," said Elkhorn. "You'll never know what a close call that really was."

I looked at Barney. "We agreed we'd come straight to the airport."

Barney elbowed Foster. "Our ol' buddy here took us on a little tour. Guess we covered every country road with a thousand rounds. And talk about flying! This ol' son-of-a-bitch took us so low we were cutting the grass."

"And the legs off every peasant," Elkhorn added.

"You guys were supposed to come straight to the airport," I said.

"We were supposed to follow Foster."

"Remember, Nose, I was leading the squadron. What do you say, Elk? Great day, huh? I ran my guns so hot, twisted off a barrel."

"Kohn has a point, I think you played it a little too close. A couple more minutes and the whole German airforce would have been after us."

"So what? We would have gotten a few more Krauts to our credit. Wow, they'll never forget we were there."

"Who's left to remember? Kohn, you really missed it. What a day!"

22

Beer, Bombs and the British

IT HAD BEEN MORE THAN a month since the German and Italian forces in Tunisia had surrendered unconditionally to the Allies. Over two hundred thousand troops threw down their arms without trying to jump the one hundred miles to Sicily. A wise decision. The British navy and our bombers, loaded with fifty gallon fuel drums, were eager to set fire to the Mediterranean in memory of the British slaughtered on the beaches at Dunkirk in 1940.

The 71st Fighter Squadron moved to Mateur, twenty kilometers south of the coastal city of Bizerte in Tunisia, within easy striking distance of Sicily and the Italian mainland. If there was to be an invasion of Sicily, we were ready. Three days before the move, Curtiss ran out of gas and crashed in the Mediterranean. Only five of the old bunch remained.

The first Sunday after our arrival at Mateur, a notice was posted on the bulletin board: "All personnel report 0930 in the big clearing." Underlined in bold black letters was: *"Everyone bring a canteen cup!"* signed, Captain Wallace.

I slipped a sketchbook in my leg pocket. Falzone, Smith, Foster, and I walked out to the clearing. The new replacements stood around in groups. They had quickly formed their own cliques. It was June, four months since we had joined the squadron, and it seemed as though there had been nearly a complete turnover of pilots.

We waited in the sun, the group personnel and administrative officers chatted about the food, construction of a new latrine, stolen supplies, techniques of engine maintenance, letters from home, and

221

news of the war. They spoke as though pilots didn't exist. We were transients. If a pilot failed to return, their lives went on.

The base had been straightened up for the occasion, though none of us knew what we were waiting for. Planes had been backed squarely in their parking spaces, loose tools collected, and gasoline cans neatly stacked. I sketched until the order came to fall in. All personnel arranged themselves in rows, some of the men sitting on the ground. My freshly laundered coveralls prevented me from joining them. Tex surveyed us from a makeshift platform. We waited.

Soon, five command cars, the lead car flying a red flag with the white star of a brigadier general, made a sweeping turn in a cloud of dust and parked behind the platform. Military and civilian service personnel spilled out of the cars and quickly funnelled the high-ranking brass toward the platform. Two civilians dressed in the plain uniforms worn by war correspondents, their faces hidden behind large speed graphic cameras, crouched between the rows of men, then flitted about, dropping to one knee to shoot angle shots of the Group with the VIP's in the background.

Tex introduced a short, stocky, middle-aged man named General Jimmy Doolittle. His name was familiar but I couldn't remember why. The general spoke for ten minutes, congratulating us for the Porto Torres mission, and said everyone in the squadron could be proud of what the 71st had done that day. The success should be shared; it took teamwork, the combined efforts of all the men on the ground and in the air. The entire 12th Air Force was to be praised. What we had done could significantly affect the outcome of Mediterranean operations. He was recommending a Presidential Citation for us. The men listened quietly.

"And now I have a surprise, something you've all been asking for," he said. "It wasn't easy, but I got it. I hope you brought your cups. I have some honest-to-goodness, ice-cold beer waiting for you. Real American beer!"

A roar went up, caps flew in the air.

"See that jeep over there, the one with the heavy tarpaulin, guarded by a couple of trusty GI's? That's right, underneath that canvas is a keg of beer packed in ice. I got it from a U.S. Navy ship's store. We traded the ships you sank for fifty gallons of beer. I figured one good turn deserves another. After all, that's what generals are for, right?"

"Right!" came the response.

"Your commanding officer says you won't be flying today, so when we're finished, we'll have a drink together."

Since we'd been in Algeria, a glass of cold beer had become synonymous with America, home; it shared equally with sex in daily conversation. The African heat, the intense humidity, the rationing of distilled water, the magnified sunlight under the plexiglass canopies, all had conspired to make beer the prime motivation for fighting the war. To take over their breweries was sufficient reason to invade Germany.

"Now, gentlemen, I have the honor and privilege of introducing one of aviation's all-time greats," Doolittle continued, "a man whose name means 'Fighter Pilot,' the greatest ace of World War I, Captain Eddie Richenbacher. He's come to talk to you today and I'm particularly glad he's here to share this important moment with us." I wondered whether he meant Porto Torres or the beer. Doolittle stepped aside and stood at ease.

Eddie Richenbacker was a tall, thin, fiftyish gentleman in a business suit, bareheaded under the hot morning sun. He reminisced about his old outfit, the 94th Hat-in-the-Ring Squadron, and rambled on about shooting down German fighters, 'Huns,' he called them. He said the American people wanted aces, and fighter pilots were the heroes of the war. It was our superior skill and ingenuity that would bring victory. He admonished us to be brave, aggressive, to blast the enemy from the sky.

I knew he was trying to inspire us, to raise our morale, but he was simply a stranger from a different time and place, a time that knew nothing about modern specialized flying technique, about tight formation, disciplined bomber escort, dive bombing, squadron concentration for effective fire power. On the ground, I didn't know the names of replacement pilots, but in the air, their planes meshed within the rigid framework of the squadron. There were no heroic aces chasing after enemy fighters on their own. The squadron was the strength. Each plane was a part of the whole, connected to the same machine. If a piece was defective, it was replaced.

The sound of the old man's voice was barely audible past the second row. My attention wandered. The image of a cup of cold beer was overpowering. I salivated and wet my lips. My gaze was drawn to the covered jeep. Nor was I alone in my lack of attention.

Our rows were taking on a wavy effect. Gradually, all the pilots stood less straight. I hid behind Elkhorn and distracted my thirst by sketching the men on the platform. Falzone gazed at distant moving clouds. Smith looked at his shoes and scuffed dirt. Foster maintained a whispering commentary about the needless delay in getting to the beer. Bodies began to sway and incoherent mumblings rippled through the ranks. Tex, sensing our inattention, swelled his chest, threw his head back, and set his jaw, swamping us with authority.

When at last Richenbacher finished and stepped back, a Chaplain moved forward, raised his arms toward the group and said, "Let us pray."

"For the beer," muttered Foster.

Sunlight reflected from silver crosses on the Chaplain's lapels. Automatically, all the men bowed their heads and closed their eyes.

"Living Lord Jesus, help us break the prejudicial barriers..."

"...that we may have our fair share of beer," Foster said.

"Father, forgive me for passing judgment on others..."

"...who would steal my beer," Foster said.

"Purify my heart, that I may bring people to share in Christ's undying love..."

"...for beer."

"Come on, Foster, knock it off," Smith breathed from the corner of his mouth.

"Your Holy Spirit lives in my heart and comforts me. Oh Lord, my Savior, in humble adoration I praise thee..."

"...and a keg of beer," Foster said.

"That's enough," Smitty scowled.

"Bless these brave men, give them courage to face the battles of life. In the name of the Father, the Son, and the Holy Ghost. Amen."

Eyes turned toward the sound of grinding gears and the jeep with the beer pulled up about a hundred yards away from us.

General Doolittle's voice didn't carry like the chaplain's. He thanked the speakers and addressed us.

"We don't know how far fifty gallons of beer will go with a couple hundred thirsty men, so regardless of rank, it's going to be first-come, first-served. ATTENTION! DISMISSED!"

The announcement caught us by surprise. There was an instant without movement, then a screaming, laughing scramble toward the jeep, a mad waving of aluminum cups held high. Smith unhooked his long legs and got to the jeep with the first twenty men. Falzone sacrificed dignity and squeezed his way in the wavy line behind dozens of enlisted men. Foster and I got a slow start, then were absorbed into the line. Every shirt was stained with patches of perspiration. Foster was breathing hard.

"That's swell! Seems a lousy nineteen pilots ought to rate some priority."

We heard the bung pop and a cheer went up as the soldier drove in a wood spigot and tipped the barrel on its side. The line pressed close to the jeep and its precious cargo. The chaplain moved alongside, speaking to the men, his arms overflowing with prayer books, which he distributed freely among the pilots.

But each man was straining to hear and see the beer pour.

"I'm sorry I haven't visited your base before. I'm permanently attached to the 32nd Bomb Group, administering to over five hundred flying crew personnel...."

The G.I. controlling the spigot dispensed no more than a third of a cup.

"...but I'm available," the chaplain said. "Make a note of my call sign, 'The Word.' Contact me by radio. If I can't come, I can talk with you, suggest chapters for study and discussion...."

Beads of condensation formed on the metal sides of each man's cup, and white bubbles foamed to within an inch of the top.

The Chaplain stopped in front of Falzone. "My son, the word of God will comfort you. Remember, every day is Sunday to God. You can have services any day of the week. Take turns administering to one another. Please, take these," he said, pressing a booklet in Falzone's hand. "Bless you. You are not alone."

"No disrespect sir, but you've never been in a fighter."

The chaplain moved on. Falzone fanned pages of the scriptures. "Probably gets all the business he can handle from bomber crews. Who's ever heard of a wounded fighter pilot getting back for last rites?"

There were only six men between us and the keg of beer. Each man held his cup under the spigot, careful to catch the last drop. The G.I. rapped the barrel with his knuckles, listened to the thud, and announced, "Won't be long."

But, as if by magic, beer continued to pour. Foster and I got our shares. I cradled the aluminum cup in both hands, delighting in the coldness. Falzone and Smith were saving their beer until we joined them in a toast. Raising and clinking our cups, we brought them to our lips. I held a mouthful of beer without swallowing and watched the others drink it down. A thin white line formed on Smith's upper lip. "What's with you, Nose?" Smith asked. "You look funny."

"I don't like it," I said.

"What?" they shrieked.

"You guys can have mine. I guess I never developed a taste for it."

*　　*　　*　　*

At dawn the next day, Brooks took the squadron on a mission to Sardinia. Within two hours Washboard radioed that one of our planes was down and a British Sunderland flying boat was on its way to pick up the P-38 pilot in the water. Falzone and I raced to our planes and caught up with the stubby plane and circled continuously while he chugged fifty feet above the water all the way to the Sardinian coast.

On the way, Brooks radioed that the pilot in the water was Smith.

The big sea plane homed in perfectly on the downed pilot, who was waving, bobbing, and splashing around in his yellow Mae West. The Sunderland skimmed the calm sea, landed close, pulled the man onboard, and, almost without stopping, bounced across the water and was airborne again. I wanted to cheer his courage and skill, touching down within sight of a German fighter base and in shooting distance of enemy shore batteries. Instead, I imitated the conservative English behavior I had heard so many times over the radio.

"Hello, 'ello there, Scoopy Five, this is Doorknob Five Two. Good Show! How's our wet friend?"

"Doorknob Five Two, Scoopy Five here, Sorry, he's not one of yours. We've plucked ourselves a Jerry!"

*　　*　　*　　*

Something was up. Running feet pounded past our tent. Unintelligible voices rang from all directions. The lights came on. My watch showed 0530. I grabbed my jacket, shoulder holster, gun, helmet, and goggles, and ran for the briefing tent. Pilots converged in a hubbub of excitement and speculation. In a few minutes, Shorty strode in, raised his hands for quiet, and announced proudly,

"Sometime during the night British and American armed forces invaded the island of Sicily."

"Hot damn, we're on our way!" someone called out.

"Next stop Rome!"

"Berlin!"

"Cleveland!"

"Minneapolis!"

"We don't know yet what kind of resistance we're running into or how much ground we've taken, but the landing parties are going to need all the help we can give 'em, so don't make any plans for the next few days," Shorty said.

The invasion came as no surprise. It had just been a question of when. For weeks we knew the island was being softened by the type of targets we had been hitting.

"They expect our squadron to put up two missions a day," Shorty continued. The pilots responded with curses and low whistles. But I was glad. That meant I could be on my way home in three days since I had only five more missions to go. Out of the squadron, out of the war, and out of that goddamn tent number eight. The absence of Smitty's cot gave me a knot in my stomach. I remembered how young he looked. It was better after Falzone and Foster rearranged their cots, closing the empty space once occupied by Smitty. Why Smitty? Why couldn't it have been Foster? With the others dead, my hate for him intensified, as though he represented the evil force that killed them.

I jerked my head at the sound of my name. "Yes, sir?"

Shorty pointed to the map. "There's no way to know for sure where the invasion forces are, so to be on the safe side, we've drawn a line. Take a good look. Above that line is fair game, anything to the south could be our men. You're not to hit any targets below that line.

"And you flight leaders, there's the possibility some of our tanks may make extra good time and bust past that line by this afternoon or tomorrow. So we've drawn a code to prevent error. British and American tanks will be flying a colored pennant or you'll see colored smoke."

"They gotta be kidding!" Falzone said, slapping Foster on the back. "Can you imagine getting close enough to see what color flag a tank is flying before deciding to shoot?"

Shorty ignored their laughter and spread his hands for attention.

"O.K., O.K. This is serious business." He referred to the sheaf of orders from Wing. "Your planes were loaded during the night. Each of you will carry a five hundred pound bomb for your primary target, Caltagirone, a town in the southeast portion of Sicily. After that, it's a rhubarb. Strafe targets of opportunity. It's a short hop. No belly tanks. So be back by 1200 to refuel and get your second assignment. You're going to be low all the time and it's going to be a scorcher, so dress light." Rhubarb missions got their name in World War I when fighters flew so low their wheels touched the flat rhubarb fields of France. Over the hilly terrain of Sicily, the name was no longer appropriate.

Every operational plane in the 71st was on the board. Falzone, Foster and I were listed to lead flights, with me leading the squadron on the first mission. Thereafter, squadron leadership would rotate. Takeoff was scheduled in forty minutes. As usual, there was no tea, and I passed on the black coffee, regretting that I had eaten my last Tootsie Roll. But it would be a short mission and I had a full pack of Luckys. I would have breakfast when I got back.

*   *   *   *

I climbed into the cockpit, leaving my sketchbook and leather jacket with Chad. Twenty minutes after sun-up I brought our squadron of twelve planes over the beaches of Sicily between Licata and Gela. We had remained low since takeoff, giving dozens of U.S. naval ships a wide berth. The shore was cluttered with landing craft and heavy concentrations of equipment. Countless numbers of troops swarmed the beaches. Ships and shore batteries maintained a continuous barrage of antiaircraft fire at unseen targets, including us. We skimmed over and disappeared into the hills, heading for Caltagirone.

Shorty had said heavy enemy concentrations were reported east of the city. Our orders were to avoid enemy aircraft, stay as low as possible, and take targets of opportunity on the way, strafing troops, convoys, and trains where we could find them. I made a low pass over the road leading out of Caltagirone, circled a railroad marshalling yard, but saw no signs of troops or heavy military activity. A few boxcars didn't warrant five hundred pound bombs. We strafed the yard setting a few of the trains on fire, then headed for Lentini just skimming the tree tops.

The road ran parallel to the railroad tracks on the right, flashes of the Caltagirone River blinked through clumps of trees on the left, then the hills flattened and we began crisscrossing in large sweeps across open plains. My flight leaders were experienced pilots, and they were right with me when I pressed the wheel forward and dropped low over a river. Huston tucked in tight at my wing, Long and his wingmen slipped in behind us, and the other two flights followed in-trail.

The narrow river several feet below broadened when it joined a tributary and snaked ahead toward the bridge between Catania and Augusta. Intelligence warned of concrete pill boxes with fixed guns along the bank facing south, so we remained north of the river and safe from their fire. Orders were to leave bridges alone for possible use by the advancing allies.

I hauled back for altitude and a good look. The plane shuddered from lazy flight into a hard steep climb. The squadron followed. The bridge and the road to the north suddenly showed the longest convoy I had ever seen, altogether unaware of our presence. It would be easy. We could wipe them out before they had a chance to return fire. I imagined the moment they would see us, vulnerable, with no place to hide, the terror of being hunted.

Thank God, I thought, I'm not down there.

Twenty-four hours later I was walking on that hostile road.

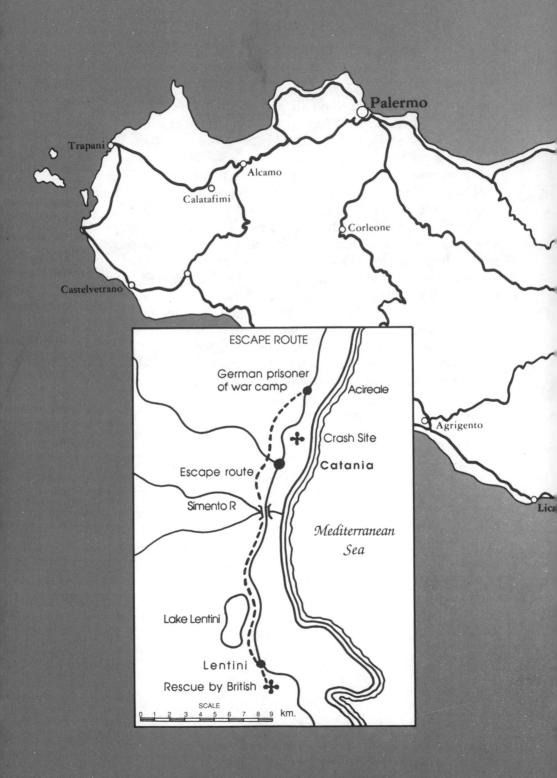

Palermo

Trapani

Alcamo

Calatafimi

Corleone

Castelvetrano

ESCAPE ROUTE

German prisoner
of war camp

Acireale

Crash Site

Agrigento

Catania

Escape route

Simento R

*Mediterranean
Sea*

Lica

Lake Lentini

Lentini

Rescue by British

SCALE

0 1 2 3 4 5 6 7 8 9 km.

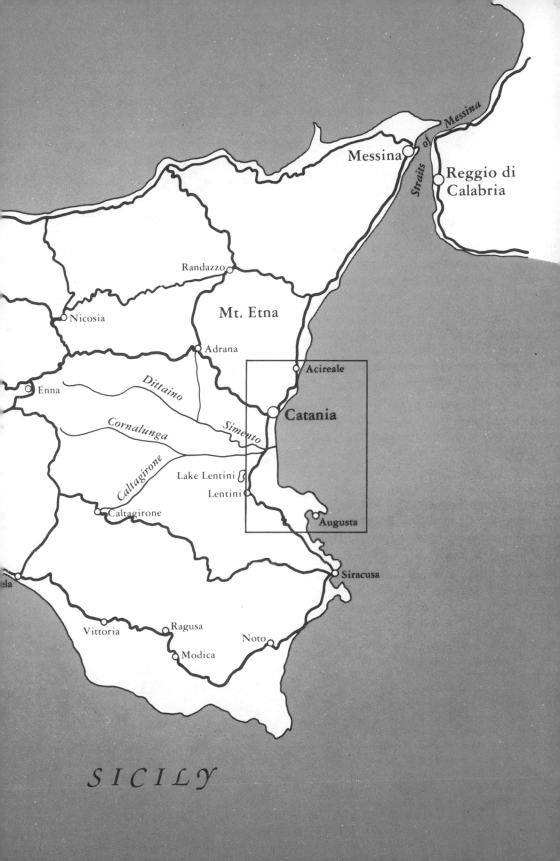

Messina

Straits of Messina

Reggio di
Calabria

Randazzo

Mt. Etna

Nicosia

Adrana

Dittaino

Acireale

Enna

Catania

Cornalunga

Simento

Lake Lentini

Caltagirone

Lentini

Caltagirone

Augusta

Gela

Siracusa

Vittoria

Ragusa

Noto

Modica

SICILY

23

Sicily—July 12, 1943

THE SUN ROSE AND THE distant sounds of artillery grew louder, flooding the landscape with noise. I had flown my last mission twenty-four hours earlier. It was the second day of the invasion of Sicily, and I had no idea whether I was walking back into my captors' arms. As far ahead as I could see, the roads and the fields were empty. The German tanks and troops had left during the night. I saw no one.

I moved from the stream and crossed a rock-strewn field carpeted with white and purple flowers. A pleasant scent rose from the field, a welcome relief from the pungent odor of raw manure clinging to my clothes.

I established a brisk pace and made good time along the open road. Several flights of low-flying aircraft roared overhead. There were those who could tell from the sound of the engines what type they were. To me, they all sounded alike. I kept my head down and continued walking.

Sunlight splashed the hills, bathing the olive and citrus groves and spreading its warmth over ancient vineyards. Isolated cottages tucked in the hills reflected the light. There were no people. Still, every curve in the ever-winding road made my pulse race with fear of what lay beyond. Even so, I walked quickly and felt strong and fresh.

Over the crest of a hill lay a large town. From its center rose a black column of smoke. There was no way to go around. I would have to walk through the village. Sooner than I wanted I passed the first two houses, staying in the center of the road, behaving as though I knew exactly where I was going and had every right to continue. The pavement changed from macadam to cobblestones. I watched my toes move through the opening in my shoes and read-justed the wicker baskets hanging from my shoulder. Keep a steady gait, shoulders stooped, head bent forward, I cautioned myself. Shutters at the windows were closed, door alcoves were shallow. There was no place to hide, no option but to continue through the town and out the other end.

Behind me I heard the opening and closing of a heavy door, and then I saw the black-stockinged, black-skirted lower body of a woman hurrying in my direction. She whisked past me. My disguise was a success! I could have been a peddler, a displaced person, she didn't care. There was nothing about me that prompted her to look twice. My heart beat fast. I nearly smiled with relief.

Rounding a corner I was confronted with a frantic spectacle. The dense black smoke I had seen from the distance poured from the second-story windows of a burning building a hundred yards ahead. A large flat-bed truck stood in the center of the road with a canvas covering a bumpy, irregular cargo. In front of the truck, the road was strewn with bed springs and mattresses, chairs and tables, and a large ornately framed family photograph. Several women rushed back and forth, bundling in their skirts the precious belongings they carried out of the house. A very old woman stood watching, crying, waving her arms and talking out loud to no one.

I moved closer, unnoticed. Several more women arrived to help. The pile of objects on the ground grew. A few feet from me stood two old men, one who appeared blind and another leaning heavily on a gnarled cane. An Italian soldier, coughing, his eyes tearing, emerged from the burning house carrying a large chest of drawers. He lowered it to the ground without looking at me. I moved to one side of the activity, deciding to wait until the soldier returned to the house and then squeeze past the truck and make a run for it.

Behind me, I heard a sound that started as a faint rumbling vibra-tion, then grew to a loud, roaring, ear splitting cascade of mech-anical noise. The ground trembled. The dirt in the joints between the cobblestones shimmied. The women talked faster and louder. I pressed close behind the two old men, feeling afraid. A motorcycle with side car came down the road, followed by several enormous German tanks. They stopped in front of us, impeded by the mound of personal possessions and the canvas-covered truck.

A German officer in the sidecar waved to the women to get out of the way. The Italian soldier stood at attention. The women started to move objects to the side of the road. The two old men were led away. I was left exposed. I turned my face from the officer's view, pressing my cheek against one of the wicker baskets on my left shoulder. The Italian soldier pulled himself into the truck and tried to start the motor. Hurriedly, two women began to pull the heavy chest away from the front of the truck.

The crews of the tanks and the German officer watched the commotion, laughing and offering suggestions. Smoke and flames broke through the roof of the house. The women worked in a frenzy. A corner of the chest caught in a cobblestone, tipped, the drawers slid out and crashed to the ground, scattering clothing all over the street. The Italian soldier jumped out of his cab to help. Screams rose from the women. Laughter swelled from the German soldiers. A large woman motioned for me to help. I stood motionless. She spoke to me rapidly in Italian, beckoning for me to approach. Each time she repeated her plea, she ended a note or two higher, almost reaching a shriek. I felt the German officer looking at me. I stared blankly at the woman. She glared back and spat more words through clenched teeth.

I couldn't speak. I shuffled toward her, dragging my feet on the stones. I tilted my head toward my shoulder, twitching my right eyelid. My lower lip and jaw sagged. The act came surprisingly easy. I became my father. Anything to hide my terror and save myself. It would be fatal to be caught, an American out of uniform pretending to be an Italian. I reached toward her with my right hand cupped and trembling, wordlessly pleading. Her eyes showed doubt, then the furrowed brow relaxed and compassion spread over her face.

I whispered, "Mama. . . ." She shook her head slowly side to side, crossed herself, and breathed, *"Madre mia."* She reached deep within the folds of her dress and extracted two dried apricots, which she placed in my open hand, closed my fingers, and gently pushed me back. Then she attacked the German officer with a barrage of Italian. I was forgotten, invisible. No one looked at me, no one returned my glance. I held my newly acquired countenance and watched as everyone's interest returned to the problem on the street.

The woman stood in front of the German officer, arms crossed over her big bosom, snarling disrespect. All the women grumbled hostilely, anger and hatred in every move. The officer barked a command. A wave of laughter rose from the German ranks.

The Italian soldier returned to the truck, mounted the front bumper, and climbed over the hood onto the top of the cab. He stood a moment listening to the laughter, then reached up with both hands and yanked the tarpaulins. They sailed to the ground uncovering his grisly cargo of dead bodies in German and Italian uniforms, neatly stacked, one on top of the other. Silence. Someone coughed. The Italian soldier slipped down onto the running board and climbed behind the steering wheel, backing the truck out of the way. The women moaned and sobbed as pieces of furniture that had leaned against the truck crashed to the cobblestones.

The tank column began to roll. Furniture splintered beneath the wheels and iron tracks. The crying women stepped back out of the road, tears running down their cheeks, then stooped and picked up stones and sticks, which they threw at the tanks as they rolled slowly by.

I followed the departing tank convoy with my eyes as they picked up speed past the village. Far ahead, I recognized the river and plains. I knew those landmarks from the air. I was on the right road. It would lead to Lentini and I would find the British.

Before the bridge, the convoy turned in the direction of the foothills and was quickly lost from view. I placed one apricot in my breast pocket with my cigarettes and ate the other very slowly. I hadn't eaten anything for two days. Saliva rushed into my mouth. I munched on minute bits, savouring them with my tongue for a long time before swallowing. I promised myself I would not eat the last apricot until I reached safety. I started off slowly down the road.

When I reached the place where the convoy had turned off, I came upon a truck tipped over on its side. Inside the smashed cab I saw a broken, tangled body. Further on was more wreckage—a confusion of Italian soldiers, mules, peasants, their bodies cruelly torn and ripped, organs exposed, limbs missing—scattered among the twisted metal remains of bombed vehicles. The tattered contents of a cardboard suitcase was flung haphazardly on the dusty ground. Death was everywhere. Bits of death blended into the ground I walked on.

News of the invasion must have caused this hysterical exodus.

And now, under the hot Sicilian sun, the air was heavy with decay. Swarms of flies covered exposed flesh. I pressed the burlap sack against my nose, inhaling the stench of manure to disguise the stench of decay. I sidestepped quickly to avoid stepping on a severed hand. Suddenly, my stomach objected and I vomited undigested bits of apricot.

Bent over, I continued to dry heave. Out of the corner of my eye, I noticed three soldiers standing on the road ahead. I forced my stomach muscles to relax their spasms and tried to look like I was interested in something on the ground. I reached for a bright shell casing. There were many scattered on the ground next to the road. Stamped on the base I read, "BBG Bridgeport, Mass." An American shell casing. From our guns. Maybe my guns. I can't think about that now. Beyond the bridge the road led to Lentini. That was my goal. Nothing else mattered.

I dropped the empty shell and went on. Something about the road became too familiar to me. I'd seen it before. It was the same road we strafed after Caltagirone. We were responsible for these tangled bodies! I must not think about that. Survival, getting past the soldiers up ahead must occupy my thoughts. Had they seen me yet?

The dead lay in grostesque attitudes embracing the embankments, distorted mannequins baking in the sun. The hot still air was weighted with the smell of death. Our squadron did this. We killed them, we. . .I. . .killed them.

Formaldehyde disguised the smell of death. It was a special assignment, Riddle had said. The newspaper wanted sketches from the morgue. There were five bodies, four had died from illness, one from an accident. I forced myself to commit to memory the dismembered body on the slab so I could sketch it accurately later. I was a professional, a newspaper artist. Concentrate on the truth. I was a professional pilot, skillful, I did my job. That was the truth.

I came abreast of the soldiers, a German on the right and two Italians on the left, each guarding the entrance of a compound. I heard the telltale sounds of military activity on both sides, but I kept my eyes focused straight ahead and walked between the soldiers. Everything else within my visual field seemed deserted. The road was clear of activity. I avoided the dead, held my head down and tilted, eyes on the pavement, arms and wrists cocked in still angles, and shuffled along. A voice said something in Italian. My heart pounded. I ignored the voice and kept sliding one foot in front of the other.

I concentrated on the bridge ahead. South of that bridge, maybe at Lentini, I would meet the British. On both sides of the bridge were concrete pill boxes. This was the Simento River. Doorknob Squadron had strafed this road yesterday. Now it was completely quiet. It would only be a matter of hours before I'd be picked up by the British.

At the south end of the bridge I encountered an odor so revolting, so overpowering, I held my nose and breathed through my mouth. More torn bodies, parts of bodies were piled at the foot of the bridge. They were uniformed paratroopers, infantry, German and British. I hurried past. Paratroopers dropped at night. We never flew at night. What drives a man to jump from a plane into a black night? I wondered if the men at the foot of the bridge died in the dark.

I saw a flight of 38's before I heard them. They came low, off the Mediterranean, turned up the river, snaked over the western hills, ducked down, and disappeared. I wondered if Foster was in one of them. They didn't fire. Those pilots must have been unaware of the heavy troop concentrations below them. Why had no one fired? I thought of the many times I had crisscrossed that area, feeling invincible, unaware I could have been destroyed. What military logic permitted our planes to sweep freely across the hills of Sicily, with German troops below? Now the hunted watched the hunters. Why hadn't anyone fired?

I noticed long gouges in the macadam road, as if it had been clawed by a giant rake. The ground glittered with more bright metal shell casings. Wide tracks of a heavy vehicle pressed deep ribbons into the earth, traced a path through an open field to the edge of a citrus grove, and ended where an enormous flat-bed carrier supported an artillery piece half the size of a railroad car. Under the pivoting gun mount dozed the gun crew, safely hidden by the trees and invisible from the air.

Then, as though by prearrangement, only moments after the Lightnings had passed, trucks rolled—gun carriers and armoured vehicles, half tracks, wheeled contraptions of every description flowed onto the road from both sides. Italian and German soldiers seemed to materialize from all directions. I slunk away from the road, crawling over a carpet of dead soldiers, until I butted against a stone wall fifty feet from the road. I could go no further. I curled within the tangle of bodies, keeping close to the ground, and watched.

The barrel of the great cannon raised skyward, each crew member in action, and shells fired in rapid succession at something I couldn't see. No shells came earthward. No one seemed concerned. Hundreds of soldiers marched past, so close I heard them talking, their eyes avoiding the carpet of dead bodies where I hid. They were disciplined, orderly, well organized, certainly not fearful, as they moved north toward the bridge. I hoped it was a retreat. With them gone, my worries would be over.

The steady flow of troops lasted almost an hour. Then came a lull, some stragglers, and the road was empty. The British must be close behind and I'll be safe, I thought. Strange, I noticed the bodies around me didn't smell. I raised up on one elbow and saw another column approaching. I froze instantly, staring ahead, afraid if I shut my eyes the movement would be seen. A soldier looked at me, then looked away. I lay back, wriggled between bodies, and vowed to remain motionless until I actually saw a British soldier.

I lay there for hours, while intermittent lines of German soldiers and equipment passed, isolated convoys, valuable military targets. If the 38's returned I'd be in the middle of a bull's eye. The huge cannon continued arcing missiles toward the south. The marching soldiers moved easily, with determination. This was no retreat, they were relocating. They must be establishing a concentration north of the bridge. I'm in the middle, hiding like a scared rabbit. Something terrible is going to happen. I didn't belong there. I clawed at the ground, flipping dirt over my legs.

Three tanks abruptly left the road and shuddered to a halt in a grove of trees. In less than a minute, a squadron of 38's flew over without firing a shot. How had the Germans been warned of the approach, I wondered. How easily they avoided detection, their camouflage blending with the terrain, just as I was undetected in the mass of bodies that surrounded me.

The tanks rumbled on, irresistibly making their way, rolling over bodies that lay in their path, plowing steadily through stone walls and giant cactus as easily as a boat glides through water. I was lucky that I lay parallel to the direction the tanks moved. As a precaution, I propped my head against the wall so I could see them coming, ready to fling myself from their path if necessary.

The worst was over, like pulling off the oxygen mask before ten thousand feet, I thought. I was on my way home. I'll kiss the first

British soldier I see. I bit a small piece from the last apricot, saving the rest for a celebration with the British. If tanks come first, I'll let them pass and wait for foot soldiers. Adjust my helmet and goggles, show empty hands. Hi there, I'm an American pilot. Want a cigarette? Watch out, heavy concentrations up ahead. I'm tired, can't fly any more. I want out.

One of our new pilots quit and nobody said a word. A shell exploded in his cockpit wiping out his instrument panel. But he didn't get a scratch. After that, he never completed a mission. Got off the ground a few times, but something always went wrong. His guns didn't work, no radio, temperatures in the red. He never made it to the target. We were glad when he was transferred. No one wants a guy you can't count on.

It would be easy—headache, bad sinuses, pains in my teeth. It's in my medical record, they'd have to believe that. The first time I went to 25,000 during training I had trouble trying to descend. Excruciating pains shot through my jaws. I had to descend a little at a time so I could tolerate the pain. The army dentist reasoned the pain came from a leaky filling. Not knowing which one, he drilled them all out. He'd guessed right. But they could hurt again and no one could say otherwise.

There were guys in World War I who cut off their trigger finger. I couldn't press the cannon button without my right thumb. I think my knife could go through bone, but I'd have to do it lefthanded. I'll try it on the dead man. I must be crazy! *Schmuck*, Just quit! No one can make you fly. Take back your goddamn medals, payoffs, bribes! Forty-six missions is enough. I can't do fifty. It was twenty-five when I enlisted, you sons-of-bitches. I'll make a deal with the British. I'll throw away my helmet and dog tags, keep up the nutty act, and they'll send me to a hospital in England for the duration.

For a long time I heard nothing and saw no one. With the deepening shadows, I felt more secure. I could rest. I stretched out. The man who lay beside me couldn't have been dead long. He didn't smell. His skin was rough and pale yellow in the glow of the dying sun. He lay stiff and frozen in the moment of death, like a sand statue I had seen on the Lake Michigan shore.

*   *   *   *

I'd ducked in around legs to see it. The artist was sculpting the form of a sleeping man, lying on his back, his arms clasped over his stomach. I watched for hours, unmindful of the burning sun. I found a rusty tin pail behind the boathouse, and in the days that followed, I molded sand statues of heads and figures. My friend Hubby came by.

"Look what I found," he said, brushing sand from the shell of a large turtle.

"Let me see, please?" I asked.

Hubby held it close to his body, in a way that kept me from getting a good look. "Beat it, you little punk. I found it," he said.

Hubby pushed the turtle along the sand, imitating a speedboat. The creature's head and legs were drawn inside the shell.

I returned to my statue. When Hubby tired of the turtle, I would be able to examine it. But when he lost interest, instead of putting it aside, he threw it with great force against a rock. I ran to the turtle.

"Don't do that! Leave him alone!" I said. Hubby smiled. He placed the turtle on the rock, picked up another rock, and smashed it against the shell. I grabbed at him, screaming and crying, digging my fingernails into his cheeks, "I'll tell my brother! He'll beat you up." He shook me loose; threw me down in the sand, and ran away.

I picked up the cracked shell and imagined the turtle's pain. He kept his head and legs inside. I dug a shallow hole in the wet sand and cradled the shell gently in the depression. Broken, jagged sections of shell interrupted the regular pattern on the turtle's back. One fragment pressed into the body, exposing moist yellow flesh. I gently moved the piece to try to relieve the pressure he must feel. The piece fell inside, releasing a putrid odor, and in the dark hole I saw a pulsating mass of white maggots. I recoiled and jumped, wiping my hands in the sand.

*   *   *   *

My eyes adjusted to the darkness. The stars seemed unusually bright and the moon unusually large. A patrol passed single file along the edge of the road, unaware of my presence. There came a reddish glow on the horizon and sporadically the entire sky brightened with explosions. The battle was in the north and south. I lay under an umbrella of safety in an intermediate zone, in the quiet eye of the storm.

The Germans will be gone during the night and the British will arrive. I need only wait. I searched two bodies next to me for canteens. They had none. My skin was covered with mosquito bites. More buzzed around me. I killed them easily. They had no survival instincts.

I woke with a start. Stupid! I had dozed off. I can't let that happen again. I heard night sounds, crickets and something else, very faint but growing louder. The familiar throbbing of aircraft engines, expanding to fill the black sky, an orchestra building to a crescendo, setting a vibration in my teeth. Voices rose in German from the other side of the road, agitated shouts of alarm. I lay perfectly still, listening but hardly breathing.

A new sound, like backfiring explosive snaps and pops and cracks in rapid succession, interspersed with the engines' drone. A flare startled me. It snaked its way toward the sound, and for a moment it was daylight. A half dozen parachutes reflected the light before they were absorbed in the earth, so close I heard branches splinter and the grunts and gasps of painful landings. The engines continued on, seeding their human cargo down the road.

A voice, words unintelligible but undoubtedly English, and then another in response. Instantly, small arms' fire broke out, another flare burst, and several men were illuminated, clawing at their parachute harnesses. Machine gun fire swept the field, and they were killed in the dying light of the flare like seed sown in a fire. Gunfire continued in the darkness, shouting in German and English, the sound of boots pounding in my direction over the hard ground, and then no more sound.

The dark shapes of a German patrol moved against the night sky, the stillness punctuated by spitting flame and red tracers from their guns directed into the bodies they passed. I was rigid with fear. Please, don't come any closer! My heels dug into the ground: my head and shoulders pressed hard against the stone wall. I stared wide-eyed, straining to see the men moving in pairs through the carpet of corpses, a few yards at a time.

A figure rose from the ground, running hard in my direction. Several others followed. A terrifying guttural moan came from his throat. I grabbed my knife, gripping it with both hands, pointing the blade toward the rushing figure. Bullets shattered stone chips from the wall behind my head. I could not be a part of this nightmare! I must be outside looking in. I couldn't see the image of myself dead.

A high-pitched scream bounced inside my own head, rising in volume. It was coming out of my throat. A silhouetted head and body towered over me, rocking unsteadily on its feet. I tasted blood, my legs jerked violently.

I gripped my knife with aching fingers. In the next moment there was an explosion and the night sky blinked through a large hole in his chest. The body toppled onto me, swallowing my knife without resistance. The patrol passed within yards, firing short bursts in my direction.

I lay beneath the weight of the body, its chin resting on my forehead. Great quantities of warm liquid poured from the chest cavity. The hogs were angry, throats cut, they snorted in rage and fear thrashing against the chain. A crevice divided the tip of mother's nose, thin black-pencilled lines formed eyebrows. Riddle asked if they died in pain. No, fear. The knife is too sharp to feel pain. Pencilled lines of cows in wide-eyed terror, blood drained while butchering. A moan nearby? They slaughtered efficiently, hogs dangling from chains clamped to rear legs, blood exhausted. Riddle liked the sketches.

A flame, nostrils filled with the stench of burning body hair, searing. Hogs, strangely white, inverted fat and naked, tracing the breast lines, pressing my brow to concentrate on the delicate detail, stifling a twelve-year-old's budding sexual urge. Another moan. Spreadeagled on me. My hands, wet and sticky, still locked about the handle, the blade buried below the waist. The blood no longer flowed. Screwed up, didn't you, *schmuck!* Zigged when you should have zagged. I moved the knife. No sound. Dead. But I was alive.

I pulled up on the knife, saw the butchers reach within fat naked bellies, swift sharp cuts up the intestines, red hands, blood-stained boots and aprons. How deftly they disemboweled. Cows stampede in panic; hogs are smart and understand; frightened sheep follow the Judas goat until he slips away, leaving them huddled in fear. The knife came loose. I slid from under the body. The dead were everywhere, corralled, metered through runways, gates slamming behind, too narrow to turn back, prodded on, trapped in a box canyon. A sixteen-pound sledge hammer smashes between the eyes, the animal's stunned to its knees, the floor tilts, a panel lifts, the animal slides out, is quickly chained and swung high. A sharp knife finds the jugular, blood spurts faster than the gutters can swallow, the butchering begins while the heart still beats.

24

The D.F.C.

A SOLDIER WALKED CASUALLY ALONG THE side of the road. Thirty yards behind him, other soldiers, all wearing tin helmets with flared brims. British uniforms!

Tears streamed down my cheeks and I sobbed as I had in my father's arms. I felt as if I were floating, so drained of energy I could blow away with a breeze. I lay still and silent, waiting, knowing I was safe now.

How many days had it been? Garrett had agreed to wait four days before he mailed the letter. If I don't get back soon enough, Dad will never talk to God again. He wasn't worried. He knew Bob and I would be safe. He'd made a deal with God. That was the best insurance you could have. I should have told Garrett to give me more time.

Eight men walked past. No hurry. I can wait. More men and tanks rolling at a snail's pace followed. Several men separated from the group and fanned out to survey the area. Two approached where I lay. For the first time I noticed the grotesque postures of the dead. When the soldiers came near, I called, "Over here!" One soldier jumped back a few paces and crouched, pointing his rifle. "Where's that?" he hollered.

"Here, next to the wall." I waved my arm and smiled.

"Mike!" He called over his shoulder, "Have a look! I'll cover." The man, his rifle ready, carefully stepped over bodies, stopped in front of me, and stared. Two buck teeth appeared, the corners of his mouth making large creases in his freckled cheeks. "Well now, wot do ye make o' this?" He nodded to his buddy to join him.

I held up a hand. "Glad to see you guys."

He stiffened. The buck teeth disappeared and he shoved his carbine against my throat. His buddy came alongside. He frowned. "He's not one o' ours." Mike pushed the barrel harder against my neck.

"I'm an American," I coughed, showing him both my empty hands.

Mike hesitated, then lowered the gun. "If so, you're the only one 'ere who is!"

He pulled the twisted sweatband from my head and studied my short-cropped blond hair and blue eyes.

"Come on, guys," I pleaded. "I'm an American pilot, look . . ." It was incredible the dream wasn't over yet. I reached inside my coveralls, "Move easy, matey!" Mike glared, raising his gun again. Slowly I extracted my helmet and goggles from inside my coveralls and then pulled them down over my head.

"I don't recall the American star being yellow."

"Look at my I.D.," I jiggled my dog tags, "I couldn't make that up."

Mike slipped between corpses and leaned close to look. Then he nodded. "Can't be too careful, you know. Where are you hit?"

"I'm not," I said, surprised at the question.

"Maybe you are and don't know it. You're covered with blood." I looked down and saw the blood had dried a large reddish brown, a stain that covered the entire front of my coveralls. I removed a crumpled pack of camels from my breast pocket, still clean by some miracle, and offered them.

"American cigarettes! Guess you are a Yank. Keep 'em, we 'ave our own." He lit mine and one of his own. I pinched its sides to draw air past the tears in the paper. Mike looked at the body next to me. A low whistle passed through his teeth, "This one's not a German either. Wonder what hit him? You could drive a lorry through that 'ole. Frank, take a look, he's a British officer!"

Mike rolled the body on its side. On the upper arm of the jacket was a red and yellow triangular patch.

"A Leftenant in the Royal Lancers . . . Communications . . . Wot d'yel suppose he was doing 'round 'ere?"

That insignia. My fellow prisoner. The helmet pressed down over the dead man's eyes and nose. Above the rigid open mouth was a well-trimmed moustache. I began to sob. Soothing hands were on my back and arms, patting me. Gentle voices. Mike and the other soldier helped me to my feet. "Don't you think nothing of it, laddy. Let it all come out. No one ever gets used to seeing things like this."

*   *   *   *

Garrett was at the wheel of the jeep when the big DC-3 dropped me back at my base. I leaned against the propwash, awkward in the ill-fitting English soldier's shirt and pants, bare ankles visible above the tops of my shoes. "Hey there, Lieutenant! The radio shack said it was Five Two that called in. How ya been?"

"Beat." I slid onto the seat alongside him. "I want to hit the sack."

"Easy, I'll drop you at your tent and tell the C.O. you'll report later. After dinner O.K.?"

"Tomorrow morning." We rode across the dusty field. Most of the parking spaces were empty. The 71st was away on a mission.

"Any change in my status?" I asked.

"No, you're listed as undetermined. We guessed you were down for repairs. We lost Jensen and Lloyd in a midair the same day you reported engine trouble. HQ don't want any official announcements about missing or killed for a couple of weeks.

"Hate to tell you this, sir. Lieutenant Brooks hasn't come back yet, and it's three hours past his fuel supply."

I clenched my teeth, unable to answer. It's insane.

"Sorry Lieutenant."

I don't care, I thought. I'm going to make it, damn it. No more for me. I'm going home.

The tent flap was tied open. A few flies cut lazy eights in a shaft of sunlight. Inside, my few possessions were just as I had left them, an untouched still life—sheepskin jacket spread across the taut canvas cot, folded blanket, valpack, writing papers and letters, my barracks bag knotted and tied with white rope. I was home. Taped to the bottom of the mattress was my contingency letter to the folks. That's it, Dad, I'll never fly again. I tore up the letter, cleared off the cot, and fell asleep.

It was morning when I awoke. The tent was empty. My head was crowded with the same thoughts I had before I had fallen asleep. No more missions for me. Forty-six was enough. Let some new pilot do my last four. They're younger, eager. My mind was made up.

The fiber mat close to the stove rippled. Then I heard faint scratching and digging. Leppy was probably making tunnel repairs. I barely breathed, hoping he would come into the light. I had glimpsed him fleetingly at night, scurrying madly across the floor under cover of flickering shadows cast by the pot belly stove and pulsing bare lightbulb. I lay still. Movement under the mat traced a path to the center of the tent. Where two mats met, dirt began to cave in, like the pouring sands of an hourglass. A nose and whiskers appeared, followed by two beady black eyes. Without once looking around, Leppy patted, pushed, and prodded the dirt at the opening. Had I been a cat, he would have been a dead rat.

He eased his sleek grey body up through the narrow opening, standing like a conductor in a pit, his long paws and thin fingers working rapidly against a rising dirt mound. He emerged fully, followed by a furless tail longer than his body, then turned, ducked his head and forearms into the hole, and rapidly continued his work. I broke off a Tootsie Roll segment and tossed it toward the hole. He whirled at the sound, sniffed the candy a few times, then disappeared. I heard him scratching in the tunnel under the mat. Then he was back, a shiny metal object in his mouth, which he deposited in trade for the candy and disappeared.

I leaned over the side of the cot and picked up the metal object. It was an Air Corps lapel insignia, gold wings and a propeller. I got out of bed and lifted the fibre mat covering Leppy's shallow tunnel. Inside were six blind and furless newborn rats, climbing over each other's bodies. An escape route led from the nest into the ground at a sharp angle. Her home was decorated with bits of string, spent matches, pieces of foil, a sardine can key, and the brass second lieutenant's bar Foster had lost. So Leppy was a mother, and a survivor, too.

I neatly folded the borrowed shirt and trousers, put on freshly laundered coveralls, shaved, slipped my sketchbook in my pocket, and went to get some breakfast. The mess sergeant prepared a plate of powdered eggs and grits. It tasted better than I had remembered. Fortified with my first meal in three days. I was ready to deliver my well-rehearsed resignation from combat and squadron. I had no more to give.

Tex shook my hand. "Ko-han. Well now, we're mighty glad to see y'all. Say hello to Captain Crawford, the new Executive Officer from HQ. Say, buddy, you look tuckered out."

Shorty was there too. I shook hands with him and the Captain. I was disappointed Tex wasn't alone. I would have to delay my resignation. Tex motioned for me to sit down. "Garrett said it was you that came in on that Gooney Bird. Get enough sleep? You're O.K., aren't you?"

"Yep, I'm O.K."

"I suppose you heard about . . ."

"Yep."

"We're averaging two missions a day . . . Bad luck . . ." Then his voice brightened. "I like your style, Ko-han, DC-3 transport, door-to-door delivery."

He noticed I didn't smile. "You're O.K.? Sure you don't want to see the Doc?"

"No. I'm O.K."

"You're too damn thin. Lose anymore weight and you'll blow away. Where did you leave the plane?"

"Crashed in Sicily."

"No shit! We thought you landed at Cape Bone or Malta. Well, I'll be goddamned. How the hell did you get back?" Shorty and Crawford looked up from their papers.

"Walked," I said. They laughed.

"Goddamn!" said Tex.

Shorty leaned forward, very serious. "Did you see any enemy activity?"

"Yeah, lots." I didn't want to talk to Shorty. I only wanted to tell Tex I was finished.

"Germans? Italians?"

"Both."

"Command Intelligence, will want to see you pronto for debriefing. And you may be eligible for R and R before finishing up your missions."

That's a laugh, I thought. It's going to be permanent R and R for me.

"Give me a minute, Tex." Shorty said, motioning for Tex to join him at the far end of the tent. He opened a folder and spread some papers. They spoke in low tones. Crawford offered me a cigarette.

"You pilots are something!" he said. "Gives me goose flesh when I read the things you guys do."

I sucked on the cigarette, while I looked at my feet.

"You're lucky, being in there where the action is. I'm stuck behind a desk. Saw the Germans, huh?"

I nodded.

Tex spoke without looking up from the papers in his hand. "Ko-han, we have an administrative pouch that has to go to Twelfth Air Force HQ. Shorty says you're required to report to their intelligence anyway, so you can drop the pouch and bring back some medals. Feel up to it?"

"Where is it?"

"Lamarsa, a little to the east. Figure fifteen minutes each way. The pouch goes to Major Crowley. Get back before noon and we'll schedule you a mission for tomorrow."

"Sure, but I need to talk to you this afternoon when I get back."

"You got a date." He pointed to a slip of paper clipped to the bag. "That's where you'll find Major Crowley. Take the piggyback and Captain Crawford can go with you. It'll save him a three hour jeep ride."

"Any of you ever meet Major Crowley?" Crawford asked smiling. "No? You're in for a surprise, Lieutenant."

Tex reached inside the pouch. "Here, Ko-han. Congratulations." He held a pair of silver bars in his hand. "Wear these. Your promotion to First Lieutenant came through on the tenth."

"Thanks," I said, "I can use the extra money."

The piggyback was a P-38 modified to carry a passenger. The mechanics had removed everything behind the pilot's seat, including the radios. Shorty had given me a terrain map, safe to carry now that North Africa was in Allied hands. Crawford was as excited as a kid. It was close with him breathing on my neck. I prayed he wouldn't get sick.

When we landed at Lamarsa, Crawford slapped my back. "Lieutenant, that was great. You guys know how to live!" We parked and he ushered me toward a group of small buildings. "I'll take you to Major Crowley," he said, smiling each time he said the Major's name. So that's it. Aside from checking with Intelligence, I'm going to get a medal. I was tired. I didn't care anymore.

A sentry brought his heels together and slapped his rifle in salute as we walked past. The sign over the doorway read, "HEAD-QUARTERS NORTHWEST AFRICAN AIR FORCES." Captain

Crawford led me into a small smoky room where three enlisted men hunched over typewriters.

"Thanks again for the ride, Lieutenant. Wait here. I'll tell Major Crowley you're here." He pounded me on the back and left. Again, that knowing smile.

The men at the typewriters, one of them with a pockmarked face, gave a quick nod of recognition to Crawford as he left the room and then continued their work. I took the sketchbook from my leg pocket. It was almost filled, a graphic record of my missions, a fighter pilot's illustrated guide to technique and survival, interspersed with caricatures of the men in the squadron. I opened the book to a blank page and traced the lines of the pockmarked face and lost myself in the convolutions of his ear.

Several minutes passed. It was a word or a phrase that caught my attention, like a shift in the steady sound of an engine that brings a new awareness.

"Either of you guys working on general orders number 155?"

"Yeah," said another. "I have two that go with the others."

"Have you used 'zeal and courage' yet?"

"No. I've used 'courage and resourcefulness' and 'outstanding courage and devotion.'"

"O.K., take three more out of the box. Use 'skilled and aggressive leadership'...," The man took notes, "'outstanding skill and gallantry' and, let me see, 'his skill as a fighter pilot and his eager and faithful performance of duty.' Get on it right away. They have to be dated today and mimoed before 1800."

"Hey Sarg," said the third man. "I got a problem with this one, a bomber co-pilot. Nothing in his file. Finished fifty and his C.O. wants him to get the medal. I'm drawing a blank."

The sergeant thumbed through some papers. "Here's a perfect one for a co-pilot. Listen...a great opening, 'Lieutenant So-and-So has displayed outstanding endurance, fortitude, and professional skill on many high-altitude missions which resulted in great destruction to enemy personnel, shipping, and military installations.' Then wind up with 'his calm judgment in combat and his consistent, alert efficiency in assisting his first pilot frequently have insured the completion of his plane's mission. His unfailing devotion to duty, et cetera, et cetera....' and let me have a copy. It's the kind of piece I need for a chicken colonel. Went on three missions and the General promised him the D.F.C."

"A full Colonel? Be sure to include 'coolness under fire' or they'll send it back for rewrite."

Bastards, sitting on their asses. What do they know? What would they write about Cominski and Smith?

The sergeant turned to me. "That pouch for us?"

"No, for Major Crowley," I replied. His face went grey. The three men looked up.

"Sorry, Lieutenant, thought when you came in with Captain Crawford you were with Intelligence. Crowley, huh? You a pilot?"

I nodded.

"I'm sorry, Lieutenant. We kid around but we don't mean any disrespect. Major Crowley, huh? Geez, I'm sorry." All three went to pounding on their typewriters, no more talking.

The name on the door read, "J.E. Crowley, Major." My escort said I was expected, and I entered without knocking. Seated behind a large wood desk, wearing a freshly ironed khaki shirt and matching tie, was the major. The major was a lady. Aside from the nurses aboard the *Susan B. Anthony,* she was the first military female I had met. I forgot to salute. I put the pouch on her desk. She stuck out her hand.

"You're Lieutenant Kohn. Thanks for bringing the reports. Please have a seat. It'll be a few minutes."

I sat down and watched her examine the contents of the pouch and make some pencil notes on the file covers. Embarrassed when she looked up and caught me staring, I returned to my sketchbook and busied myself with the sketch of the serviceman, accenting the man's fat earlobe and adding swirls of hair to the back of the neck.

Some minutes later she patted the pouch. I'll leave this for you to take to your squadron when you're ready to go." She came around the side of the desk. "May I see what you're drawing?"

As she leaned over the pad, her hand shot to her mouth and she gasped. I followed her stare back to my sketch, really seeing it for the first time. It was the ear, the curly hair, half a contorted face emerging from under a helmet—the last picture burned in my memory of the dead Englishman.

Confused, I covered the drawing with my hand. A buzzer sounded. The Major picked up a small blue box from the corner of her desk and a page of typewritten copy. "Please come with me." I followed her into the adjacent office. A two-star general behind a desk didn't look up when the lady Major approached, saluted, and said, "Sir, we have a presentation. Lieutenant Kohn, a flying officer of the 71st Fighter Squadron."

She placed the blue box in front of him. He laid his pencil alongside a note pad, picked up the box, and came around the desk toward us. He stared thoughtfully into the distance, cradling the box in both hands, while the Major read aloud:

> *Under the provisions of AR 600-45, as amended, and pursuant to authority in Circular No. 126, Headquarters NATOUSA 2 July 1943, the Distinguished Flying Cross is awarded to the following named personnel, Air Corps, United States Army, in the name of the Commanding General, NATOUSA. . . .*

She took a breath and continued:

> *Fredric Kohn, 0732274, 2nd Lieutenant, Chicago, Illinois. . . .*

The D.F.C. for Killer Kohn. . . I wonder what adjectives the boys in the back came up with to describe the bodies, the pieces, the stench. . .

> *. . .for extraordinary achievement while participating in aerial flight in the North African Theater of Operations as pilot of P-38 type aircraft. While leading his flight on a low level bombing and strafing mission over Porto Torres Harbor, Sardinia, on 14 May 1943, . . .*

I remember that place. I remember what we did there. . .

> *Lieutenant Kohn, though unable to jettison his belly tank, flew in the face of intense antiaircraft fire, to drop his thousand pound bomb squarely on a dock where two enemy vessels were moored. Continuing on to Alghero Airdrome, he destroyed a machine gun position and crew which was firing on his comrades, and enabled them, unhindered, to destroy eight aircraft on the ground, damage two others and to set fire to two hangars. He shot up a pill box as he crossed the coast and brought his flight home safely. On many combat missions, his skilled and aggressive leadership has reflected great credit upon himself and the Armed Forces of the United States.*
>
> *By command of Lieutenant General Spaatz.*

. . .how about that, Dad. You remember that flight. You know the truth. . . .

The general silently shook my hand, handed me the box, walked back around the desk, and sat down. I thanked him and followed the major out of the office.

"Congratulations, Lieutenant. You must be very proud." She smiled and offered me a cigarette. I was being bought. I pressed the little brass button and opened the box. The Distinguished Flying Cross, a four-bladed propeller, hung from a red, white and blue ribbon. The D.F.C. The big one, Dad. I placed the paper from which she had read inside, closed the lid, and slipped the box into the leg pocket of my coveralls.

"It's rare when the general can make a personal presentation. It gives him a great deal of pleasure. Orders for the air medal and oak leaf clusters for other pilots in your squadron are being cut now. You can take them back with you when you go. I see you are to report to Intelligence. You can do that while the orders are being typed." She cranked a field telephone and asked the mouthpiece to send Captain Spears to her office.

"How many sorties have you completed, Lieutenant?"

"Sortie? Sounds like a date to the senior prom. You mean missions?"

"They're really the same."

"How do you define a sortie?"

"If a flight enters enemy territory or is exposed to potential attack, that's a sortie. Five gets you an air medal and fifty is a ticket home. Combat hours don't count, only the number of times you fly out to meet the enemy, whether you engage him or not." She sounded like a lawyer.

"Can I get credit for a sortie if I'm not attached to a Fighter Group?"

"Sure. As long as it qualifies under the definition of a sortie, I can't see why not."

"I've flown 46 missions with the 71st and several others while attached to the 328th."

"That's a training outfit."

"Yes, but the flights were vectors into the Atlantic to escort incoming convoys and protect them against enemy attack. Add four of those missions and my tour's over."

My heart began to pound. I looked into her soft brown eyes, pleading. Her expression remained unchanged, but we held each other's eyes. It was several moments before she spoke.

"Have you discussed this with your C.O.?"

"I asked him about it when the number of missions in a combat tour was changed from twenty-five to fifty."

She thumbed the pages in front of her. Very slowly she said, "You've shown yourself to be an aggressive Squadron Leader with an extraordinary combat record. I'll review your 201 file. See me again after you're finished with Intelligence. Would you please leave your sketches with me?" I shrugged and put my sketch pad on her desk.

There was a knock at the door and a Captain entered the office. Like the Major, Captain Spears was a non-flying officer, neat and well-groomed. His attitude was pleasant and he listened respectfully to Major Crowley. "Captain, Lieutenant Kohn will go with you. When you've finished interrogation regarding his contact with enemy ground forces, brief him relative to returning combat personnel."

Could it be? Why brief me for going home? Was she going to give me credit for those four missions?

Captain Spears worked in a tiny partitioned cubicle. He typed three or four lines and asked, "You were shot down in Sicily?"

"Yes, sir."

"Captured?"

"Yes, sir. By Italians."

"Did you put up a fight?"

"No, I didn't." I raised my chin.

Captain Spears looked at me kindly, "I have to ask these questions."

I nodded.

"And then?" he asked.

"I was turned over to the Germans at a detention center near Catania."

"Were you interrogated?"

"Yes, sir. Just name, rank, and serial number."

"Were you part of an escape committee?"

"No, sir. A British officer and I did it on the spur of the moment." Please, I thought. Don't ask about him.

"How did you escape?"

"We walked out when they weren't looking."

"How did you get back to Africa?"

"I was picked up by the British 8th Army and got a ride on a plane out of Noto."

"Where's that?"

"Southern Sicily. It's a German airfield that was occupied on the day of the invasion."

"See any enemy troup activity?"

"Yes, sir. All types of military equipment north of the Primisole Bridge."

"Anything else you can add that you feel could be helpful to our operation?"

"No, sir," I said, wondering if it would help for him to know how many bodies I saw, that the British officer was dead, that I was going to quit.

"I will forward your report to British Intelligence. They may wish to conduct their own interrogation."

He referred to a notebook. "So you're going back to the States?" he asked, not expecting an answer.

"Am I?"

Captain Spears looked up. "Of course. I assume you've completed your tour of duty. These bulletins will be made a part of your 201 file. I will read their contents to you so you'll have a clear understanding of what is expected of you. When I have finished, you will initial each page.

"The material covers 'Combat Experience and Return to the United States of Combat Crews and Pilots.' I am sure, Lieutenant, you can appreciate how important it is that returning personnel be cautioned regarding what they say back home." I nodded and waited.

He flipped pages in the notebook and read out loud: "Loose, thoughtless talk by returned personnel returned from active theaters can do great harm. There have been public arguments back in the states over the performance of our aircraft, which led to interviews of returning pilots by newspapers and the radio, innocently increasing that contention by their statements. There have been incidents of improper conversation, thoughtless and dangerous."

He looked up. "You must not discuss any contact you may have had with the enemy on the ground or any other activities until you have been instructed what you may say by the Intelligence Section of the command to whom you report for duty. Any questions?"

"No, sir!" I snapped in dead earnest. Let me go home, I thought, and I'll say anything.

"You understand, Lieutenant, we know you have the utmost confidence in yourself, your fellows, and the equipment you've been using and have a burning desire to fight the enemy relentlessly."

He looked up for agreement, I nodded hastily. He began to read again. "As a former fighter pilot with combat experience, you'll probably be given duty as an instructor. There is need in our training units in the U.S. for your kind of zeal. It will provide a strong personal incentive among our young pilots in training to engage the enemy in actual combat. You must impress upon our trainees some of the glamour of war and the great personal satisfaction to be derived from actually hitting the enemy between the eyes. Proper discussion of your experiences in actual combat will boost morale and enthusiasm.

"The Air Forces are proud of the fighting spirit of men like you. Everything possible must be done to build the same enthusiasm in the new units being formed. This can be done through men like you who have the proper attitude toward combat. The benefits of your action will be reflected in the efficiency and enthusiasm to fight on the part of the replacements."

"Yes, sir, you can count on me." Easy now, no sarcasm. Make him believe me. I've got to get away from this gnawing at my gut, the killing, and Foster. No more. Can't handle it anymore.

"You are going to be entrusted with the serious task of training new pilots. . . . The very fact that those men will have the honor and privilege of learning from men like you who have been through the thick of combat and who have returned with decorations for their outstanding work is in itself an excellent morale builder. You must exercise great care to insure a continuous enthusiastic reaction through discussions of your combat experiences."

"Yes, sir!" I squared my shoulders, my jaw set, eyes drilling into him. Poor man, you're an egg, you haven't been born yet. You don't know anything.

Captain Spears handed the papers and a pen to me.

"Lieutenant, a great responsibility is being placed in your hands and one which your commanding officers have taken into consideration in recommending your return to the United States.

Your record in this theater is in itself a guarantee that you will ably and wisely carry out your new assignment."

"Yes, sir!"

I walked back with Captain Spears to Major Crowley's office. Spears laid two copies of my escape report on her desk and said goodbye. Slowly, she read the statement and handed it to me. "If this is substantially correct, please sign the original. Were you told the British may wish to interrogate you?"

"Yes." I signed the report. She punched two holes in the top and slipped it over the metal prongs of an inch-thick file folder. That's me, I thought, my 201 file, my life in her hands. Several minutes of silence passed while she reread the report. I lit a cigarette to hide my anxiety.

"I reviewed your flight time," she began, "and the six flights you made while with the 328th. They were recorded as 'combat time,' not as sorties."

Damn it, they're going to cop-out! "But according to your definition, ma'am . . . ."

"Allow me to finish."

"Yes, ma'am." I drew deeply on my cigarette, resolving not to react to anything she said. Whatever the decision, it was done.

"It is also true, Lieutenant, you've been credited with only the forty-six sorties you flew with the 71st." She referred to a note pad. "Of the prior six flights you flew at Marrakech, two were listed as 'simulated combat formation.' They don't count. Of the remaining four, one was a vector to the Straights of Gibraltar, which we have classified as scouting for submarine activity. Gibraltar isn't enemy territory. There was no risk of enemy attack nor was the flight in response to an alert. However, the three vectored flights into the Atlantic were different. Enemy bombers were reported in the area, and it was your mission to intercept, engage, and destroy the enemy."

She was a pretty lady, even without makeup. She slid the pouch and my sketch book across the table to me.

"I showed your book of sketches to the General. He was impressed and feels, as I do, your artistic talent and skill as a fighter pilot complement each other and have potential value to our training command. It's an unusual combination and a recommendation is noted in your 201 file suggesting your capabilities be used to good advantage." She assumed a formal air. "The General has directed, in accordance with military definition, your flights into the Atlantic be recorded as sorties and, as such, duly noted in your flight log; a total of forty-nine."

"I must fly one more?" In a pig's eye, I thought. You fly it, sister! "Major, I have to level with you. I appreciate what you've done, but . . ."

"Lieutenant, I must insist you wait until I'm finished."

Lady, you're playing with my life. Forty-six or forty-nine, it makes no difference. I wasn't going to fly another one. She placed a mimeo form and a handwritten note on top of the pouch.

"You understand, the additional sorties cannot be counted as credit toward oak leaf clusters to your air medal. Even completion of your last mission will not add to the decorations you have been awarded. . . ."

I couldn't concentrate on what she was saying. I didn't give a shit about their medals. All I could think about was that they expected me to fly another mission. Not a chance! A trace of a smile tugged at the corners of her mouth. Her eyes burrowed into mine, as though to communciate something more than what she was saying.

". . . However, they count toward completion of your tour. I had hoped to wish you bon voyage but it cannot be stretched further. One more and you'll be finished." She raised a hand to stop me from interrupting, pointing to the papers resting on the pouch. "I am confident, very confident, your last mission will be without incident and you'll be on your way home. Make certain your commanding officer reads my note. I've endorsed your file and recommended your reassignment to the states. . . ."

I was tuning her out, thinking of all the guys that had been killed, all the missions I had flown, that Foster would never die and leave me alone, and with all the fancy talk it still meant they expected one more mission. I had to get out of there. I started to rise.

"Wait," she said. "The 71st has sustained substantial losses and we note there are very few left of the original replacements. We want you to finish the required fifty. When a pilot goes home, it's a morale boost to the remaining members of the squadron."

She patted the pouch again. "I've included a copy of the latest definition of sortie. You'll fly your last mission as a 'spare' and receive credit for a 'sortie'. . . *even if you don't fill a vacancy*. Do you understand?"

I sat back, afraid to relax.

"It's possible, Lieutenant, you are suffering from combat fatigue."

"You mean I'm getting a free one?"

"It's in my note, explained in detail. A technicality. Your C.O. will understand. Have a safe journey home."

She returned my salute. I would have liked to kiss her. Instead, I took the pouch and left.

25

The Last Sortie

"CONGRATULATIONS, LOOTENANT!" I HEARD CHAD SHOUT as I cranked down the side window. "We heard about your promotion." I flipped open the canopy, stepped onto the wing and slid to the ground.

"Guess it won't be long before you'll be leaving the squadron."

"Don't give it a *kenahora*," I said.

"A what?"

"If you talk about it, maybe it won't happen. I love you guys, but I'm ready to go home."

"Your citation for the D.F.C. was posted after you took off. Wow! I asked Sergeant Garrett to make copies for the ground crew. You don't mind, do you?"

I smiled. "Grab my chute, will you, Sarg?"

"Mind if I ask a question, Lootenant?"

"Fire away."

"We heard you sprung a coolant leak and lost the plane. Can't understand it. It's a closed system, no hoses or clamps . . . you don't think we fucked up, do you?"

"Hell no, Sergeant. It was lead poisoning. I got shot down. Lost the other engine too."

"Then when I get a new plane, you'll fly it? I'll decorate it just like 'Mr. Arnold'. O.K., Lootenant? With all those medals and planes to your credit, they ought to make you a captain."

I was his pilot, his hero. It was his plane. I'm going home promoted and decorated. I'll tell them what they want to hear. I didn't kill anyone; I destroyed the enemy. I couldn't look him in the eye. They want to believe in it, be a part of the big game. Each tells his own stories, changing it according to the reaction he gets, editing, adding, refining until it's fine-tuned. Vicariously, they all become heroes. No one wants the truth. If you tell them you don't deserve the medals, they'll nod knowingly, warmed by your humility and modesty, a heroic trait in the finest tradition. And if you don't talk at all, your silence is a symbol of strength.

Intelligence hadn't bothered to ask how I felt; their interest was purely clinical: Can others use my escape route? What did I learn about the enemy? And tell them back home how wonderful it was, no dirty business. Fuck 'em. I'm going home.

"Almost forgot, Lootenant. The C.O.'s waiting for you."

Tex took his time. He separated the citations and the medals into two piles, filed the miscellaneous reports in their proper folders, then leaned back on his cot to read the material I knew applied to me. I sat crosslegged on the floor and finished a cigarette before he spoke.

"Real interestin', Ko-han. This here definition of sorties. Can't say I disagree with them. I just never had the authority to give any of your felllows credit for missions prior to joinin' our outfit."

Liar. He'd refused to forward the question to headquarters.

"It's an interestin' technicality. I'm not sayin' they weren't missions, just not the same as we fly. Hell, if the general says they count as sorties, that's good enough for me. But you gotta admit, Jewish people do have a knack, you're clever and I'm saying that as a compliment 'cause if its good for you, it's good for all the rest of the pilots. Did you meet Major Crowley? They say he's a ball buster."

"Sure is."

"Now then, suppose y'all know about this new setup regardin' spares?"

"Not exactly."

"Says here y'all are goin' to fly your last mission as a spare and get credit. It says here, 'If a spare doesn't fill in but stays with the squadron until over enemy territory or enemy attack is possible, he receives credit for one sortie. A pilot may not be assigned duty as a spare more than once in every twenty missions.' Guess you're home free. And listen to this note, somethin' personal, Major Crowley wants no slip up, no chance you might have to fill in. Says here you're to go as one of three spares and be the last one to fill in. That's money in the bank, a ticket back to the old U.S. of A. Want a few days' rest?"

"No, the sooner the better."

"You don't look so hot. Sure y'all O.K.?"

"I'm ready."

"O.K. Tomorrow soon enough?"

"Yes, sir!" It was guaranteed mission credit without risk. Even if the impossible happened and all three spares had to fill in, I could make something go wrong, lean it out, burn it up, or shut it down. I'd never fill in as tail-end-Charlie on my last mission...not I...not my ass.

"O.K." Tex shuffled papers. "We're going to escort a squadron of B-26 bombers. The target will be an airport on the coast of Italy. I'll have confirmation which one in the mornin' My guess is it'll be Reggio Calabria. Their planes are providin' the strongest resistance in Sicily.

"The 26's will go in low and they promise to get in and get out fast. I don't like puttin' our planes in flak that low, but it can't be helped. You know our boys, they would rather spend their time on the deck shootin' up Sicily. Elkhorn will lead Doorknob."

Tex looked at his watch. "You'll lead the spares. They gotta fill before you do. All you gotta do is get your toe across a line within three miles of the coast, and when the belly tanks drop, come on home and pack your gear."

He reread the note from Crowley. "They sure want you to make this one. No big deal, no risk, they're just tryin' to make it legal. I suppose it's a good idea. When one of you guys makes fifty, it makes everybody happy.

"Suppose you heard the 14th quit. From tail-end-Charlie to the C.O., they up and quit. If that news gets out, it'll hurt all of us. I'm not sayin' they're cowards. Don't know the details and it's true they got beat up pretty bad. But goddamn, what the hell we out here for? Nobody says you gotta be a fighter pilot, so when someone cops-out, it frosts me."

Tex looked at the handwritten note again, "You can use my plane. I'll have it towed over so your crew can preflight it. The gun sights were set special for me, but don't worry, you won't be needin' 'em. Any questions?"

I had the feeling once again that Tex was asking if I were willing to go. I had no choice. I had made a deal.

"What time's the mission?"

"Briefing at 0600. Foster and Falzone will be the other two spares, but you're the boss. Who knows, maybe it'll be a free ride for tent number eight.

*   *   *   *

Just before lights out, Foster called to Falzone, "Suppose you heard we'll be chaperoning Nose on his last mission tomorrow. He's getting a free ride."

Falzone nodded, "So will we, if we don't fill in."

"I say if you want a free ride, quit."

I felt Foster's eyes on me. I stretched my legs to the end of the cot, folded my hands under my head and closed my eyes. One more mission and I'll never see him again. I imagined my arrival in the United States, the flow of street traffic, crowded beaches, puffy white clouds, ocean breezes and mounds of sand. The clouds pulsated into everchanging forms of horses' heads, whales, colossal faces, hands, . . .

Falzone's voice intruded. "Pretty good Kohn, picking up credit for those extra three. How did you pull it off?"

"Didn't you hear?" Foster laughed. "He brown-nosed that Major Crowley."

. . . the sand reshaped from hills and valleys into torsos, arms, legs, corpses . . .

"Seriously, Kohn. How did you do it?"

I shook my head, freeing my mind of the cascade of visions. I stared at Falzone. His lips were slightly parted, I saw him dead . . . I forced my thoughts back to reason and logic and answered, "Check your logs . . . read the definition . . ." Foster lay with his arms across his thick white chest, his broad shoulders crowded the edges of his cot as though pressed within the sides of a narrow coffin. I heard his words without seeing his lips move. "Sounds just like one of those shyster Jew lawyers . . ."

Slowly, I sat upright, swung my legs around, and pushed away from the cot. I have no recollection of how I crossed to where Foster lay. I remember standing over him, my hands, palms down, reaching out to quiet him, hush, it's over, the dead don't talk. A question in his eyes seemed to ask, "Why me?" He reached up,

grabbed my arms. I felt the vise-like grip of his fingers overlapping
my thin wrists, the pressure of his thumbs bent my arms back,
drawing me down, forcing me to kneel and join the dead. He
pressed his face close to mine. Words seemed to come from his
eyes. "I could break you in half. . ." Falzone was behind me. "Why
don't you guys grow up?"

"He started it!" Then Foster released his grip and pushed. I fell
backward. Falzone's hand caught the back of my head. "You
all right?" he asked. "Did you eat? How do you expect to fly
tomorrow if you don't eat?"

"I'm O.K."

"He ever comes at me like that again, I'll let him have it."

"You know what happens when you start with those Jew
remarks. Don't let him get to you, Kohn."

"I'm all right."

"I'm not so sure. I'll bet that crash landing in Sicily was no picnic.
You should rest, stay in the sack and not fly tomorrow."

"No. I feel fine. Really."

"I'm going to talk to Tex."

"No, don't do that."

"Are you sure?"

"Yes, I'm going tomorrow."

I heard Foster roll over. "Remember, Falzone? He outranks us. He
gives the orders."

Then the lights went out.

*   *   *   *

Tex's plane was fresh and spanking new. There were two instruments on the panel I had never seen before and the shape of the
control wheel was different.

When the last plane of the squadron left the ground the next
morning, I followed with Foster's and Falzone's planes behind me. I
missed the familiar odors of my own cockpit. Quickly, we formed a
V-formation, Foster on my left, Falzone on my right. I couldn't look
at Foster's face. I would check his position by viewing his plane as
an object relative to mine. The squadron tightened up in less than a
half turn and went into a steady climb, levelling at 8,000. I hung
high and behind all the way to the rendezvous with the 26's. They
were a sleek bunch—menacing, and highly manueverable. Those

powerful radial engines looked like they could keep themselves airborne without wings. We called them flying prostitutes, no visible means of support. And they moved fast. The faster the better, I thought. The sooner I get there, the sooner I get home.

Doorknob Squadron cruised over Halltree, the code name for the twelve bombers. They held a disciplined formation as we flew over Sicily. The seemingly quiet patch of terrain below that had taken three days to traverse on foot, slid past under my wing in seconds. I held my breath as though I were flying through the smell of death.

Then a wingman from White Flight turned back. Promptly, Falzone banked away and slid into the vacated position. It's O.K., Dad. There's still Foster left to fill in.

The Italian coast appeared as a dark pencil line on the horizon. Twenty minutes to go. Then, tail-end-Charlie of Red Flight peeled off and headed back. Foster slipped into the vacated position and I was glad. I would never see or hear that son-of-a-bitch again.

I was the last spare. If another plane returned, it would be my turn to fill in. I had the feeling I'd lived this before. Destiny, fate. It all seemed so familiar, meant to happen. I'm programmed, indoctrinated to move on cue, to fill an empty slot like pouring water in a crack.

My engines purred, all systems normal. What excuse could I use? I swung from one side of the formation to the other, watching, threatening. Please. Don't any of you sons-of-bitches go home. This is it, the last time. Only one little Indian left. So, Tex? Where's the free ride?

I prepared myself for another dropout. I throttled ahead, readjusted my seat, shook my shoulders to get ready, and relaxed my grip on the controls. Here we go again, Dad. Let's do it right. Concentrate on the moment, forget what could have been. Warmth spread throughout my body from my pounding heart.

And the bombers? Cattle steadily plowing a furrow toward the Italian coast, low at 6,000 for bombing accuracy, themselves perfect targets for enemy flak. Guts! We covered the herd from above, weaving from side to side, watching for enemy fighters, protecting them only as far as the target, and then they were on their own.

Ahead, spatterings of black and white flak appeared above the coast at our altitude, like visual notes rising from an orchestra pit before the main performance.

"Doorknob Squadron! Look alive! This is Blue Leader. Bogie coming in at six o'clock! Watch'um. He's closing fast! Get ready for a break left."

The plane coming in from the rear started to oscillate, swinging side to side, exposing his belly. "It's me, Harper!" a voice shouted frantically. "Doorknob Six Seven. Got a wrong reading on my coolant. False alarm. Everything's O.K. I'm rejoining my flight. O.K.?"

Foster pulled away and returned to my wing.

"Thought you lost me, huh Nose?"

"O.K., knock it off!" Elkhorn ordered. "Keep the air clear."

The lead bombers were into their run. Columns of smoke and fire rose from the target and Elkhorn gave the order to drop tanks. All the empties tumbled away like bowling pins, one after another, falling toward the sea. I was free to go home.

I lowered the nose, and with Foster close behind my right shoulder, pulled ahead of the Doorknob squadron. I wanted my last communication to be something memorable, but all I said was, "This is Doorknob Five Two, see ya back home." Looking back I could see both squadrons in perfect formation against a background of blue sea, white surf, and green rolling hills. Beautiful, huh, Dad? I did a half loop and pushed the plane into a screaming dive, levelling off a few hundred feet above the Mediterranean with Foster a half a dozen plane lengths behind. Someone called, "Good luck, Kohn. Give our regards to Broadway."

In fifteen minutes, the northern coast of Sicily appeared on our left. We'll stay low and fast, Dad, and we'll be home in thirty minutes. One day I'll punch a channel and listen to country music, fly my plane to Frisco for dinner and then home again in the still night air, wrapped in a blanket of stars and twinkling lights. I'll tune in to newscasters, laugh at the comedy hour, my wheels will squeak on concrete, I'll scuff my heels on solid pavement still warm from the heat of the day, someone will put her arms around me, and I won't be alone. I made it, Dad. It's over.

Foster's voice made me jump. "Lookie, lookie, Nose. Twelve o'clock level. BINGO! We did it again!"

Straight ahead, on a converging course, closure within less than a minute, I saw four German Junker transport planes stuck on the horizon like thumbtacks on a bulletin board. Above them a single fighter escort, a Messerschmidt 109, kept a lonely vigil. They hadn't seen us yet, our green paint blending with the dark water.

The transports were awkward, slow, and overweight, apparently struggling under the load of evacuating German troops. I thought of the men jammed inside, their sweating bodies, compressed and held upright by their own numbers, squeezed inside the stifling heat of that metal packing case no different than carloads of Jews shipped for extermination. The cries of the dying, the sounds of the Rabbi beating his breast, the wailing of the congregation as they tore at their clothes, gripped my brain. How many are there? Fifty, sixty to each plane? Over two hundred Fosters, I was bathed in a feeling of euphoria, I need only to will it and they were dead. Like the blood of circumcision, rivulets of perspiration flowed from under my helmet, past my eyebrows and forked at the bridge of my nose.

"How about it, Nose? Like shooting sheep tied to a post."

"What about the 109?"

"Let's pick him off first."

"And while we're busy with him, the transports'll run for the hills."

As though reading my thoughts, the 109 banked quickly into position between us and the transports who arranged themselves into a tight vee formation. Surprise was gone. They had seen us.

The 109 flitted side to side like a sheepdog protecting its herd. It was the first time I had seen a 109 in a defensive position. We can take it easy, Dad. Take them one at a time. I throttled back and we flew over, a thousand feet above, the 109 glued to the line of sight between us and the transports.

Foster moved closer, crowding my wing. "Well? What are we waiting for?"

"Calm down," I ordered. "We're going to do this right."

I needed time to think. Five planes. Over two hundred men. I couldn't do it. I turned and we dipped our noses toward the formation. The 109 flipped his nose and guns toward us. I understood. Nervous, aren't you, buddy. I continued to the far side of the formation, unable to go after the transports without a head-on attack by the 109 and they were too close to the water to attack from below.

"What's the plan, Nose? We going to escort them to Germany or are we going after them?" I felt Foster's eyes drilling holes in the back of my head.

A new voice crashed through my headset so loud it pained my

teeth. "DOORKNOB FIVE TWO! THIS IS ADLER EINS!" Instinctively I twisted the volume control, shocked to hear the German accent.

"You playing games, Nose?"

"Shut up, Foster. This is Doorknob Five Two. Go ahead."

"This is Adler Eins. You remember me, Doorknob, jah?"

"Karl Muenster?"

"So? I thought you were on your way to Germany."

"Where are you?"

"We meet again." The 109 rocked his wings.

"How did you get one of our radios?"

"We have friends in North Africa."

"What in the goddamn hell is going on?" Foster screamed.

"That's the 109 who shot me down in Sicily. He hears and understands every word we're saying."

"So why don't you sing the Star Spangled Banner while I put a cannon shell up his ass?"

"Karl? Never saw a Messerschmidt so far from land."

"When the Junkers are safe, I return."

"Not a chance, I can follow those transports to Germany and back, but you and your Mickey Mouse airplane are going to end up in the drink if you don't start back soon."

"I do not understand. Say again."

"Karl, you don't stand a chance. You're finished, kaput."

"O.K., Nose, so now what?"

"Doorknob?" The German spoke softly. "Come after me but do not attack the transports."

"Say again?"

"The transports carry American and English prisoners from the camp."

"And you're a tour guide."

"I tell the truth."

"Nose, we've got him and he knows it. Don't chicken out."

"He could be telling the truth."

We flew along, stacked like a wedding cake, the transports on the bottom, the 109 in the middle, and the two of us on top waiting for the ceremony to start. Karl spoke again. "Doorknob. The prisoners do not concern me but the transport pilots and crew are German. I have more experience. If you attack. I will destroy you both. What are your intentions?"

What *chutzpah!* A dead man and he demands to know my intentions.

"How about it, Nose?"

"What if there are Americans on those planes?"

"Bullshit! You want to go home and show off your medals."

We continued in slow flight, ambling along like Indian scouts watching a group of covered wagons. Several minutes passed.

"Well?" asked Foster.

"Doorknob Five Two. I do not lie."

Getting worried, Karl? Hang around too long and you go in the drink. Leave, and we get four boxcars. Don't know whether to shit or go blind, do you? We continued for several more minutes, maintaining the advantage of altitude. Karl's position remained constant, between the two of us and the transports, a dedicated defender. How many times had I sat where he sat now, waiting, unable to leave the bombers, tempted to turn, to end the constant threat of attack, always the mouse. Now I'm the cat.

"Well, Kohn. When are we going after that son-of-a-bitch? That fucking radio of his buried a lot of our guys. If you don't take command, I will."

"How do we know he's not telling the truth?"

"Doorknob Five Two. This is Adler Eins. Over."

I didn't answer. He said that meant Eagle One. Some Eagle. A fucking vulture! It must have been he who ordered Shaker into a break right, and then attacked us from the left. We'd lost two men. Now he was caught. We were riding herd on five German planes with all the time in the world. And he knew it. I wanted to believe him. I wouldn't kill anymore. Then he called again.

"I give proof," said the German. "Fly close to the Junkers. Look in the windows. You will see for yourself."

"That's O.K. with me, Nose. I'll go down and take a look."

"You don't move Foster until I give the order."

"Doorknob. I am low on petrol. I leave the Junkers without defense. You look in the windows, jah?"

The guy was trying to make a deal.

"I have your word?" he asked.

"O.K., Karl. If you're telling the truth, it's a good trade. Go home. I agree."

And then I saw an amazing thing. The transports awkwardly

reformed in line, like circus elephants following the tail of the one ahead and the 109 moved away, up and far to the left.

"There! That is proof, yes?" He sounded so convincing. "I cannot interfere. You are free to fly close to the transports."

I looked back over my left shoulder. Foster was gone. Far below, I saw him. His plane was in a dive heading straight for the transport last in line. Too fast, I thought. He'll never be able to see anything at that speed. His belly tank whipped away. He was zeroed in on the last transport. He was attacking! "Wait!" I screamed. "Foster! Pull up! We're going to do this together."

"Screw you. This is like shooting fish in a barrel."

The 109 flipped on its back, reversed course and dove after Foster. It was madness.

"Break off Foster! We made a deal!"

Gunsmoke streamed around the nose of Foster's plane. The last transport exploded, cracked in half like a broken egg, bodies spilled out and splashed into the sea. Who were they? Americans, Germans, Jews, what difference did it make? I watched, horrified, transfixed on the sidelines of insanity. Foster pulled up coming around for another attack. The 109 anticipated Foster's turn and closed the distance.

Just like my fantasies, Foster with a Messerschmidt on his tail and, in my dreams, I would save him and he would thank me and say he was sorry. But I was too far away, and even though I was helpless, I didn't care.

Karl's shells poured into Foster's plane and the cockpit disintegrated.

Foster's P-38 rolled over and crashed in the sea. In less than ten seconds, there was no trace of what had been a Ju-52 and its human cargo, or Foster.

The 109 pulled up and headed south.

"I told you I was good," Karl's voice was calm. "And I spoke the truth. Your friend destroyed a planeload of American and English soldiers and a few Germans. A bad exchange. And now I have only a few gallons of petrol remaining. I go now. Do as you like."

I circled back, dropped low over the water and came up alongside one of the remaining transports. Karl remained high on the horizon.

On the side of the transport's fuselage was painted a six-foot black swastika, outlined in white. I edged closer, so close I could count the rivets securing the rectangular windows. Each window framed frightened faces, waving hands, noses flattened against the panes, fingers flashing V-signs, and American and British caps. I could have been a passenger on that plane. The transport pilot sat erect in the cockpit, his eyes on the tail of the transport ahead of him.

I pulled up into a climb and followed Karl.

"Doorknob Five Two. I have only twenty-three minutes of petrol left. Not enough to reach my base, but enough for one more fight, if that is your intention."

"Haven't you had enough, Karl? Bail out. I'll call Washboard and have you picked up."

"That is not possible. I do not carry a raft."

"If you agree, Washboard will direct us to the closest American airport we have in Sicily."

He had slowed to conserve fuel. I was catching up with him.

"I agree," he said.

I drew closer. "Turn to two one zero degrees. I'll show you the way to Kansas."

Smoke streamed back over his wings as he emptied his guns, dumping ammunition to reduce weight.

"Do you have channel B on that fancy radio of yours?" I asked.

"Affirmative."

"Change to channel B now." Then I called Washboard.

"This is Doorknob Five Two. Two planes, low on fuel, airspeed 240. Vector us to the closest friendly field."

"Give me a long transmission."

I counted forward to ten and back, and in half a minute Washboard fixed my position. "Lean it out 'til it's shaking. I can vector you to an airstrip ten miles south of Palermo just taken by Patton. It's 78 miles from your present position, about 19 minutes, but that's an active combat zone."

"Give me a heading."

"Watch out for the west end of that strip, craters big enough to swallow a Mack truck. They answer to Burnin' Bush on D channel."

"Washboard, give me the heading."

The prospect of hedge-hopping ten to twenty miles over Patton's army filled me with a sense of impending doom. I remembered Palermo and I squeezed my mind to see the map of the town and the terrain—the harbor, the gold church dome, the crowded white stucco houses that formed steps against the surrounding hills. The army airfield must be close to the main road. I gave Washboard another transmission and he pinpointed us on course.

The propeller of the 109 caught the sun's reflection. It seemed for a moment to stand still and then go backward. For a terrible second, I thought Muenster's engine had quit.

"There's the coast, Karl. Go to channel D now. Burning Bush! Burning Bush! Do you read Doorknob P-38? Over."

No answer. I repeated the call.

"Probably out to lunch. Karl, how you doing on petrol?" He didn't answer. Damn, now what? I punched in B. "Do you hear me, Karl?"

"Doorknob, I do not have channel D."

"O.K. Follow me. I can take us right to the field. Stay on B. I'll talk to them and come back to you. Do you understand?"

"I understand."

I gradually pulled ahead of the Messerschmidt and called repeatedly to Burning Bush, my eyes squinting to sharpen their focus, searching to pick the field from the crazy quilted countryside below. Then I saw it. The field was a mile and a half ahead, next to a congested road jammed with American armoured vehicles and tanks.

"Burning Bush? Mayday! Mayday! Do you read?"

"This is Burning Bush. Say your name and go ahead."

"This is a P-38 fighter plane. I have an emergency. A German fighter plane out of fuel will land at your field. Over."

I looked back to see gasps of black smoke streaming from Karl's exhaust, and a windmilling prop.

"This is Burning Bush. You say a German fighter is coming toward our field?"

"Affirmative! Clear the area!"

"You bet your sweet ass we'll clear the area."

"NO. The German plane is unarmed. He's out of gas! Let him land!"

"No shit!"

"Burning Bush! Do you understand? His engine's dead. We'll be there in less than a minute. He's gliding in dead stick. I wouldn't be in front of him if his guns were loaded. Clear the goddamn area!"

I returned to B channel, "You O.K., Karl?"

His voice came back strong, confident, "I see the field. No problem. I have made many such landings. Thank you, Doorknob."

"O.K. See you in the States."

I got back on D channel. Burning Bush asked, "Who did you say you are?"

"Listen, you asshole, we're running out of time! You know what a P-38 looks like?"

"Take it easy, buddy, this ain't the Army Air Corps. We're radio control for the 67th Armoured Division. I'm not located at the airfield."

"How do I let them know the plane's unarmed and not to fire on him?"

"You can't. I'll crank 'em on the phone. Relax, you got nothing to worry about."

Karl was about a hundred yards behind me as he turned into final approach, waiting until the last moment to lower his gear. He had it made, money in the bank, his timing exquisite. It was thrilling to watch a 109 without dread, in the hands of an expert, operated with delicacy and perfection, sensitive to the touch of the stick. The black crosses and squadron markings belonged there, like a top hat, white tie, and tails. The plane was beautiful stripped of superfluous accessories, trimmed to the best flying weight, a strong, agile, functional design.

The sun's rays formed a halo round him. For an instant he seemed motionless, pirouetting on a wingtip. Damn, he was good! Then, as if pointing at a star, three fingers of light, brighter than the rays of the sun, rose from the stiff barrels of three Sherman tanks and focused on him, a dancer caught on the converging beams of three spotlights. The tanks stood, rooted rock hard, pumping a stream of hyphenated shells. They found their mark, transforming the 109 into a multicolored splash against the blue sky.

I was numb, stunned, in a trance. Raucous voices filled my earphones.

"Charlie Two, Charlie Two, we got the bugger!"

"Come in, Burning Bush, Burning Bush, this is Charlie Four. We jus' had ourselves a turkey shoot!"

"This is Burning Bush."

"You see that motherfucker blow?"

"What happened?"

"Saved that Lightnin's ass!"

26

Coming Home

"MOM, IT'S FREDDIE."

"Freddie? Oh my god, Dave, it's Freddie! Freddie, Where are you?"

"In Maine. I just got back."

"Maine? What's in Maine? You're coming home, aren't you? Oh, how we've missed you...Dave, wait. Oh, he's so excited. He's crying. Wait a minute, Freddie. Sit down, Dave. Careful, you'll fall. Look, he's trying to come to the phone. So, what would you say? I'll hold the phone for you. Freddie, say something. It's Papa. Let him hear your voice."

"How ya doin', Dad? I'm home! Everything's O.K....Come on, Dad, take it easy...I hear you. I'll try to get to Chicago today...Come on fella, easy now...Please, put Mom on."

"Freddie, wait...hang on the phone, I'll help him. Don't go away."

I waited, so choked up I didn't think I could talk.

"Mom, listen. How's Bob?"

"He's on one of his trips. He always calls when he gets back. How wonderful to hear your voice," she sobbed. "Thank God you've come home."

*   *   *   *

The taxi turned into Belmont Avenue. My heart began to pound. I moved forward in my seat to see better. I could barely make them

273

out. They were sitting on the lawn. My father was in a wheelchair. My mother was looking up and down the street. Then she saw our cab. I could see her squinting, trying to see through the glare on the windshield.

"Looks like you've got a reception committee, Lieutenant," the driver said, as he pulled the flag and stopped at the curb. I jumped out and hugged my mother, picking her up off the ground. She was crying.

"Freddie, Freddie . . ."

Through blurring eyes I saw my father. His emaciated body trembling, he raised himself on skeletal arms in an attempt to stand.

"Wait, Dad . . ."

He held up a bony hand to stop me, and with total concentration and effort, he willed himself to stand up. He shuffled toward me. We embraced and we cried.

"Freddie, Freddie. Thank God you're home," my mother said. "You don't know how bad it's been. They're rationing everything . . ."

"You must be proud of your son, Mr. and Mrs. Kohn." Parks said above the sounds of my father's sobs.

"Mom, this is Captain Parks. He's with Public Relations."

" . . . we can't get gasoline for Ginnie to drive us to the doctor . . ."

"Captain, I'd like you to meet my mother and father."

"He's a hero, Mr. Kohn, an ace . . ."

"It's been so difficult taking care of your father. You can't imagine how terrible it's been . . ."

"Good luck, Lieutenant." The driver put my val-pack on the ground.

"Wait," I reached in my pocket.

"Oh no, you don't," the driver said, patting me. "I owe you."

" . . . your father's impossible. I have to do everything for him, feed him, bathe him . . ."

"Destroyed seven planes, look at all those medals," Parks said.

" . . . thank God, you're home. What did I do to deserve this? Why didn't you write more often?"

"Did you know he was shot down?"

My father looked at Parks, as though hearing him for the first time. Then he placed his trembling hand on the ribbons I wore, moaning and shaking his head. I held him close.

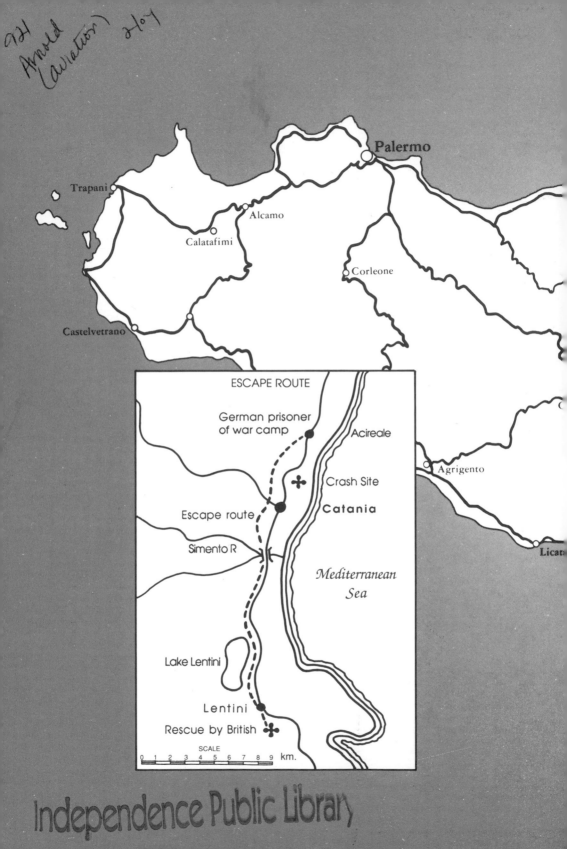

ESCAPE ROUTE

German prisoner
of war camp

Acireale

Crash Site

Escape route

Catania

Simento R

Mediterranean
Sea

Lake Lentini

Lentini

Rescue by British

SCALE
0 1 2 3 4 5 6 7 8 9 km.

Palermo

Trapani

Alcamo

Calatafimi

Corleone

Castelvetrano

Agrigento

Licata

Independence Public Library